DESTINATION EARTH

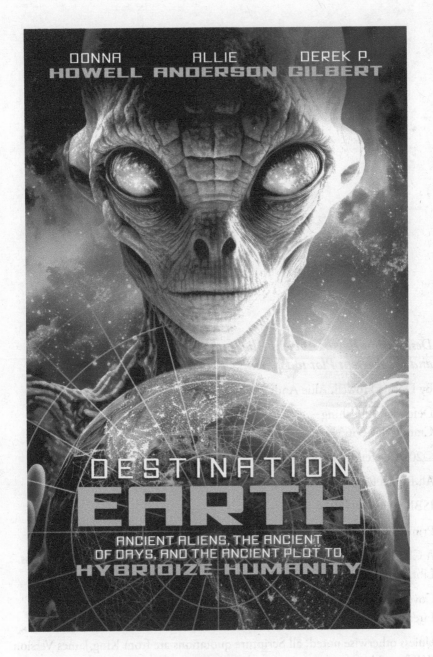

DONNA ALLIE DEREK P.
HOWELL ANDERSON GILBERT

DESTINATION
EARTH

ANCIENT ALIENS, THE ANCIENT
OF DAYS, AND THE ANCIENT PLOT TO,
HYBRIDIZE HUMANITY

DEFENDER
CRANE, MO

Destination Earth: Ancient Aliens, the Ancient of Days, and the Ancient Plot to Hybridize Humanity

By Donna Howell, Allie Anderson, and Derek P. Gilbert

Defender Publishing
Crane, MO 65633

©2024 Defender Publishing

All Rights Reserved. Published 2024.

ISBN: 978-1-948014-82-3

Printed in the United States of America.

A CIP Catalog record of this book is available from the Library of Congress.
Library of Congress Control Number: 2024943164

Cover designer: Jeffrey Mardis
Interior designer: Katherine Lloyd

Unless otherwise noted, all Scripture quotations are from King James Version (KJV): public domain.

DEDICATIONS

From Donna Howell:

First and foremost, this book, like all others I've written, is dedicated to God and to the lifting and maintaining of His Truth in an increasingly secularized world. May the writings herein lead eager, spiritual souls closer to Christ and away from the perverted alien gospel currently using His Name as a means by which to merge the miraculous events of the New Testament with the fallen angels of old.

Second, to my dear husband, James, who has been my best friend and ministry partner for eighteen glorious years, and to my son, Joee, and daughter, Sissy, my "young scholars" who have already surrendered their lives to the Lord's will and to the study of His Word.

From Allie Anderson:

To my precious and beloved father, known to the world as Dr. Thomas R. Horn, but to me as "Daddy." Not a day goes by that I don't miss you terribly and thank God for the assurance that I will see you again.

To my beautiful and selfless mother, Nita Horn, who, with strength and fortitude, is an inspiring model of unwavering faith and determination. I love you with all my heart, without even a piece of it off.

From Derek Gilbert:

For my father, Paul Bailey Gilbert (1935–2005), who decided that believing Von Däniken required more faith than believing the Gospel of Jesus Christ.

CONTENTS

CHAPTER 1

REACHING THE LOST: YES, EVEN THOSE GUYS!

By Donna Howell

The well-known acronym "UFO" stands for "unidentified flying objects." Despite the technical association with an object left "unidentified"—thus entirely unknown and not necessarily anything of extraterrestrial origin—the term is almost always used humorously as a synonym for an "alien spaceship." (That is also true for the more recently preferred terminology, "UAP," or "unidentified aerial phenomena.") We haven't yet ventured even beyond the first paragraph of this book and a major point has already been made: Things we see but don't understand are often spoken of as if we have, in fact, "identified" what we're observing.

What is that in the sky? It doesn't look like a bird, a plane, or Superman, so it must be an alien craft…

I recall a number of months ago when a friend woke me up early in the morning, flooding my smartphone with TikTok videos and photos of what could only be described as a slow-moving saucer in the skies of New Jersey the day before. She wasn't alone in her concern. Hundreds of folks had captured the UFO on camera, and the audio accompanying the shaky, freelance video feeds several times featured quivering, scared voices yelling about how they didn't know what they were looking at, though many appeared to be interpreting the craft as bad news. The footage exhibited a near-complete stop on a major highway; one car after another had been parked at the edges of the road while drivers emerged, cellphones pointed toward the clouds just over the hill. Those still attempting to get somewhere that day were inching along, carefully trying to weave between both human and vehicular obstacles as men and women wandered the highway on foot filming the object in the sky as well as the chaos on the ground.

My friend was a little panicked, but because she is fully aware UFOs have held their place in my typical research wheelhouse (though she hasn't read my books), she texted me a bazillion times in a row with shock and awe over the fact that this "saucer" had been captured on film by so many, and she pleaded with me to produce answers. As I calmly watched the videos and perused the images over a morning cup of coffee, skeptical that what had been captured was anything more than a weather balloon or something, this friend continued to text questions almost faster than I could read them: Were we all going to be abducted? Would we be strapped to chrome gurneys and chipped against our will while the bulbous-headed greys used their psychic powers to render us paralyzed and vulnerable to unthinkable experiments? Would there be a war between us mere earthlings and interstellar travelers? Had the day finally arrived when Earth would become the next mineral or vegetation reserve for beings of high intelligence from another world whose home planet had been tapped of all its natural resources? How much time did we have until they all landed here, and where could we hide if their arrival was *not* accompanied by the Hollywood-esque "we come in peace" mantra?

Was this it, the end? Were we all gonna die?

Try as I might to reassure her the UFO probably had a perfectly reasonable, human-origin explanation, her anxiety propelled her in a theological direction, leading to more fear-derived questions: Were these otherworldly wanderers demons, fallen angels, or something else? Was there *any* verse in the Bible that addresses alien visitors? Were we officially entering the seven-year Tribulation prophesied in the book of Revelation? Wait a second—could *Antichrist, himself,* be on that ship?!

One—*single*—search online for the story (outside those posted by the people on the road that day) yielded several articles by journalists local to the area in question who thought the public reaction was humorous. As it turned out, the "alien spacecraft" was a blimp hovering over a nearby outdoor sports stadium. Closer, clearer, and more steady-handed photos alongside video footage by various weather and traffic cameras throughout the city showed the Goodyear Tire and Rubber Company logo displayed on the side of the craft.[1]

Unless Antichrist and his False-Prophet pet stooge had some indeterminable reason to make their great eschatological entrance into human societies from literally one of the slowest and most underwhelming aircrafts humankind has ever made, while simultaneously endorsing Goodyear's prized rubber road-grippers, no, it wasn't likely this flying machine was about to usher in the apocalypse.

When I sent my friend three or four of these articles, she was able to calm down and accept that she had reacted far too soon. Though she felt a little silly that she hadn't thought of looking it up herself before joining the fray of premature worry, we were able to share a good laugh over the whole ordeal.

Was the blimp a UFO?

For a time, *yes*, as it was technically "unidentified" at first.

Was it an alien spacecraft?

In a word: no.

But the next text that lit up my cellphone screen took a turn I didn't expect. The friend messaging me is a true and honest Christian who reads her Bible, prays, and has a relationship with God. Imagine my surprise when I read the following words—and yes, I do have her permission and blessing to share this private text with you all:

> Wait a second, Donna… Is it possible that God IS an alien? Don't just dismiss the idea. Think about it for a sec! If God is an alien, and Jesus is His Son, then everything Jesus did in the Gospels can be explained! If the people who have seen the *real* UFOs (not a Goodyear blimp) are correct in describing how they zip around in the air in ways none of OUR aircrafts can mimic, then aliens (or whatever they are) have access to a much higher level of intelligence and tech than we do. What if Jesus was just "doing tech" instead of "doing miracles" in the Gospels? Have you ever thought of that?

Of course I had thought of that…and I had written about it several times before, showing how and why such a theory is theologically impossible after considering what the Bible says about them.

This story illustrates our aforementioned inclination to blame the paranormal for anything we don't *immediately* have an answer for, but there is an additional, underlying lesson in this example as well that begins with two important questions: Will the God of the Bible really someday be characterized as an alien among humans? And, if so: Will the Church be prepared to respond to such a claim, or are there people in the Church right this minute who will be deceived?

I personally believe the answer to both questions is, sadly, *yes*. (For the record, my friend and I had a phone call immediately after the text that cleared everything up on her end. Between my conversation with her and her doing a bit of digging through literature available by ministries that *dare* to address this subject with respect and compassion, she is now beside me as one who will be able to engage in this topic with others who have the same questions but who can't get answers in today's Church—the Church that incorrectly assumes there will never be a serious "ET religion" threat to contend with.)

Shortly after conversations with my friend, I was lying in bed one night, well into the process of falling asleep, thinking about this conversation about whether God could be an alien. In my mind's eye—which, I *must* clarify was only my human imagination in a mid-sleep drift and *not* a vision, sign from God, or anything supernatural at all—I saw something alarming. I was on my back, looking up from a first-person perspective, as three of the classic "alien greys" as depicted by Hollywood influences bent over me. They didn't say a word, and there was no telepathic communication with literal sentences like in many abduction accounts, but a message swelled in the air between us, inaudibly pressing the conclusion: "We are God. Humans have always had it wrong."

In this…"imagining" (if you will)…I tried to speak, but couldn't. I tried to jump up and make a dash for it, but my body wouldn't move. While I lay there, completely incapacitated, I began repeating the Name of Jesus in my mind—and *not* the "Jesus" of what the New Age circles call "Christ consciousness." I pled the blood of my personal Lord and New-Testament Savior over my mind, my body, and my soul, until imaginary me faded away and real me was in my bed next to my husband again, eyes open, wide awake, and covered in a thin layer of nervous sweat. (Thank God—literally—I was able to stop what was about to become a seriously disturbing dream that would no doubt strap me with frightening images not easily forgotten!)

Back to real life now, I started saying His Name in a whisper so as not to wake Mr. Howell. My thoughts very quickly moved on to something else, and I fell asleep. The next morning, after a cup of coffee and with a refreshed mind, I thought about the scene I had visualized the night before, and it drove me to pray about it off and on throughout the day. Although I'm not one to always think of everything as a sign, I wondered if the Lord was prompting me with a new outline for a book, so I emailed Tom Horn (CEO of Defender Publishing at the time). I explained what I had imagined the night before and how it evidently scared my subconscious to the point that I physically broke out in a sweat, and he agreed *this* book needed to be written. It's not enough that I had tackled whether the "alien Jesus" theory could be correct in past titles. I needed to produce one that directly addressed the issue—thus, the book you now read.

How many others—including staunchly faithful Christians—had imagined the same or a similar thing but without a theological understanding of why this kind of scene would inherently be a lie from the Enemy?

As stated earlier, I had written about this subject before. But you know what I hadn't yet done? Produced a book solely on the topic that tackled all three points: 1) God the Father, the Son, and the Holy Spirit are theologically incompatible with what we currently know to be aliens; 2) despite this, the world will soon embrace one or more members of the Trinity as aliens, as the world is currently being psychologically groomed to do; 3) such an embrace will be an eschatological deception of epic proportions, flipping the world of religious thought on its head and ushering in the "bad guys" as "gods" while the Church sleeps on the sidelines. Allie Anderson and Derek Gilbert joined me in this project to make this Tom Horn/Donna Howell outline a stronger, three-fold argument in light of Tom's passing.

As it stands in this moment: If you're a believing Christian, this question of whether the God of the Bible would be associated with aliens likely inspires a good, old-fashioned, throw-your-head-back-and-laugh response. And whereas that reaction in times past would have been understandable and common, we've already entered an era wherein this "alien God thing" can be considered a leading explanation of all events and teachings the Bible describes in its Old-Testament cosmological and New-Testament supernatural narratives. (This branch of study has even been assigned a name: "exotheology.")

Ask yourself this: If the lost suddenly did champion the theory that God is an alien, or is somehow directly associated with aliens, would you be able to provide a compassionate, learned response that could help them draw closer to God? If yes, then congratulations for making the souls of the lost *so* important that you would risk being seen among your peers as "on the fringe" while you tackled the "preposterous." The Lord will reward you for responding to the needs of real people with real thinking brains out there who are also doing the best they can to parse various "fringe" mysteries of the cosmos, just as the apostles did for the pagans around them who believed in the "preposterous" Greco-Roman pantheon and other "fringe" religions of the first century that appear bizarre to us now. The apostles never poked fun when their neighbors hailed the many-breasted goddess Artemis/Diana as the source of every successful hunting trip in the woods that provided meat on their tables for dinner. The apostles didn't gibe and sneer when the men and women they were sharing the Gospel of Christ with feared that words about this Jesus Messiah person might offend the listening ears of Priapus, the hermaphroditic (meaning both male and female) god of androgyny and abnormal sex. The apostles chose to remain approachable and kind when their listeners argued whether this Christ fellow's words about healing in His Name trumped those of Asclepius as they made clay molds of their own genitals as offerings hung from the ceiling of his sanctuaries and temples to rid themselves of sexually transmitted diseases.

Yet, the apostles were not "crazy" for maintaining an open ear to their neighbors about the true identity of the false gods and the lies that had been embraced regarding them in their time. For what would we do if we didn't have the New Testament in its current form, which is a product of the apostolic response? Are we—Donna Howell, Allie Anderson, and Derek Gilbert—"crazy" for keeping an open ear to and responding to *our* neighbors concerning the true identity of the false gods and the lies being embraced about them in *our* time? Despite the last twenty straight years of blasting insults from many in mainstream Christian circles asserting that we're wasting our time discussing peripheral topics within a minority group while a whole world of lost souls is in need of a Savior, we wholly believe the ET religion of *tomorrow* has already sprouted deep roots *today*, and what Christians so often assume to be a "minority" will become an enormous population in a very short time. This entire book points to repeat evidence of that, as a fact, and not only is this alien-God idea developing rapidly among secular theorists, a growing number of people currently identifying themselves as Christians are beginning to link the God of the Bible with aliens as well. If the terms "alien" and "extraterrestrial," stripped down to their most basic definitions, simply mean a being who dwells in some location apart from Earth's surface (a dangerous word game addressed in Chapter 4), then you can quickly see how this deception has, even now, begun to place its sticky, convoluted grip around the throat of sincere seekers. The glaring problem with that approach, however, is that it *will* associate the God of the Bible with contemporary cultural concepts of aliens, including (but not limited to) abductee testimonies, stories of crop circles, and the appearance of frightening and malevolent entities. (And if that was the connection we were attempting to make in this book or any others we've released on this topic, I would understand why naysayers and skeptics would respond harshly. Most harsh feedback we've historically received in this area has been from people who haven't read what our books are truly saying. They hear a Christian drop the word "alien" and, if the speaker isn't clearly poking fun, they are guilty of these associations by default—even when their goal is the same as that of the listener: to debunk these hazardous correlations.) No matter how hard one might try to responsibly draw a thick, solid line between our pop-cultural ideas and a true reflection of the God of the Bible, these two worlds between God and pop-culture aliens *will* collide, and many will be deceived...both the secular and the elect saints alike, as the Bible says (Matthew 24:24), whether or not any high-tech craft ever touches our soil.

Good luck finding the Bible verse that says, "Thus sayeth the Lord: 'Jesus isn't an alien.'" It doesn't exist. Meanwhile, the theories do exist; the Bible is *not* silent on the issue as many assume, and the souls who subscribe to the "alien God" theories are as precious to the Lord as anyone else.

To answer my own question: No, we are not "crazy." The writing is on the wall, and we're trying to avoid assuming, in that know-it-all tone so heavily associated with Christians, that these tough (and important!) questions are so ridiculous we can't be bothered to address them. Over and again, when the lost asked questions in New Testament times, those who set the grandest example of Christian love (just under Christ, Himself) responded with compassion, not ridicule, and every Christian who follows that standard is likewise showing compassion—regardless of whether doing so makes us look a certain way among the sheep of the fold. Winning popularity contests is a lost cause (Matthew 10:22); winning *souls* is a biblical command (1 Corinthians 9:19–23; Matthew 28:19). Consider the parable of the sower. I don't normally include longer quotations from Scripture in my books, but this instance is important enough that it is deemed worthy of taking a moment to absorb the fullness of what Christ taught:

> Behold, there went out a sower to sow: And it came to pass, as he sowed, some [seeds] fell by the way side, and the fowls of the air came and devoured it up. And some fell on stony ground, where it had not much earth; and immediately it sprang up, because it had no depth of earth: But when the sun was up, it was scorched; and because it had no root, it withered away. And some fell among thorns, and the thorns grew up, and choked it, and it yielded no fruit. And other fell on good ground, and did yield fruit that sprang up and increased; and brought forth, some thirty, and some sixty, and some an hundred. (Mark 4:3–8)

Like some readers who are perhaps less familiar with the Bible and Christ's teachings, the disciples didn't immediately understand the meaning of this parable, so they asked for clarification, and Jesus interpreted it for them:

> The sower soweth the word [the Gospel]. And these are they by the way side, where the word is sown; but when they have heard, Satan cometh immediately, and taketh away the word that was sown in their hearts. And these are they likewise which are sown on stony ground; who, when they have heard the word, immediately receive it with gladness; And have no root

in themselves, and so endure but for a time: afterward, when affliction or persecution ariseth for the word's sake, immediately they are offended. And these are they which are sown among thorns; such as hear the word, And the cares of this world, and the deceitfulness of riches, and the lusts of other things entering in, choke the word, and it becometh unfruitful. And these are they which are sown on good ground; such as hear the word, and receive it, and bring forth fruit, some thirtyfold, some sixty, and some an hundred. (Mark 4:14–20)

Some ministers of the Gospel are scattering seeds in quite shallow soil when it comes to the millions who wonder how aliens fit into the biblical worldview. Whereas it's true the Gospel holds power for all times and in all cultures, if it remains *unaddressed* by the Church, the word "aliens" may become the satanic voice that steals the truth from the hearts of some; the factor that causes the "immediate gladness" reception might stop short from rooting any deeper in rocky soil; or the distracting thorns that choke out fresh growth within a new/young believer might take hold. All it takes is one single Goodyear blimp to fly above a sports stadium, and everyone on the highway who believed in Christ five minutes prior will be tempted to think, *My pastor said aliens and UFOs don't exist, and the Bible says nothing about it…but I just saw one! Is it possible Christianity is wrong (or irrelevant)?*

We *must*—as witnesses of the Risen Christ—be prepared to respond to our culture's questions regarding the character and nature of God at all times, especially when those questions are related to subjects of the supernatural or paranormal. In this moment, there isn't a demand to explain how God is not a cat or dog…but if the telltale signs of secular society and culture were to produce evidence tomorrow that this was the latest trend in spirituality and/or syncretism (blending multiple religions into a customized amalgamation of beliefs for the individual who otherwise wouldn't follow a single religious system), then make no mistake: Tomorrow, Christians would be required to explain how God is not a cat or dog, and flippantly disregarding that need would be nothing less than shameful negligence of the very same people we've been called to love and minister to. We are called to be fishers of *all* people, including those whom most Christians perceive to be within the "minority."

Even then, the word "minority" in this application is no longer accurate. It's not just a few conspiracy theorists wearing tinfoil hats and living on military rations in a bunker in the middle of a desert wasteland anymore. The association between the God of the Bible and aliens as we know them is becoming one of the leading responses of the secular world in regard to how we all got here; even well-meaning folks who don't have an inflammatory or provocative bone in their body are finding this thread of thought a quite reasonable explanation for supernatural and cosmological events that regular humans cannot otherwise account for in the natural world.

Let's tackle one more item while we're on the subject: Why do Christians so fear opposing questions, anyway? Often, as I've observed, when Christians are confronted with a question or issue that doesn't immediately align with their own interpretation of the Bible, they tend to toss it away as total nonsense unworthy of a response (how arrogant!) or start reiterating common opinions of church members around them without even investigating the subject or what Scripture truly says about it. Laziness could certainly be the cause of such a reaction (if a Christian simply can't be bothered to participate in the Great Commission), as well as reverential fear (that their answer, or lack of one, might sway a person away from God), and likely several other potential explanations...but I believe the universal reason for avoiding uncomfortable discourse with folks who hold to beliefs we deem unusual (at least for Western Christians) is that it threatens our *traditions*. The beliefs each Christian holds are almost always some-how influenced by our background, which is a personal, human, and finite framework—*not* a divine one. God is divine and His Gospel is divine—of that there is certainly no doubt! But the big picture our traditions paint so long as we're stuck in this mortal coil can (and will) have errors in the final strokes within the picture's margins because

God's Holy Message is subject to such vastly differing interpretations. If we cling to "what pastor [so-and-so] said" or repeat the reaction offered from the Christian majority in that comfortable circle of fellow scoffers, we're *not* maintaining a readiness at all times to provide a gentle answer to seekers regarding what we believe the Bible says about who and what God is in relation to us. We are essentially donning a corporate attitude that says, "Let someone else figure it out and provide an answer," which goes against the teaching of 1 Peter 3:15.

According to Princeton Theological Seminary's 2024 report through the Overseas Ministries Study Center, there are more than forty-seven *thousand* Christian denominations in the world today![2] The essential doctrines of the Christian faith, as well as the identity of the Messiah and the work He came to do here on Earth, are the same throughout almost all of these denominations! It is only in their *human traditions* that they differ, and many have turned their back on an inquiring lost soul to protect these traditions from being challenged, even though the Bible identifies such an act as terribly wrong (Mark 7:7–13). (Having traditional beliefs is not innately wrong, as Paul stated in 2 Thessalonians 2:15, but abandoning nonbelievers for the sake of holding to those traditional beliefs is sinful, as the verses from Mark just referenced say in absolute terms.)

What is it about traditional interpretations of Scripture that must become the new sacred cow of our faith that cannot be touched or challenged? Is God the all-powerful or not? Is His Truth really *true* or not? Can we, like Elijah on Mt. Carmel (1 Kings 18:16–45), boldly *embrace* the challenges from the outside world and allow God to prove Himself to skeptics? Or does He need our help? Acts 17:24–25 makes it pretty clear that God doesn't need us to protect His Message, or what some would call His "religion." But, this only frees us from the obligatory feeling that God cannot provide whole Truth without our involvement. It does *not* free us from *sharing* that Truth. It is our duty to study the Word of God responsibly (2 Timothy 2:15) and confidently deliver it to others (Matthew 28:19–20), while we let Him take care of the rest (Isaiah 41:13; Luke 1:37).

Furthermore, if God's Word is true, then it's true no matter what is discovered, observed, or believed by finite humans, anyway. What's the worst thing that could happen if one were to confront their own traditions in pursuit of providing answers to others whose beliefs or worldview is different? One quick example of this is science. I can't count how many times I've seen that classic, nervous look exhibited on the face of a fellow believer when someone outside the Church questions the Bible's validity in light of human scientific discovery and progress. (Don't get me started on the age of the Earth…however, if that's something you're interested in, I just published a book last year alongside Dr. Thomas Horn addressing this very issue. It's called *Before Genesis*, and one of our chief goals in writing that book was to show how the evidence overwhelmingly stacks in favor of the harmony between science and theology, but seeing that harmony requires us to set aside our traditions!) The key word here is "human," meaning imperfect and flawed. At their very core—after setting aside all human errors that arose during the gathering and reporting phases of scientific observation—science and religion do *not* clash. They cannot disagree, because God created the Earth and everything on it, including the men and women who approach scientific observations in the first place. He is *the* God over science, the Master Scientist (as *Before Genesis* continually credits Him to be), and since He cannot disagree with Himself, we're ultimately not as threatened by science as many of my fellow believers thought we were as I grew up in the Church. So, the worst thing that could happen while questioning our own traditions is finding our traditions inferior to truth and thus growing all the more in God's Truth!

That's a *good* thing, isn't it? I personally want that, and I imagine you do, too, so where is the threat? Why put off being more enlightened about who God *really* is and what His Word *really* says just to hold to a lifestyle that won't last longer than a vanishing vapor in the light of eternity anyway, as James 4:14 identifies?

I beseech you, readers and listeners, to sincerely let the following sentence sink in:

Don't fear the "crazy people" who ask "crazy questions"; fear NOT having the answer to those questions while a soul hangs in the balance.

I, for one, want to hear my sweet Father say, "Well done, My good and faithful servant" (Matthew 25:23), not, "I put hundreds of lost and wandering souls in your path and you failed to reach any of them because you were too stuck in your own limited denominational/interpretational traditions that you refused to help My children."

Yikes. Talk about a "wet the pants" moment. (Dear Lord, please let me always be available to reach Your people!)

But if your answer to my earlier query about your ability to provide an informed answer to the lost about God and aliens was *no*, this book may be more important to your ministry (personal or professional) than you thought.

With that in mind, let's take a look at where we might be headed in light of the coming alien deception, the recent shift toward widespread belief in aliens, and how suitably this all fits into Antichrist's end-times schema.

CHAPTER 2

YESTERDAY'S ABSURDITY: TOMORROW'S EMBRACED DECEPTION

By Donna Howell

The majority of the non-Christian world could be separated into categories ranging from a) those who are skeptical of everything that smells of the paranormal/supernatural and instead grab the first natural-cause explanation for everything that occurs, no matter how unbelievable, to b) those who tend to accept/embrace any extraterrestrial or ancient astronaut theory as an explanation for what humans always historically interpreted to be God, and c) everywhere in between those extremes.

Consider the shift in society's consideration of the topic.

Only decades ago, a vast majority of people across the globe would have landed in the first category (skepticism), while, more recently, the second category (acceptance) has inflated to unthinkable proportions in only a short time. According to the statistical analysis group, *Statista*, in a survey examining one thousand Americans in 2022, the number of people willing to accept that any unidentified aircraft is of alien origin has increased from 20 percent in 1996 to 34 percent in 2022, while just under 60 percent of *all* respondents affirmed their belief in extraterrestrial intelligent life in general.[3] The Pew Research Center also weighed in on this topic in a survey conducted just before the US government's assessment of alien life in 2021. Their findings similarly testify that 65 percent of adults in America believe in extraterrestrial life in general, and 51 percent admit to the belief that military-reported UFO sightings might be evidence of life on other planets (11 percent said they "definitely" were), while 46 percent of all respondents believe they are of some level of threat to US national security. The report goes on to show that the largest demographic to embrace theories of extraterrestrial intelligent life is young Americans between the ages of eighteen to twenty-nine,[4] supporting the idea that these numbers will only increase even more in coming generations when these young people raise their children to have minds equally open to that possibility. Meanwhile, according to the National UFO Reporting Center, as reported through *Statista*, the number of global sightings of unidentified flying objects has dramatically increased, along with progressive improvements in and ready public access to more advanced observation technology (such as cellphone cameras). We had merely 346 reported UFO sightings to fear in 1990—a sum that climbed to a staggering 8,779 by the year 2015; a dip in this activity occurred between then and now, but by 2022, we were back up to 5,035 sightings per year and climbing.[5]

Of course, all these reports, statistics, and ruminations assume we will not be confronted with a future visitation by these beings, for if our planet Earth did—irrefutably and undeniably—become the landing pad for extraterrestrials, it would no longer be a matter of whether we believe in their existence, but what we make of who they are and what they want.

Will extraterrestrials eventually land on our turf to invade?

That depends on what exactly that question means. If we're asking whether the Hollywood aliens of such films as *Independence Day* starring Will Smith are on their way down, we don't believe that for a second. Now that *is* preposterous! But, if we're asking whether something incredibly wicked will one day arrive from the great "out there" and malignantly influence our world toward great evil, then we not only believe that to be a true and imminent possibility, but we also believe the Bible's teachings show they've *already been here*, and a someday return is a near guarantee, though they will not be anything close to what our current society imagines when the word "alien" is spoken. Christians don't question whether demons would ever be present here (both historically and currently), as the Bible is clear on that matter, so why do we so often dismiss the idea that something demonic/satanic from the place called "space" would ever be present here—especially when such a scenario would play so perfectly into the eschatological events foretold in the book of Revelation?

Read on. The entities we refer to as "aliens" are more related to the subject of demons than most think.

But just because a growing majority in the Western world is rapidly coming to a belief in aliens doesn't necessarily mean they will automatically someday confuse them with God...right?

Not so fast. It is the opinion of these authors that this is exactly what people will do—and the speed at which they embrace that connection will increase if or when reports of extraterrestrial activity (visitations, good, bad, or spiritual; abductions, etc.) likewise increase.

Though many voices cloud the proverbial aliens-and-God discussion board with conflicting speculations and opinions, in general, public concern for what the theoretical arrival of aliens to Earth would do to human religions (including, and *especially*, Christianity) tends to boil down to two perceivable scenarios: 1) we revisit theology in light of confirmed extraterrestrial intelligence and adapt as needed, providing answers (including interpretations of Scripture) as to who/what they are, how they fit into the ancient past (involving theological interaction with Christianity's Creation narrative from Genesis), and what that means for us in modernity; 2) we abandon all earthly religions and their historical interpretations in trade for whatever these beings claim to be truth, while either figuratively or literally worshipping them as all-knowing gods in the meantime (what many will do, we believe).

At this point in our consideration of these groups, many of our conservative readers likely just thought, *I would absolutely never abandon my belief in Christ—even if our planet was bombarded by aliens over- night!* And we agree. However, specific to those brave—and few and far between—Christian voices who are a) willing to entertain discourse on this subject in the first place, and b) confident their conservative faith and values systems would remain steadfast upon the arrival of interga- lactic visitors, the question becomes *how* we might adapt our theology of Christ and the Godhead to fit with the confirmed presence of non- human entities from space. Within this sphere, we likewise often see a split between two interpretations: 1) aliens cannot be anything but evil for fill-in-the-blank reasons (many of which are valid and will be discussed throughout this book); and 2) because all things were created by God (Colossians 1:16–17), the alien visitors were an equal part of His creation, and though they may, like humans, have a history of their own regarding how they interacted with the tension between God and Satan or good and evil, they should be embraced as fellow creations of God and therefore siblings in this temporal realm we call "life."

The questions this latter approach forces upon Bible scholars are immense, but the overwhelming majority of folks tend to begin with the following basic ponderings: What does that mean for redemption? Did Christ have to die on other planets as well, or was the gift of redemption solely for humanity's benefit and not for that of the "little green men"? And if Christ's sacrifice *was* for humankind alone, does this render aliens unredeemable and damned? *If so,* how is that fair to them? How could our fair and loving God create beings that never have a chance to be saved?

(Spoiler alert: God *did not* create aliens…at least not in the form people believe them to be in now. That warped form, assuming it's real when it is spotted and not therefore a hallucination or fabrication, was of their own doing. Certainly, it's true that God created all things perfectly and beautifully *in the beginning* [Colossians 1:16; John 1:1–5], but when sin entered the picture and warped what He first intended to exist, we should never claim God was responsible.)

Or…could it be that they never fell in the first place? That would *either* make them morally perfect (a theological disaster on unthinkable counts—see Romans 8:19–23) or creatures who were never designed with intrinsic free will, because the introduction of sin into our universe occurred as an exercise of free will in the Garden of Eden in the first place. Since every other intelligent creature God ever made has demonstrated free will, it must be that they either *are* inheritors of redemption in some way/capacity, theorists say, or they are, in fact, morally perfect…and, therefore, they are like gods themselves. It is the latter of these two conclusions I fear the most, as I see humanity is already well beyond the beginning phases of embracing a demonic, alien, ET religion that *will* bring Jesus Christ into view as a god-alien who wore a human-flesh suit during the events of the New Testament narrative.

Alien religions are nothing new. Aside from a growing number of people who don't belong to any official group but who ascribe to the ancient astronaut or panspermia theories (which view life as having been "seeded" from another planet), spiritual alien cults have already risen up to draw in many followers in the recent past, including, but not limited to, organized cults that rely on mystical, human-history revelations delivered through extraterrestrial contact, including (but not limited to) the following:

- Swedenborgianism, founded by Emanuel Swedenborg after he astral projected to Mars, Venus, Saturn, and Jupiter to confer with spirit-beings;
- Theosophy, as taught by the mother of New Ageism and the popular I AM movement, Helena P. Blavatsky, whose body and voice were completely surrendered to the control of the "Lords of the Flame" (giants from Venus) while they "channeled" insight regarding the mysteries of the universe

through speech and automatic writing (a movement that carried on through many sub-cults and is highly active today in New Age circles involving members who often don't know the roots of their practice);

- The Urantia Foundation, founded by a psychiatric doctor who recorded the utterings of one of his patients (called "trance-channeling"), which claims to be the most accurate source of both theology and human history in its teachings regarding the "seven trillion inhabited planets and many gods";

- The FIGU Society, founded by Eduard ("Billy") Albert Meier, one of seven leading prophets in the society whose "Contact Notes" apparently originated through telepathic conversation with extraterrestrials in Switzerland claiming the historical Jesus never existed (ignoring much from the colossal stack of evidence in support of Him);

- The International Raelian Movement, founded by Claude Vorilhon, who has successfully gained "tens of thousands of international followers" through perpetuating his panspermic teachings that life was seeded on Earth by extraterrestrial "Elohims" (plural of the Hebrew *Elohim*, an Old-Testament name of God), as Vorilhorn's telepathic contact with an alien established in 1973;

- The Unarius Academy of Science, founded by Ernest and Ruth Norman following Ernest's telepathic conversations with "Space Brothers" in the 1950s who confirmed reincarnation and humanity's current need for past-life psychotherapy to "awaken the individual to previous life encounters, the clairvoyant aptitude of the mind, and the reality of one's spiritual connection";

- The Aetherius Society, launched in London by quasi-New-Ageist George King, whose teachings, originally stemming from the telepathic "Cosmic Masters," claim that Jesus, following His Resurrection, moved to Venus.[6]

The chief difference between these groups and those I believe will rise tomorrow boils down to size and following. Religions like these have historically elicited jests and jeers while the adherents are viewed as either lacking in some area of their sanity or willingly participating in nonsense (whatever motive they may have had in doing so, such as to exploit other cult members, or what have you). But the alien religion of tomorrow will posture itself as the answer to every universal mystery, including key events from the Bible, because they will, like the *nachash* in the Garden of Eden who tempted Adam and Eve, carry *some* truth in addition to the lies while the lies can be fluid and malleable, responding almost immediately to any curious question one might think to ask a leader who is "in contact" with the beings who hold every answer. (Would you expect anything else from a religion built on constant incoming telepathic messages?)

Don't scoff just yet. I'm not alone in my observations, and, as I said above, it's not only the "tinfoil-hat crowd" that sees the writing on the wall in this regard.

Despite having earned himself the (unsurprising) reputation by his peers of being an eccentric for his willingness to engage in discourse on the subject of extraterrestrial life (and who wouldn't be at *this* moment in time, while "aliens" are still considered a hypothetical reality?), one example of a well-educated individual who views humanity's eventual embrace of an alien God is astrophysicist, cosmologist, and Harvard professor Avi Loeb. In a filmed interview with *Fox News*, as shared in the article, "Harvard Physicist Searching for UFO Evidence Says Humanity Will View Alien Intelligence Like 'God,'" Loeb says: "A very advanced scientific [extraterrestrial] civilization is a good approximation to God because: Just imagine a cave-dweller visiting New York City and seeing all the gadgets and technology in terms of the lights appearing as a miracle to the cave-dweller, so a higher level of intelligence may not be easily understandable to us." He goes on to use Moses' account of the burning bush in the Old Testament as an example of how we might interpret something as a supernatural act of God when it otherwise had a perfectly natural, scientific explanation (such as the surface temperature of Moses' bush and the energy emitted from it instead of miraculous fire).

"You can imagine," Loeb says, "that a superhuman [or alien] civilization that understands how to unify quantum mechanics and gravity might actually be able to create a baby universe in the laboratory—a quality that we assign to God in religious texts."

The video ends with Loeb's endorsement of seeking a higher intelligence than that which we have here, on our own planet, Earth.[7]

Scientific American ran a similar story, sharing first the third law of fiction writer Arthur C. Clarke's popular three laws (regarding the future of science and humankind)—"Any sufficiently advanced technology is indistinguishable from magic"—as evidence for why humanity will view "members of such a civilization [i.e., aliens]…as a pretty good approximation to God."[8] In other words, humanity will be so inferior to this intelligence that we will see the wonders these beings produce and—*regardless of whether those wonders are legitimate miracles or merely advanced technology we don't yet possess*—view them as godlike. From there, it's only a small leap to start attributing the identity of Christ (and possibly also the Father and the Holy Spirit) to extraterrestrials.

But aside from having just diluted the miracle of God speaking through fire in Moses' burning-bush experience, Loeb is onto something. If we imagine ourselves, as he suggests, as mere metaphorical cave dwellers introduced to the tech of New York City when imagining our future reactions to extraterrestrials, it all clicks into place…and it's not even clever. It's obvious. A being could appear tomorrow performing signs and wonders that look like those performed by Christ in the New Testament, illustrate supremacy over the laws of nature, claim to be God in the flesh (or claim to be working on His behalf), and many people (including Christians) would be hard-pressed to come up with evidence to refute the being's assertions. How could we? What proof would we have that the being is *not* God or Christ, perhaps outside of the Holy Spirit's voice internally warning us (which will matter little to folks in the outside world who are not in tune to His voice)? Since we don't have a long history of studying where that kind of power could have come from via science or technology and have always viewed those categories of demonstrations as "miracles" only God is capable of (demonic supernatural activity aside), we would be as ignorant as babes. And what if everything this being did was interpreted as good and beneficial for humanity?

While we're on the subject, let's take it a step further and imagine how we would interpret a great leader who appears on the scene in, say, Israel/Jerusalem, carrying out great wonders of healing, resurrecting of the dead, and exhibiting authority over lightning, thunder, winds, and natural laws like gravity. As he leads and shares his incredible ideas with humankind, he provides an answer to the maladies that have long plagued our history and teaches us how to *finally* restore peace in those areas, such as world hunger, war, poverty, terrorism, human trafficking, persecution of all kinds, drug cartels, international migration and border issues, matters of public safety, and healing of disease and pandemics. He even instructs us how to eradicate "fake news" from our society so everyone will at last "receive only the truth, always" from all service media outlets. Overnight, earthly governments begin to apply his world-fixing objectives and, lo and behold, they prove to actually work!—not just in theory and on paper, but in application. Never before have we seen a leader like this...and every country on the globe is all in. Whatever *that guy* says goes, because he is providing, at lightning speed, reparations our fallen nature has never been able to produce, while commanding the storms to cease. Just imagine.

Then, when he has gained our trust on a global scale, uniting all governments toward a common goal for the good of humanity, he just happens to share that he is *also* God, Himself, and always has been. He explains that all world religions are essentially telling the same story; Islam, Hinduism, Christianity, Judaism, along with *all* of their denominations and sects, and even influential philosophies (that folks often call "religions") such as Buddhism, are all pointing to one and the same God (a perfect example of the fallacy of syncretism). Contradictions between these belief systems are expertly washed away as he calmly and gently visits the Holy Bible alongside all other sacred texts of the world, explaining how the only incompatibilities between them are only *perceived* inconsistencies—a matter of finite, human (and therefore faulty) interpretation. If you look at them the way he does, they suddenly fit together and unify into a big picture: All this time, every religion among humankind had been describing *him*. (Think back to the last time you heard a verse taken extremely out of context and saw an entire community of people accept that teaching as the "teacher" expressed it; then, you will start to see this scenario is not at all implausible. There always will be folks who follow false leaders, as there always have been. It boils down to which false teachers tell the most sensible stories, and the one who can tell such stories while illustrating miraculous power will get the attention of even the hardest skeptics.)

At the same time, this leader also shows the error of our interpretations regarding concepts of "aliens" or "extraterrestrials." It was *us*—the humans who have been limited both in our intelligence and in our powers of comprehension—who came up with terms like "little green men" and "the greys." He will say *we* were those who mistook these "creatures of outer space" as merely another civilization of life on other planets when, this whole time, they were the angels of the Bible (or the spiritual beings of other world religions) who ministered to humanity just like our holy books describe. And when the Bible says Jesus performed many signs, miracles, and wonders, it was true all along—but Jesus was actually an alien in a human-flesh suit, and He even spoke of His extraterrestrial brethren in Luke 21:25–26, when men's hearts fail them from the fear of "things which are coming on the earth." Jesus' miracles and healings were expert tech, the being from the sky might say; His Resurrection was the reanimation of otherworldly body tissues we can't begin to wrap our brains around even in the most advanced human laboratories, as their biology is not governed by the same earthly laws as our own; His Ascension into the heavens in front of the apostles was simply a demonstration of His authority over gravity until He could reach the craft He would then ride to the right hand of the Father—our human word for the Uber Alien of the Skies. It wouldn't matter if it were truth or lies; an explanation for everything we attribute to Jesus could be wrapped up in this "theological response to who God really is."

So far in this rumination, your mind has probably filled in the blanks on what this guy looks like, and perhaps you pictured him as human—and though he may have chosen to appear in that form and then remain that way so as not to alarm us at his appearance (as I imagine he likely would, considering the implications of Daniel 7:20), he wouldn't necessarily have to. If he shows up on the scene claiming to come in peace to bless us all, fix all of our problems, and repair our world, in the long-term, who would care if he admitted he was what we had always interpreted aliens to be and looked different from us? If his head was bulging from a giant brain, if his eyes were bigger than ours and black as night, if his skin was grey...heck, if he outright announced that he was a Zeta Reticulan, what would that matter to the secular mind in light of the healing and goodness that he would be bringing to us? By this time, many people would believe he was some kind of savior, or *the* Savior, Jesus, who "came back, just as He said." This leader would have so much support he could usher in a legion of other beings as his advisors and our superiors, and it wouldn't matter if the whole lot of them looked like alien greys, bipedal reptilians, or insectoids. As frightening as it might have been at any other time in our planet's history to see droves of bizarre creatures marching up on the White House lawn for a State of the Union address or gathering in the holiest landmarks of Israel for a power-hour of prayer, by this point, we would have been groomed to accept that they *do* come in peace and they *do* represent only goodness for us always, regardless of a past and primitive fear of the unknown or whether or not a spaceship is involved in their arrival.

As to the true identity of this being and any others he brought along with him: Would they be who they said they were? Or would they be satanic?

If you've read the book of Revelation and believe what it says, then you already know we're going to see the manifestation of all kinds of spiritual and supernatural activity in the last days, and they will be otherworldly. The biblical Antichrist and False Prophet of Revelation will do for world politics and social issues just what I have described to this point, and do so in the "angel of light" fashion. As I wrote in a previous work, *Dark Covenant*:

A deceiver would be far more convincing if he, like Satan, appeared as "an angel of light" (2 Corinthians 11:14).... Antichrist will be a man, but he'll also be the "seed of the serpent" (Genesis 3:15). Just as Christ was (and is) the Son of God, Antichrist will be the son of Satan. Therefore, just as the Son of God exercises power from His Father in heaven (Matthew 9:6, 8; 21:23ff; 26:64; 28:18–19; Daniel 7:14), so, too, will Antichrist receive his power from his father in hell (Revelation 13:2, 4). Nothing about his intelligence will be limited to a single lifetime or one mere man's powers of articulation. As he will be filled with the unbridled influence of all the authority in hell, Antichrist's capabilities of misleading the masses and appearing as an "angel of light" will result in his display of *ultimate*:

- **Speaking presence:** "There was given unto him a mouth speaking great things" (Revelation 13:5); "and a mouth speaking great things" (Daniel 7:8); and "a mouth that spake very great things" (Daniel 7:20).
- **Political power:** "Ten kings...shall give their power and strength unto the beast...and give their kingdom unto the beast" (Revelation 17:12–13, 17; cf. Daniel 9:27).
- **Military command:** "The beast, and the kings of the earth, and their armies, gathered together to make war" (Revelation 19:19).
- **Earthly wealth and extravagance:** "A god whom his fathers knew not shall he honour with gold, and silver, and with precious stones, and pleasant things" (Daniel 11:38).

- **Economic policies and organization:** "And the merchants of the earth are waxed rich through the abundance of [Antichrist's city, Babylon's] delicacies"; "The merchandise of gold, and silver, and precious stones, and of pearls, and fine linen, and purple, and silk, and scarlet, and all thyine wood, and all manner vessels of ivory, and all manner vessels of most precious wood, and of brass, and iron, and marble, And cinnamon, and odours, and ointments, and frankincense, and wine, and oil, and fine flour, and wheat, and beasts, and sheep, and horses, and chariots, and slaves, and souls of men...[and involving] all things which were dainty and goodly...[and] ships...[and] trade by sea...[and] harpers, and musicians, and...pipers, and trumpeters...[and] craftsmen" (Revelation 18:3, 12–17, 22).

- **Persuasion in self-aggrandizement:** "And he shall exalt himself...and shall prosper" (Daniel 11:36).

- **Patient, successful oppression of God's people:** "And shall wear out the saints of the most High, and think to change times and laws: and they shall be given into his hand" (Daniel 7:25).

  On top of all of this, he's going to be tremendously attractive, with features so appealing that the Word says he will be better looking than any of "his fellows" (Daniel 7:20).[9]

The only part in this theoretical future alien-Antichrist scenario the Bible doesn't directly spell out for us is whether he, his False Prophet, and his other wicked subordinates might associate themselves with our historical concepts of extraterrestrial entities in any capacity. My opinion is that Antichrist will be so motivated to deceive he will say *anything* he has to (possibly including a connection to our concepts of aliens) to lead the masses in a way that serves his satanic agenda. He will be so convincing in his deception he could remove a mask and be a giant beetle, and, so long as he remains more fascinating and/or appealing than "his fellows," he could still be Antichrist and nobody would care.

Under no circumstances am I suggesting this is an exact picture of the end-times scenario we'll someday face. What I *am* suggesting is that Antichrist will do and say whatever he must in order to deceive the largest number of listeners at once, and if it serves his purpose to put an alien spin on everything he says in a day and age when humankind is so heavily obsessed with extraterrestrial intelligence, then it's a no-brainer he would capitalize on that opportunity and pull the age-old "I come in peace" schtick…*regardless* of what skins or forms he and his minions choose to wear or appear in. If he, like Loeb said, continues to assume "qualit[ies] that we assign to God in religious texts," he can claim to be God and do so successfully, just as the Bible describes (2 Thessalonians 2:4; Matthew 24:24).

And if crowds and crowds of people see a Goodyear blimp and immediately believe it to be an alien spacecraft, how much more willing would they be to accept an alien-God explanation behind all the stories in the Bible if one were to appear with vast intelligence and claim that very thing with powers of articulate deception in development since before Earth's birthday?

But whether you are personally among a) those who believe this all to be possible or b) those who believe everything I've just written is pure science-fiction hullabaloo, one thing is certain: The Bible does say, from our race's earliest ages, the surface of our planet has been visited by inhuman beings, including God's angels and satanic entities. Just short of picking and choosing which passages of Scripture we believe and which ones we don't, or interpreting away anything that requires a supernatural worldview to believe—both of which are highly incompatible with a biblical worldview (our Lord, Christ, Himself, was born of a virgin, so good luck believing the Bible apart from a supernatural worldview)—we have little choice but to admit Earth has always been a "landing pad" for beings who did not originate here. Assuming we're agreed up to that point, the leap from such terms as "angels" and "demons" that describe these inhuman beings to such terms as "aliens" and "extraterrestrials" isn't such a wide chasm when tomorrow's lies accumulate. Recognizing the "good guys" from the "bad guys" in the context of otherworldly visitors is a crucial detail requiring far more than a game of semantics. Obviously, having a personal relationship with the Risen Christ and the Holy Spirit marked by spiritual maturity and recognizing His voice will result in that gut-wrenching "uh oh" feeling when our eyes land on something evil. But for the *droves* of people who will not have that kind of discernment in the end of days, the forthcoming alien religion (likely embedded with an alien-Jesus twist) will be a true problem. Our history is rife with tales of gods or heavenly visitors who came from space or the heavenlies to live among humans, just like the Sumerian Anunnaki (which, interestingly enough, appeared most often in a snakelike form, as reflected in stone throughout uncountable ancient archeological sites around the world).

Although it helps strengthen my case to cite from such scholars as Professor Loeb regarding the probability that people will someday confuse our Christian God with some "über alien," truth be told, we don't even need fancy intellectuals with a bunch of letters after their names to see that as a very real, looming possibility. Many in the Church would laugh at the notion that demons, fallen angels, or any other wicked and malevolent beings would arrive on our planet in the form of intelligent visitors from space and bring us unfathomable knowledge with a hidden agenda of drawing humanity away from God. Why? Because they don't believe evil entities would do such a thing? No. Because a great number of Christians *don't even believe aliens do, or ever could, exist.*

Paradoxically, neither do I—at least not in the traditional, cultural, Hollywood-alien sense; I don't believe in what the world and society are referring to when they casually drop the word "aliens," because I believe they are what the Bible describes the fallen angels to be... and, like my coauthors and countless scholars deeply entrenched in addressing exotheological concepts, I *do not* believe "the Bible is silent on this," as so many have said.

CHAPTER 3

BACK TO THE ANCIENT "ALIEN" BASICS

By Donna Howell

Historically, the terms "aliens" and "extraterrestrials" have referred to quite a Hollywood-boogeyman idea. They hover through the dark skies, land in giant wheat fields to make circles for some apparently symbolic reason, creep through our windows, abduct us in the night to perform wild experiments on our bodies, and so on. (By the way, regarding crop circles, many expert ufologists, including Jenny Randles and Peter Hough, authors of *The Complete Book of UFOs*, have repetitiously stated they are a hoax or, at the very least, have nothing to do with alien activity.[10]) We tend to always view them as traveling between planets in their disc-shaped crafts, as if, when they have finished with us on Earth, they get in their craft and fly straight home the way we would drive home from work. In the back of our minds, as influenced by cultural models, we accept that they aren't always necessarily inherently good or evil by our standards; they're just another race living and surviving the way we do, making good or bad decisions based on their superior intelligence and their own moral criteria and patterns of behavior as developed on their home planet. If one *were* to encounter an intelligent race from another world, *including* that invisible, unseen realm from which demonic entities frequently come, we expect they could either be good/benevolent or wicked/malevolent, but whichever the case, it's based on our own concepts of a moral construct as well as early-age nurturing. Of course, I can understand why that would be the general assumption, because, out of all non-machine entities in the currently known universe, human beings are uniquely gifted with *reason*, an attribute the animal and the machine cannot intrinsically possess, though another natural/biological being of intelligence would, and arrive at that position in the same or similar fashion as we have, we assume. Therefore, we compare them to our reality perhaps a little more than we should: We think of "aliens" and believe them to be born into a world of free will, and *reason* suggests choosing right or wrong as they develop in their own extraterrestrial societies and cultures. Even subconsciously, we consider them as individuals whose lives play out as ours do: Two "adult" aliens bring a baby alien into existence, and that little "person" begins to perceive the world one step at a time, gradually learning through trial and error and eventually reaching adulthood, when their decisions reflect their upbringing and experiences through emotional and psychological growth and development. When they've matured, they congregate into factions and communities with varying movements and goals. Perhaps they have among them humanitarian groups striving to end poverty or world hunger, shining as bright examples of charity and morality while others among them provoke regional wars or maintain powerful but corrupted chairs of government. Those who abduct humans from Earth are "the bad guys," while the "good guys" are the benevolent angels of space capable of bringing us unthinkable wisdom and knowledge.

Unfortunately, this is not a story of the "Bible tells me so" variety as much as it is a cartoon.

But in order to attempt to conceptualize what aliens truly are, we first have to start over with a blank slate—one uncontaminated by human-conceived and Hollywood-perpetuated perceptions from the past. As I teased at the end of the previous chapter, despite the mainstream narrative of the Church that believes the Bible is silent on the topic (other than some who view Ezekiel 1 to be a description of a UFO, which it isn't, as Allie and Derek later point out), I believe what we've historically interpreted as "space aliens" have been something quite evil the Bible has always transparently addressed. Just because the Bible doesn't come right out and say, "Once upon a time there were these little green men called 'aliens,'" doesn't mean it says nothing about them in its original languages. (Excuse my sarcasm, but you simply wouldn't believe the insane number of times I've heard fellow Bible-believers say aliens don't and can't exist because the Bible doesn't address them. Sadly, that assumption most frequently accomplishes two negative feats: 1) It fails to provide an answer for the precious souls who sincerely believe they've encountered alien activity in their lives and wish to know what that means regarding their Christian faith; and 2) it perpetuates the incorrect notion that Christianity is irrelevant to the topic of extraterrestrials and, therefore, if we ever begin to see convincing evidence of alien existence, Christianity either goes out the window completely or we're left with the only Christological response the mainstream has yet provided—and Jesus is, once again, brought into view as an alien savior. Of equal importance regarding eschatology: Many scholars have taught that the Rapture of the Church will result in a literal Tim LaHaye and Jerry B. Jenkins *Left Behind* scenario. All true believers disappear in an instant, leaving the rest of the planet to figure out where we've gone. Some who remain will recall previous teachings about the Rapture and instantly regret their former disbelief, but others will offer up alternative theories. If all of these scholars who see a literal, "left-behind" scenario are correct, "mass alien abduction" will be an easy explanation in that day, and trust me when I say those infused with the Antichrist spirit *will* find a way of weaving it all together with the exotheological claims of the "gods from space" in a way that glorifies them.)

For the sake of readers who may be just joining the conversation and for whom all of this is brand-new information (or in case someone out there needs a refresher), I will take a moment to briefly cover the basics. (For more in-depth analysis, see any of the number of previous Defender Publishing and SkyWatch Television titles that exhaustively tackle this topic.)

For a moment, imagine you've never considered the possibility that these beings exist and this is the first time you're hearing about them. Wipe out all the bulging heads, giant black eyes, reptilian/insectoid humanoids, and even the perfectly human-looking Nordic concepts from your mind. Forget about two aliens falling in love, having a baby, and raising it toward right or wrong, good or evil, and imagine the following story instead. (Also note that I'm attempting to keep one clean voice throughout the following several paragraphs, so have addressed some of the opposing arguments in the endnotes. Check them out if you're curious about where we got our information or if you're interested in others' views regarding the events of the fallen angels early in humanity's history. Likewise, though I've chosen to keep the references in the following few pages strictly canonical, please note that the apocryphal Book of Enoch *also* tells this story, merging with the biblical passages noted. Despite Enoch's eventual exclusion from the canon, many Jewish rabbis and modern Bible scholars alike still attest to the legitimacy of that account.)

Long ago, before the first human was ever formed, God created angels (Nehemiah 9:6; Psalm 148:2, 5; Job 38:4–7; 1 Peter 3:22; Colossians 1:15–16), and He instilled within them the priceless gift of free will so they would be permitted to choose their own fate. They were amazing and majestic beings, and God's affection for them was so great He called them His "sons."[11] A portion of these angels rose up against their Creator, convincing themselves they could be like (or better than) the Most High (Jude 1:6; 2 Peter 2:4; Matthew 25:41; Revelation 12:7–9; Luke 10:18). They formed a plan to usurp His rule, but they drastically miscalculated God's power and authority. Because of their rebellion, they were kicked out of their first home in the heavens, becoming fallen (Jude 1:6).

God then formed another race of creatures called humans (Genesis 1–2), giving them the gift of free will as well, along with the power of reproduction. These humans were designed to inhabit and populate Earth with their kind (Genesis 1:28).

One fateful day—despite the perfect garden God had provided for them in paradise, complete with every imaginable liberty and blessing—the humans foolishly listened to the lies of one leading fallen angel of old who visited them and deceived them into believing they, too, could be like God. When the humans turned their backs on God and rebelled, they fell as the angels before them, taking on an internal ugliness that affected everything around them, sending their home and all that existed upon it into a state of decay and death (Genesis 3). Throughout several future human generations (Genesis 5), beginning with their first son, Cain, evil erupted everywhere, introducing into the human race such vile acts of wickedness as murder and war-making (Genesis 4).

Though some humans followed the ways of their Creator God, many chose to follow the ways of His usurpers. When the fallen angels appeared amidst the human community, they copulated with human women, producing part-fallen-angel, part-human hybrid offspring known as the Nephilim (meaning "fallen ones"; Genesis 6). Enormous, monolithic stones rife with intricate carvings of the fallen angels were raised in the cities as an act of worship toward the heaven-exiled angels,[12] who perpetuated among humanity the lie that they were *like* God. Before long, the people began to view the evil angels *as* gods. The Almighty God and Creator, in His righteousness, cleansed the fallen-angel/human hybrid Nephilim from Earth's surface by bringing a global Flood, sparing only a righteous man named Noah and his family, whose blood had not been contaminated by the intermingling of fallen-angel DNA (Genesis 6–9). The fallen angels who originally participated as fathers in these unholy sexual unions with human women were bound, confined away from humankind, at least until the end-times judgment (2 Peter 2:4–5; Jude 1:6–7). Once the floodwaters had subsided, Noah and his family worked to repopulate the Earth with humanity once again through many generations (Genesis 10).

All human beings at this time spoke the same language. Those who had abandoned God used this perfect communication to work together to build a tower up to the heavens to exalt themselves in the same wicked spirit exhibited by the angels before them. In response, God confused the people's languages and sent them to various places all over the Earth, dividing them up within boundaries and appointing supervisors over them from the angels who had not participated in the earlier hybridization of angel and man (Genesis 11; Deuteronomy 32:8). But, like their brothers before them, these angels eventually rose against God as well (Psalm 82; see especially verse 8).

Another leading interpretation of Genesis 6, most often called the "Sethite view," claims these passages speak of the relationships the human descendants of Seth had with the daughters of Israel. That argument has been exhaustively tackled in many of our books already, as well as in many other books by Hebrew scholars outside Defender Publishing, so we won't visit the issue at length here. But, for a quick overview of the holes this approach creates, suffice it to say the Sethite view: 1) requires dismantling the supernatural worldview the Old Testament regularly applies to other elements of this narrative, rendering inconsistent application to sound biblical interpretation; 2) raises many more questions than it answers; and 3) still doesn't explain the origin of the Nephilim or giants in this area of Scripture that do not fit the description of the "only good" creation credited to God's doing (Genesis 1:31).

Meanwhile, as to the leading argument against the angel/human hybrids, which is rooted in Matthew 22:28–30 (Christ's teaching that the angels "in heaven" do not marry)—it's important to remember the context of this passage is a response to the question of whose wife a certain (human) woman would be among brothers in heaven; it is *not* within the context of the ancient angelic fall. It's true that the "angels in heaven" (i.e., those who still willingly submit to God's authority) do not "marry" (take wives or reproduce), but the wicked angels who tried to overthrow God's ways and kingdom most certainly *would have* done whatever perverse thing they needed to do to accomplish their goals.

Naturally, as opposers/usurpers of God, one main objective would be to thwart the plans of the Messiah as prophesied in Genesis 5:15, whose appearance on the Earth would reconcile humans to God. If the Enemy had/has *any* brains, he would know that whoever this Messiah is would be catastrophic news for the fallen angels' schemes and, since God's plans are always far more powerful than the Enemy's, this Messiah would be unstoppable. This would be significant motivation to try to prevent Him from coming in the first place, as opposed to waiting for His arrival and trying in vain to defeat Him head-on. How does a group of angry, evil angels thwart Christ's birth? By corrupting all human DNA so that no matter *what* bloodline the prophesied Messiah hailed from, it would be at least in part stained by the blood of a fallen angel ancestor. For how can a "pure" Jesus be brought into the world through the womb of a young Mary whose great granddaddy was an evil angel or Nephilim? Her very blood would be contaminated. The most effective way to terminate God's perfect plan would be to cut off the messianic line early on so Jesus could never be born into the realm of humanity, while the fallen angels' Nephilim sons became the "gods" (or "mighty men") worshipped among men and commemorated in the ancient pagan pantheons, as Ethelbert Bullinger's popular commentary volumes acknowledge:

> Moreover, we have in these mighty men, the "men of renown" [Genesis 6:4], the explanation of the origin of the Greek mythology. That mythology was no mere *invention* of the human brain, but it grew out of the traditions, and memories, and legends of the doings of that mighty race of beings; and was gradually evolved out of the "heroes" of Gen. 6:4. The fact that they were supernatural in their origin formed an easy step to their being regarded as the demi-gods of the Greeks.[13]

Remember Hercules? Yeah…he may be more than just a strong Disney character with his own line of fan merchandise; he *may not* have been made up from the imaginations of storytellers, as Bullinger connects. It's quite possible he was real, though, no doubt, the historical narratives that arose about him (and the other gods and demigods) were likely extensively embellished. You don't need to blindly accept all the legends, lore, myths, and fanciful stories to see that there might have been a real entity in Earth's early years that, at least in part, walked, talked, and performed great wonders of strength just as the tales tell.

For those who still think this approach is too sensational, consider this: Why *else* would God flood the world in the days of Noah? Why *else* would humankind be viewed in the eyes of God as so profusely and continuously evil that they were rendered entirely unredeemable (Genesis 6:5)? Since when has any human being since the time of Adam been incapable of redemption? And why would God call Noah "perfect" (Genesis 6:9), when no single human other than Christ, Himself, has ever been "perfect"?

The key is understanding what kind of "perfection" is in view here. Even in English, the Bible doesn't say God called Noah *morally* "perfect"; it says Noah was *tamim*, Hebrew meaning "whole," "without blemish," or "unimpaired." Despite some translations today that frequently imply this is a moral *tamim*, even going as far as to render this important word as "blameless," Hebrew scholars know that isn't what is going on here. Bullinger states:

> The Heb. word *tamim* means *without blemish*, and is the technical word for bodily and physical perfection, and *not moral*. Hence it is used of animals of *sacrificial purity*. This shows that Gen. 6:9 does not speak of Noah's moral perfection, but tells us that he and his family alone had preserved their pedigree and kept it pure, in spite of the prevailing corruption brought about by the fallen angels.[14]

Likewise, readers of the Word don't need to go further than this same verse to see the word "perfect" qualified and defined by another telling definition. The next words are "in his generations" (Hebrew *dor*), meaning among his genealogical bloodline. If, by "generations," the Bible is only meant to point to an *era of time*, or to Noah's own fellows or neighbors, then we have the theological mess of having to discover what other mere humans were perfect in different times or regions, and we're round about back to the beginning: What human has ever been perfect other than Christ, because now it appears we have multiples? If, on the other hand, "generations" here can refer to bloodlines, the context takes us to something that occurred in the blood and body of humanity in the days of Noah, recorded *only a couple verses after* these bizarre Nephilim giants were born upon the Earth when the "sons of God" (angels—fallen, in this case) procreated with human women. Albert Barnes, a renowned Bible scholar and author of the widely celebrated *Barnes' Notes on the Whole Bible*—despite allowing for the possibility that Genesis 6:4 *may* be referring to ancient warriors of a wicked nation (and not necessarily fallen angels or their hybrid offspring)—interprets the "in his generations" of Genesis 6:9 in this way:

> "In his ages"… This phrase indicates the contrast between Noah and the men of his day. It is probable, moreover, that he was of *pure descent*, and in that respect also distinguished from *his contemporaries* who *were the offspring of promiscuous intermarriage between the godly and the ungodly.*[15]

Barnes, whose work is antiquated in our day, wasn't completely settled on any of the varying interpretations of who copulated with whom in Genesis 6:4 that made God angry enough to destroy all of humanity. He therefore simply referred to the "good guys" and the "bad guys" here as "the godly and the ungodly," thus avoiding permanent association to *either* the Sethite view *or* the fallen angels view regarding the identity of the ancestors of the Nephilim giants. As such, his treatment of the Hebrew *dor* ("generations") is entirely free of the bias that could potentially be inherent in backing one view over another—i.e., he had no agenda behind the study of this word. He was strictly reconstructing the meaning of *dor* for his English readers so we would understand what kind of perfection was here attributed to Noah. His conclusion is therefore quite valuable today, when *moral* perfection is so often assumed over the likelier reference to undefiled human blood. It's as if Barnes said: "I don't exactly know if we're talking about Sethites or fallen angels here, but I *do* know Noah's generational perfection is describing a family lineage kept pure and undefiled from intermarriage with the ungodly who walked the earth in those days." If we're correct in understanding the big picture so far: Noah's family was the only one left whose DNA was uncontaminated.

As to how the fallen angels could have physiologically done this—a delicate but fair question regarding the "equipment" needed to reproduce—note there were certainly moments, as recorded in the Word of God, when angels took on human form, and in some cases they even ate human food (Genesis 18 and 19). Overall, though there are some inherent mysteries behind these interpretations, it's only "new to Christianity" in recent times. Jewish literature established among rabbis since before the time of Christ, including the Book of Enoch (a paramount book in this version of events!) and the study thereof, openly supports the supernatural worldview of fallen angels and their procreation among human females. If it were to boil down to the earliest texts that weigh in on these events, the roots of Christianity—Judaism—most often treat these interpretations as fact (as Dr. Michael Heiser's 2017 book *Reversing Hermon* also shows).

Often, Christian teaching overemphasizes a single account of a fall—primarily that which occurred in the Garden of Eden when Adam and Eve listened to the deceiver at the Tree of the Knowledge of Good and Evil (Genesis 3)—to the exclusion of the others. However, as our "once upon a time" overview above shows, there are at least two more: when the angels took women unto themselves and produced a hybrid offspring (Genesis 6), and when the angels delegated to watching over humanity after the Babel confusion (Genesis 11; Deuteronomy 32:8) rebelled, leading to the "courtroom scene" of God presiding as judge over them (Psalm 82). We thus have *three separate* fall accounts originating from the narratives in Genesis alone, showing the angels *have used and can use* their free will to fall away from the ways of God and mislead humanity.[16]

And if they've successfully done it at least three times in the past, each instance resulting in a deception of epic proportions, why wouldn't they do it again in our (perhaps very near) future if such a thing fed into their satanic agenda? The bottom line is that they *would* do such a thing again, and, based on the trends I'm seeing in secular alien parlance, that mission has already been launched. Earthlings are buying into the lies as we speak…and rapidly so. It's almost as if we're so resolute in avoiding the moral accountability the Gospel drives that we will have built the satanic, alien-religion platform for them in advance, so all they have to do is land on it and preach whatever we want to hear. At the very least, Paul saw such insanity coming, and said people in the end times will leave sound theological teaching behind in trade for whatever "gospel" best flatters their individual circumstances and suits their own lusts, regardless of its legitimacy (2 Timothy 4:3).

With the slate refreshed on our former Hollywood ideas of little green men, do you still think the Bible is silent on the topic of what we call "aliens"? Perhaps not as much as mainstream Christian teaching assumes. The authors of this book believe the identity of these intergalactic beings are clearly of the fallen-angel variety, and as far as whether they look like greys (or insectoids, or reptilians, etc.), they've already proven to engage in sickening cross-breeding tactics producing hybrid weirdness in times of old (the remains of which have been baffling scientists for ages, as many of our former books have shown[17]). So, the smartest thing we could ever do is *not* assume to know every form they would take if or when they decide to interact with humanity in modernity as they did in ancient days. Quite to the contrary, we should fully expect them to possibly warp themselves further, as is their recorded Genesis-6 *modus operandi*. As to the many sightings throughout history of flying discs that appear and disappear in the sky, defying everything we know about aerodynamics and airborne craft—if those sightings in fact *do* point to these beings and their activity—we are speaking of a race of beings who were personally present at the time of

Creation (Job 38:6–7). They have had a *long* stinkin' time to develop mind-boggling tech—and, as is their wicked nature, they would be thrilled if we saw something evil they created and assumed it was a space vehicle containing naturally born "people" of the skies who will one day bring us incredible knowledge and wisdom for our benefit. It is also assumed aliens travel between planets casually, like humans used to go door-to-door selling vacuums, but considering the *mountain* of problems innate to the concept of interplanetary space travel (at least regarding the most advanced human-conceived scientific hypotheses and the responses of those communities to the question of whether such a thing is possible), it's more believable that these "aliens" and their "spaceships" (UFOs/UAPs) would be passing through some kind of interdimensional—not interplanetary—portal. Since Christians have no problem believing demons (who, according to Hebrew scholars, are the disembodied spirits of the once-physical Nephilim[18]) pop in and out of our realm invisibly to torment (and even possess) unprotected humans, it's not a leap that their fallen-angel ancestors would be capable of something similar, and suddenly "space travel" is no longer the only explanation of "alien presence" here on Earth.

CHAPTER 4

WORDS FROM THE SCHOLARS: "IS GOD AN ALIEN OR EXTRATERRESTRIAL?"

By Donna Howell

So, *is* God an alien? In the context of what *our* culture means when we utter that term, and as the previous reflection on their ancient origin and malevolent dealings amidst humankind's earliest days has no doubt imparted: No, God is not an "alien." That word, once we divorce our perceptions from Hollywood and look at what is actually *there*, "out in space," is reserved for beings of a fallen-angel nature, essence, and substance. And to address the elephant in the room, just in case you think the alien-savior approach has merit, it doesn't: Since angels are created beings and Colossians 1:16–17 makes it clear Jesus is the One who created them, then Jesus is not an angel; He is God. He cannot be an alien, good *or* bad.

But if we remove the fallen-angel context and biblical context from the argument and just look at what "alien" and "extraterrestrial" mean in their purely technical definitions, we spot an area of vulnerability the Enemy of God might exploit. When consulting word-study sources and dictionaries, we see they objectively describe something we recognize as different from ourselves, or someone/something that exists outside of planet Earth. From *Webster's Collegiate Dictionary's* listings, "alien" and "extraterrestrial" are defined thus:

[1]**alien**...(14c)
    1 a: belonging or relating to another person, place, or thing: STRANGE **b:** relating, belonging, or owing allegiance to another country or government: FOREIGN **c:** EXOTIC
    2: differing in nature or character typically to the point of incompatibility

[2]**alien** n (14c)
    1: a person of another family, race, or nation
    2: a foreign-born resident who has not been naturalized and is still a subject or citizen of a foreign country; broadly: a foreign-born citizen...

[1]**ex·tra·ter·res·tri·al**...adj (1848): originating, existing, or occurring outside the earth or its atmosphere

[2]**extraterrestrial** n (1950): an extraterrestrial being[19]

Other sources provide similar definitions. *Chambers' Etymological Dictionary of the English Language*, for example, says the following: "**Alien,** āl'yen, *adj.* foreign: different in nature: adverse to.—*n.* one belonging to another country,"[20] and so on. Nowhere in the initial definitions do these words require us to apply our cultural colloquial understanding of little green men to comprehend what they are describing. In fact, depending on the translation, the word "alien" is found throughout the Old Testament—though, of course, the context is synonymous to "foreigner" and applies to regular humans from other earthly territories. Even today, political spokespersons occasionally still use the expression "illegal alien" to describe (obviously human) immigrants, despite perhaps the egg-on-face effect now that the phrase is seen as politically incorrect. The immediate association with the Hollywood alien upon utterance of these terms is a very young idea. Once divorced from all context, the words are *so* innocuous that men and women heavily involved in the debate regarding the relationship between the Bible and aliens refuse to answer whether God is or could be an alien until the word is properly defined—an absolutely necessary starting point.

Such care was understandably taken when I emailed some of Tom Horn's closest fellow scholars-in-arms within this spectrum of study in an experiment I conducted just weeks before I wrote this.

When the concept of this book was in its infancy, the opening chapter was planned to play out like a conversation between a curious spectator and Tom Horn, whose lengthy list of books has already taken these God-alien concepts into mind. I, myself, was slated to play spectator in the back-and-forth, asking Tom all sorts of questions he's received from his enormous number of readers throughout the years, giving him the platform upon which he could draw from his pool of books and resources to finally tackle all of these issues in one place. From there, we had planned on addressing essentially the rest of what this book contains from this point forward.

Unfortunately, Tom Horn, the great and wonderful scholar who was among the very first to boldly go where no other modern scholar has gone in regard to this taboo topic, went to live in the presence of our Lord in October of 2023, leaving the three of us (myself, along with coauthors Derek Gilbert and Allie Anderson) to carry the project to fruition as he wished. Meanwhile, in his absence, I contacted the scholars who have also written at length on this topic, so the "conversation with Tom" chapter idea could remain in this work, even though the format is now slightly different.

To all participants, I sent three emails: First, I asked if they would be willing to take part in a quick, one-question interview for an idea

Tom had for a book (each person I contacted said "yes"). Second, I asked, "Is God an alien or extraterrestrial?" and explained that the query was intentionally without any context whatsoever to get their rawest response (in part to test specifically whether they would begin with a definition of terms, though they weren't aware of this intent at that time). Third, after receiving their initial answer, I sent them the outline of the book and its ultimate direction in case they wanted to weigh in further. In almost every case, the participants acknowledged the error of asking such a question without first identifying what's meant by "alien" or "extraterrestrial." Though I never intended to "trap" anyone (and it wouldn't have worked anyway, considering those I questioned are about as well-versed on the topic as anyone else alive today), they quickly recognized, then expertly tackled, the glaring inadequacy of the question.

To put it another way, the scholars were already so aware of the discrepancy among terms that they, like Tom Horn and me, saw the gaping word hole as an area many alien religions and cults have already exploited: "Extra," as a prefix, *only* means "outside" or "beyond," while "terrestrial" relates to our planet, Earth, and its inhabitants, Since, then, God is inherently unbound by the physical limitations of Earth's atmosphere, He is technically capable of being *extra-terrestrial*, or inhabiting regions beyond or outside of this planet. (Duh…) Similarly, He could be interpreted as "alien" only in the sense that He could be viewed as being "from" somewhere else. Technically, God, the Alpha and Omega, the First and Last, the Beginning and the End, had no beginning, so we wouldn't consider Him "from" *anywhere* specifically, but as He appeared to us initially in the Garden of Eden, He wasn't "from Earth." (Again: Duh.) "Therefore," ET religious leaders say, "God is an extraterrestrial alien. The Bible bears evidence throughout that He and His holy angels came from 'out there.' We were right along, guys. So, the next time you're contacted by these entities, listen to what they have to say. They either *are* God, or they are *from* God, sent to do His work."

Yikes…

The best lies are based on partial truths…and I can't think of a better example of how a simple game of semantics (word-twisting) could mislead the masses into confusing the character, essence, attributes, and nature of our Lord God with satanic concepts. But those with eyes to see and ears to hear will spot, like our scholars did, the error in this dangerous—and, tragically, ignorant—approach to theology. I could address this all day long with my own developed responses, but suffice it to say a more diverse explanation may help even more, so I will share the feedback I received from Tom's associates.

As he parsed the word-game trap most succinctly, I believe Mondo Gonzalez, Christian author and highly educated host of the *Prophecy Watchers* television program, is a good place to start. In response to my question, "Is God an alien?" he emailed back:

> The technical answer to this is yes and no, depending on how one defines the word "alien." If we understand the word "alien" in the colloquial sense—as another sentient being or creature from another star system based on a naturalistic and evolutionary foundation—then God is *not* an alien. However, if we define "alien" as "foreign" or "extraterrestrial," then the answer is yes. God is not from our terrestrial domain and is certainly not Earth-born as Adam was. God is transcendent of time and space altogether and the Bible demonstrates that He is the ground of all being and is the Creator of all that exists. He alone possesses aseity [existing of Himself; He does not depend on any cause outside of Himself for His own existence; He is not a "created being"].

Bingo, Mondo. Way to drive it home quickly, simply, and powerfully. If one were to apply *only* this response from Mondo, a sizeable percentage of UFO/alien cults in operation today (and in the near future) would be heavily challenged, if not effectively cancelled.

Ret. US Army Lt. Col. Robert L. Maginnis is a bestselling author who is internationally recognized as a security and foreign affairs expert (with decades of experience as an on-the-air analyst for numerous media outlets like Fox News). He supported the US Army for more than a half century and remained stationed in the Pentagon for decades. He is also a senior fellow for national defense at the Family Research Council. His latest book—*Out of This World: Are UFOs Aliens, Spirits, or Pure Hokum?*—addresses the subject of aliens in light of both theology and our government's current knowledge of their dealings in space. Maginnis also sees the coming deception, taking the "yes and no" approach while acknowledging the image of God we were made in...and adding a surprising twist regarding *our own* alien status:

The short answer is both "yes and no."

No, God is not an alien because He is our Creator and we are made in His image, albeit imperfect, thanks to sin. However, He is always with us via His Holy Spirit and, having accepted His Son as our Savior, we will join Him in Heaven for eternity to celebrate Him.

Yes, He is an alien—otherworldly—in the sense that He has characteristics that we earthlings—saved or not—will never possess: [He is] self-existent, transcendent, immanent, immutable, eternal, omnipresent, omnipotent, omniscient, incorporeal, one, creator, personal, incomprehensible, and morally perfect.

Therefore, I've split the baby in this instance. We, Earthbound Christian believers, serve an "alien" God Almighty who is radically different than us, yet we cling to the promise that we will join Him in that alien place called Heaven. Once in paradise, we will become higher than His angels and serve Him for eternity as aliens from Earth.

We humans aren't that spiritual; at least that's the case for most of us. That's why we struggle with understanding the immaterial (spiritual) world. The fact is, our sciences can't measure the immaterial and, therefore, for much of the scientific world, nothing exists beyond our five senses or our instruments that peer into deep space or into the electrons that energize atoms.

It's Satan's great deception to cause us to seek out extra-terrestrials upon which to place our hope. Satan knows our weakness is a focus on the material, the here and now. It's key for him to manipulate gullible humans into placing their hope in an ET material world rather than an "alien" immaterial God. Yes, the "religion" of worshipping at the altar of the material ET is more acceptable to modern mankind.

God is alien, but not the ET kind gullible humans seek!

Are you starting to see a pattern here? There is no "alien religion" without a First Cause and Creator at the center of it all…and there is way to claim God is an "alien" without also delicately parsing *what that means*. The specialists who spend a lot of time entrenched in sound theology and discussions surrounding beings of and activities in outer space rightly acknowledge that God, as He reveals Himself in the Word, cannot be associated in any way with the Hollywood alien of our Western cultural concepts unless you disregard the Bible entirely or annihilate its passages with grossly negligent misinterpretation.

Dr. Michael Lake, chancellor and founder of Biblical Life College and Seminary, likewise took on the matter of defining words, taking it a step further to address angels and the nature of God:

Is God an extraterrestrial?

First, let me deal with the theological elephant in the room. I do not believe in panspermia. Almighty God is not a little green or grey alien that came to Earth in a spacecraft and seeded life on this planet. Creation is more than some cosmic labora-tory experiment. This concept is a pipe dream of evolutionists who have realized their theories are not viable. However, God is not from planet Earth, either. We must examine what the Word of God reveals about our Creator.

We must ask the question of what an extraterrestrial is. A working definition would be: "**Extraterrestrial life**, also known as **alien life**, refers to life forms that do not originate from

Earth."[21] When we examine the Word of God, we discover a host of created immortals that fit this description. Traditionally, we call these beings "angels," although this term means "messenger" and cannot be applied to most of this ancient class of created beings. The prophets of Israel provide us with a wealth of information on this elder race. Some are terrifying to behold, while others are so powerful that when they shouted "holy" before the presence of God, the foundations of Heaven shook, and the Temple of God was filled with smoke (Isa. 6:4).

The powerful scene in chapter six of the book of Isaiah reveals an awesome truth about Almighty God. Hebraically, the only aspect of God that is brought to the superlative is that God is "holy." *The Hebrew and Aramaic Lexicon of the Old Testament* defines "holy" as "**holy, commanding respect, awesome,** treated with respect, removed from profane usage."[22] Dr. R. C. Sproul, in his series on "The Holiness of God," takes us deeper into the meaning of this Hebrew word by defining the holiness of God as God being "the absolute other."[23] God existed before He created the universe or the three heavens. The secret place of the Almighty is eternity, which is outside all of space-time. Unless the Father chooses to reveal Himself, He is unknowable. In theology, we refer to this as "God is transcendent" (i.e., He is absolutely beyond our comprehension and unknowable). Yet, out of eternity, the unknowable God spoke. The Word of God created all things (Col. 1:16–20). Now, we can know God through General Revelation or His creation. Then there is Special Revelation, meaning we know God through His written Word. Finally, this Word became flesh and dwelt among humanity (John 1:14). Theologically, we refer to this as "God is immanent." The Word became Immanuel (God with us). Yet, as John details in chapter 1, verse 10, God was so alien to His creation that His own did not recognize Him. Almighty God must be revealed to us by His Spirit, and He will then utilize both General and Special Revelation to reveal Himself.

Now, I have said all of this to bring us to this point: Because God is transcendent (or alien) to the entire universe, He is also a mystery to the gates of Hell. While Almighty God is consistent in His dealings with humanity so that we can learn His ways, He is tactically unpredictable in His response to the enemy. Once, He used a shepherd and his staff on the backside of the desert to bring down an empire. The next time, He would use a few lepers to turn the tide of siege on a city and chase off an army. The kingdom of darkness thought that they had won when they crucified the Word incarnate. Yet, His death, burial, and Resurrection were their most significant defeat…so far. Almighty God is the ultimate extraterrestrial for planet Earth and the universe. He will win because He is alien to His creation (including all fallen immortals). Almighty God is beyond the ken of the gates of Hell itself. When God makes His final move against them, they will never see it coming![24]

L. A. Marzulli—an internationally recognized expert author, filmmaker, and lecturer on the subject of the Nephilim giants of Genesis 6, fallen angels, and their sordid, historical interactions in the sphere of alien activity, including UFOs—comprehends more than most the confusion between the God of the Bible and the beings "out there." Of anyone I could possibly choose to include in this one-question interview, Marzulli most likely has the most personal experience in freeing folks from the satanic grip of what they believe to be "alien contact" (including abduction accounts) through the blood of Christ and the power of His Name. After granting that God/Christ could fit the technical definition of "alien," which Marzulli views as "anything that originates off-planet [Earth]," he tightens up the looser ends, saying:

But here's the catch: Because God created the heavens and earth, He is the rightful owner of *all* of this, so I suppose that would make Him exempt from an alien status as it was the work of His hands as He spoke it all into existence.

Short, sweet, and to the *very good* point, indeed, Mr. Marzulli. God would naturally be exempt not only from the Hollywood-alien status, but also from the very term "alien," itself, if and when it forces the concept of being a stranger to some planet He personally designed through the work of His hands in the first place!

In a similar vein, Derek Gilbert—renowned Bible scholar, best-selling author, expert on the gods of multiple ancient and pantheonic religions, and coauthor of this very book—replied to my question with an outright "no," having approached the subject in a way similar to that of Marzulli:

> No, God is not an alien. The word "alien" conveys the sense of someone or something unfamiliar or from another world. God created humanity because He desired family. Sadly, we've chosen to reject His household to chase after lesser gods. He may seem like an alien because we have alienated ourselves from Him.

If we're going to whip out associations that "mix God with the greys," scholars well-versed in the subject can flip that on its head, making humanity more alien than He could ever be! (Right on, Derek.)

Revelation, prophecy, and end-times expert, Terry James—who has written forty-seven books on the Rapture and the eschatological role Antichrist will play in the last days—first acknowledged the recent uptick in interest of UFO and alien phenomena and their relationship with religion, then shares what he believes may be the literal manifestation of those beings upon the Earth in the near future. His response is lengthier than others, but between his widely recognized expertise on this subject and the surprise ending to what he shared, I can't help but include his feedback in its entirety:

> Recent information issued by the US government on UFO matters is almost certainly framed in a way to cause the public to think extraterrestrial life exists. This is a strange turn of events.

For decades, government agencies have done all they could to fend off any notion that such life exists—or at least that it has in any way visited this big, blue marble [Earth]. Now, however, official government verbiage has seemingly done a 180-degree turn, and has changed the nomenclature of visitors from space they now want us to believe are here.

Now these visitors [and their crafts] are, rather than being called "unidentified flying objects (UFOs)," instead are termed "unidentified aerial phenomena (UAPs)."

No longer is there a concerted effort, like in the Roswell UFO incident in 1947, to, even through threat of physical harm, silence those within government and even private life who would bring evidence to the forefront of the question of extraterrestrial life.

It is as if governments and even the mainstream scientific community, previously extremely skeptical in UFO matters, now not only accept openly the probability of UAPs, but wholeheartedly embrace that they are here. In some cases, the lights in the sky, and however else they manifest, seem welcome in ways never before imagined.

…These *visitations* in their various manifestations have been equated to intervention by astrophysical gods into the affairs of humankind. There are cults that have, at their center, theology that harbor claimed deities from other worlds. Such have become increasingly less marginalized, as were the cults of not long ago. These today are no longer automatically considered as far out on the fringe of religious thought and activity.

The deities, to these worshippers, are considered to be descended from extraterrestrial worlds. God, to these religionists of otherworldly sorts, is an extraterrestrial, not from the eternal realm as presented in Christianity.

My study of Bible prophecy from this point in human history forward, in consideration of the above—the extraterrestrial incursion in terms of developing religious acceptance of

UAPs as god-like beings—convinces me that significant Lucif-erian purpose resides at the black heart of things involved.

All we are witnessing in the lights in the sky, now being accepted by even governments as visitors from extraterres-trial worlds, I believe, is stage-setting for a grand deception to come. That deception is found in Revelation as part of the seven years of Tribulation about which John was given to write while exiled on the Aegean island of Patmos.

The deception will be foisted upon humanity at that time by the god of this world—the one whose name was changed from Lucifer to Satan. He will install his son of perdition—Antichrist—upon the earthly throne he will try to establish on a worldwide basis. This man of sin will demand worship. All who will not do so will be hated, hunted, and killed. Surveillance controls, no doubt greatly enhanced through technological advances, will make Antichrist's regime capable of tracking and tracing the activities of every human being. A system of computer and artificial intelligence (AI) technologies will cause all to receive number codes in their flesh in order to comply with Antichrist's dictates.

The False Prophet, Antichrist's chief henchman and reli-gious leader of the false religion that will have developed, will set up an image that looks to be alive. All people will be forced to worship the image or be cut from the system of control that allows buying and selling.

The False Prophet will mesmerize most everyone on earth by performing miracles. One of these miracles will be to call fire down from Heaven. Here is what God's Word says about this satanic ploy.

> And he doeth great wonders, so that he maketh fire come down from heaven on the earth in the sight of men, And deceiveth them that dwell on the earth by the means of those miracles which he had power to do in

the sight of the beast; saying to them that dwell on the earth, that they should make an image to the beast, which had the wound by a sword, and did live. And he had power to give life unto the image of the beast, that the image of the beast should both speak, and cause that as many as would not worship the image of the beast should be killed. (Revelation 13:13–15)

…the False Prophet will call fire down from Heaven. This wicked religionist-dictator will make it look as if he will cause fire to descend from space onto the Earth.

This future deception, I believe, is why the stage is being set for deceiving the people of Earth even at our present moment in time. The entire unidentified aerial phenomena—formerly UFO—hoopla might just be Satan setting the stage for the moment the False Prophet of Revelation 13 supposedly calls fire down from the heavens.

In fact, I believe the "fire" that will be called down by the False Prophet in performing that "miracle" will be Lucifer, the fallen one, and all of his rebellious angel followers being kicked out from the heavenly realm forever. Here is God's Word on that event:

And there was war in heaven: Michael and his angels fought against the dragon; and the dragon fought and his angels, And prevailed not; neither was their place found any more in heaven. And the great dragon was cast out, that old serpent, called the Devil, and Satan, which deceiveth the whole world: he was cast out into the earth, and his angels were cast out with him. And I heard a loud voice saying in heaven, Now is come salvation, and strength, and the kingdom of our God, and the power of his Christ: for the accuser of our brethren is cast down, which accused them before our God day and night. (Revelation 12:7–10)

The prophecy then gives this foreboding warning:

Therefore rejoice, ye heavens, and ye that dwell in them. Woe to the inhabiters of the earth and of the sea! for the devil is come down unto you, having great wrath, because he knoweth that he hath but a short time. (Revelation 12:12)

The devil and his angels will apparently appear as fire as they fall from space. Rather than gods coming down to make things heaven on Earth, it will be the horde of fallen angels come to Earth to wreak unprecedented havoc on the planet.

So, in my studied view, it is highly likely that the things we are witnessing at this moment regarding the great interest in God being somehow from another extraterrestrial world is setting the stage for what in part will constitute the great lie, as Paul the apostle explained.

And then shall that Wicked be revealed, whom the Lord shall consume with the spirit of his mouth, and shall destroy with the brightness of his coming: Even him, whose coming is after the working of Satan with all power and signs and lying wonders, And with all deceivableness of unrighteousness in them that perish; because they received not the love of the truth, that they might be saved. And for this cause God shall send them strong delusion, that they should believe a lie: That they all might be damned who believed not the truth, but had pleasure in unrighteousness. (2 Thessalonians 2:8–12)

Those who refuse God's Truth right now, before the Tribulation comes upon this rebellious Earth, will, God's Word says, believe a lie that this False Prophet, inspired by Satan, will tell.

It seems a big part of that lie might be that the fire falling from the heavens are extraterrestrial gods who have come to save the planet. But the cascading lights will instead be an invasion from the enraged Lucifer, the fallen one, and his vast horde of evil angels.

God, the Almighty Creator of all that is—who is Jesus Christ, Second Person of the Godhead—is not an extraterrestrial, but is the eternal *I AM*. He will ultimately put an end to the wicked lies about His true majestic identity. And He will put an end of the deadly serpent called Satan.

Terry James' assessment of this topic shows a projected end that's similar to what we covered in chapters 1–3. The ET religion of tomorrow would fit seamlessly into Antichrist's eschatological schemes and, if Terry's right, it's going to be a bloodbath.

I want to move on to the important insight provided by Allie Anderson in the next chapter of this book, but before we go there, let's take a quick, slam-dunk look at the irreconcilable incompatibilities of God and/or Christ as a personal alien entity from a theological standpoint.

CHAPTER 5

"ALIEN CHRIST":
A THEOLOGICAL IMPOSSIBILITY!

By Donna Howell

I n my most recent book, *Before Genesis* (2023), I pointed out that the rivalry between science and religion is actually a matter of philosophy, not science:

> The statement, "Nature is the only cause behind existence," is not scientific, it's *philosophical*. Nothing is wrong with engaging in philosophy, so long as we remember never to cross the fine line between a) studying the sciences and appreciating what those pursuits show, and b) concluding that science "proves" nature to be the only cause behind everything that exists. Science can show God's handiwork, but it cannot disprove His existence. The minute that line is blurred, we've crossed over from science (demonstrable facts) into philosophy (seeking wisdom about the world and its people).[25]

Similarly, nothing about the "alien Jesus" theory can be proven or disproven, unlike the *mountain* of proof in favor of Christ's messianic claims, including the enormous number of prophecies He fulfilled in His coming. For as many answers as the alien Jesus theory allegedly provides, more often than not, it *must* rely on conjecture, not on facts or evidence, which technically renders it a philosophy, as other scholars responding to this "theology" have noted. From Don Stewart's textual commentaries series, we read:

> The alien theory is often stated in such a way that nothing can either prove or disprove it.... However, for any theory to be meaningful there must be some way in which to falsify it....
>
> Of course, if one could not tell the difference between the alien Jesus and the genuine Jesus then how do we know it was the alien Jesus? Why couldn't the Jesus of the New Testament have been the real Jesus? Why must we assume it was some alien imposter?[26]

Another source identifying the same problem is Logos Bible Software's esteemed *Holman QuickSource Guide to Christian Apologetics*, which states:

> The problem with this theory is that it actually proves too much. Any objection that can be offered against the theory is too easily dismissed by invoking Jesus' alien nature. This nature is presumed to include abilities that look supernatural to humans and that are sufficient for Jesus to pull off this charade. The result is that there is no possible way to prove the theory right or wrong; there is no test that can be performed to determine the truth of the claim. Thus, philosophers dismiss this type of flawed argument as unfalsifiable.
>
> Another weakness of this claim is that instead of weighing all the evidence and being led to this conclusion, adherents start with this conclusion and try to conform all the facts to the

theory in a favorable way. This is also a fallacy known as "confirmation bias." This leaves us with an argument that proves so much that it actually proves nothing.[27]

It is so sad that people would bet the duration of their own *eternal existence* on unprovable, philosophical speculation that even philosophers consider to be dismissible! The Church needs to be ready to respond to this for the sake of the lost—today *and* tomorrow!

I believe most Christians aren't prepared to respond to the ET religion from a *theological* standpoint. They may be able to poke holes in some presentations of ET gospel material if those they're debating include assertions that conflict with essential doctrines of the Church. And Christians may make generic statements such as, "That's just ridiculous!" But if a person well versed in the dangerous "alien"/"extraterrestrial" word game (addressed at the beginning of chapter 4) presented the average Christian with exotheological claims or teachings, would he or she know what to say, or have even the most basic foundation of a compassionate, yet educated, reply? Would that soldier of God know how to assist in staving off the ET religious cult of tomorrow so the true Church of Jesus Christ can remain "alien-free" for just a while longer?

So far, in my experience, the answer is a resounding *no*. Immediate, know-it-all reactions (often condescending) are abundant! But Christians equipped to handle this topic with knowledge of the facts are few and far between.

This chapter is in no way an exhaustive overview of all issues arising daily between responsible theology and exotheology. However, readers (and audiobook listeners) will be able to walk away from this chapter with at least a basic working knowledge of the incompatibilities between the God of the Bible and extraterrestrials.

First on the docket is something we touched on briefly before. "In chapter 3, "Back to the Ancient 'Alien' Basics," we covered the fact that there have been malevolent and evil spirits within and outside of Earth's atmosphere since its foundation. These are the angels who were once good, but fell, becoming spiritually warped for certain, and likely physically warped in some way as well. Regardless of their fallen nature, however, they are of the angelic race, and Jesus *is not*. Angels are created beings (Job 38:4–7), and Jesus is eternal—He had no creator because He *is* the Creator (Colossians 1:16). Under no circumstances can any one member of the Trinity or all three Persons together fit this racial category. This fact alone is enough proof that "alien Jesus" is an impossibility.

On the other hand, rejecting the interpretation shared herein that aliens, as we know them, draw their origin from the Genesis 6 narrative—if a person were to staunchly insist aliens are entirely unrelated to a race of angels altogether, fallen or not—we would need to focus instead on the limited information we have regarding the nature and character of these entities from space whose interactions on this planet have been *nothing but incompatible* with the Risen Christ. Though this chapter will focus more heavily on the Genesis 6 origin theology, notice that, either way, no Person of the Godhead could fit the descriptions we have of these perverse creatures.

In response to questions arising about aliens' appearances, we have little choice but to allow for an "anything goes" approach at this time. Their willingness to take on a corporeal form and copulate with human women to produce hybrid offspring to cut off the messianic bloodline shows their physical form to be malleable in some way, so it isn't a huge leap to conclude that they might appear as the "aliens" people so often claim to encounter in modern times, including greys, Nordics, reptilian, insectoids, or any other of their documented forms.

As their nature is *now* very wicked, it makes sense that any contemporary UFO or extraterrestrial phenomenon would likewise be wicked, and in ways far beyond anything physical. Over and again, abductee and "contact" testimonials describe a whole list of elements incompatible with the Yahweh, Christ, and the Holy Spirit, including:

- **Free-will restrictions:** Almost all abduction accounts involve at least a partial denial of a person's free will or control over their own body. They can't move and often can't speak, while they recall lying on their back in a room with strange beings hovering over them, speaking without moving their mouths (telepathy), and often cutting into the person's flesh for bizarre experiments or curious implantations. That we know of, no physical restraint is placed upon the person; he or she is rendered completely incapacitated and/or silent by the invisible and unknowable power of the beings. Not only is free will an irrevocable theological absolute given by our Heavenly Father to all people, no verse anywhere in the Word allows for God or His celestial servants to physically cut into a person for any reason, least of all for implants or experiments by the All-Knowing God who already knows all there is to know about the human body and its interactions with the universe. (Even circumcision under the Abrahamic Covenant was exercised by free will, and was never forced upon anyone, as the story of Moses' and Zipporah's son in Genesis 17 shows.)

- **Contradictory interactions:** Holy angels of the Bible are "messengers," and that's not solely based on the actions they carry out in the scriptural narrative (although that applies here as well)—the Greek word *angelos* and the Hebrew *malak* literally translate "messenger," so this job description of delivering information and missives from God to humans indicates who they are and what they do. Angels aren't in the business of invading people's homes by floating through windows from a craft "parked" in the sky outside and beaming them up for disconcerting adventures through space. Angels of God described in the Bible simply showed up, delivered a message, and left. Further, Hebrews 1:14 makes it clear that holy angels are guardians or "ministering spirits" for those who have accepted Christ's salvation. I don't believe it's necessary to elaborate regarding how and why a being who sneaks into someone's bedroom, telepathically controls their body and mind, plants various space tech under their skin, occasionally rapes them, and induces a lifetime of nightmares is not what we typically think of when we hear the terms "ministering spirit" or "guardian."

- **Acceptance of worship:** In addition to some especially dramatic alien-abduction accounts in which the entity demands some form of veneration or other, the "gods" of the old world who *stemmed from* the fallen angel and Nephilim narratives obviously insisted upon being worshipped throughout many epochs. As our own history reflects, this was a successful endeavor resulting in multiple pagan pantheons overflowing with gods who readily and openly accepted such worship from humans. (In my book *Before Genesis*, I visited a number of ancient archeological sites around the globe that document an ongoing, multigenerational worship of gods, often serpentine in nature, who required steady veneration and a whole gamut of disturbing rituals.) Though God, Himself, does *accept* worship, consistent with the note regarding free will above, He never *forces* us to comply with this expectation. As for the angels: The Word of God is clear that we are never to worship them under any circumstances (Colossians 2:18). When John the Revelator attempted to, the angel firmly refused to receive it, insisting that John worship *only God* (Revelation 19:10; 22:9). Thus, true, holy, and unfallen angels of the Lord wouldn't allow humans to worship them even if we wanted to, identifying yet another incompatibility between Christs' fleet of celestial servants and these fallen-angelic space beings.

- **The wrong kind of fear:** Throughout the Bible, holy angels often say "Fear not" when they show up on the scene with a message for God's children. Naturally, this infers that their presence is so commanding and authoritative that their very appearance, alone, could evoke surprise or alarm. To the spokespeople of the ET religion, this might be seen as "proof that the scary thing you saw in your bedroom last night was an angel of the Lord." However, Scripture allows for at least two applications of the word "fear": reverential (healthy and helpful) or hostile (destructive), and these should not be confused. We are told in some passages to "fear God," resulting in a positive and constructive reverence and awe—similar to a pauper being led into the inner courtrooms of his beloved king (see, for instance, Proverbs 3:7; 9:10; and 10:27). In other places (such as Isaiah 41:13), we read that we're never to fear, and that God doesn't induce fear but instead gives us a spirit "of love and a sound mind" (2 Timothy 1:7). So, although a holy angel *could* cause one to experience a feeling of awe or reverential fear, the very fact that angelic beings repeatedly try to put people at ease, telling humans *not* to be afraid of them, proves they are all about preventing alarm. On the contrary, in episode after wild episode of abduction documents, people consistently report feeling as though they were in the presence of something supremely evil; there's nothing "reverential" about it. And don't forget the test of the spirits in 1 John 4:1–6: A holy angel will *always* acknowledge Jesus was and is exactly who He claims to be; they willingly worship Him as their Lord (Revelation 7:11). Aliens, on the other hand...well, that's precisely where we're headed next.

In the New Testament, we read Christ's personal words about a kingdom unable to "stand" if it is in conflict with itself. Let's look at exactly what He said before we consider what it implies.

In the third chapter of the book of Mark, we read that, after a healing Jesus performed on the Sabbath (along with a bit of narrative detailing the growing crowds who followed Him and His appointing of the twelve to go, preach, and drive out demons), religious leaders showed up and accused Him of casting out demons—in the name, or by the authority, of Beelzebub:

> And the scribes which came down from Jerusalem said, "He hath Beelzebub, and by the prince of the devils casteth he out devils."

And he [Christ] called them unto him, and said unto them in parables, "How can Satan cast out Satan? And if a kingdom be divided against itself, that kingdom cannot stand. And if a house be divided against itself, that house cannot stand. And if Satan rise up against himself, and be divided, he cannot stand, but hath an end…. Verily I say unto you, All sins shall be forgiven unto the sons of men, and blasphemies wherewith soever they shall blaspheme: But he that shall blaspheme against the Holy Ghost hath never forgiveness, but is in danger of eternal damnation."

Because they said, "He hath an unclean spirit." (Mark 3:22–30)

Let this sink in: Jesus has just made the point that a leader of a kingdom or house cannot expect his dominion to stand firm if he is in conflict with himself. Jesus' words point out the absurdity of the scribes' accusation that Jesus could a) be possessed with a spirit of Satan, and b) use that very satanic spirit to cast out other servants of Satan. In so doing, Christ is emphasizing that, unlike the human realm that is affected by capricious and impulsive shifts in mood, whim, and even devotion, *in the supernatural realm, authorities must remain consistent in their nature and character*. If Jesus is "of the kingdom of aliens," then: 1) He is "in conflict with Himself" by being a *good* alien, as their nature just discussed conflicts with the biblical "good guys"; or 2) the *entire New Testament* is wrong in insisting that He is the Son of God, wholly good. So, what do we make of the idea that Jesus has the power to cast out demons and devils and holds supreme power over all evil, yet His nature could still merge with something…supremely evil?

And let's not forget, as recorded *thousands* of times in the documented cases of dealings with extraterrestrials, it is Jesus' own personal and powerful Name that has delivered countless tormented people from these disturbing visitations! Could the power of the alien Jesus cast out aliens? *Ahem…* Let me put this another way: Can a kingdom divided against itself stand?! Again, not if Christ's words in Mark chapter 3 are true! (One noteworthy consideration among the many documented cases provided by such ministers as Joe Jordan shows there have been people who *did* cry out to the Lord Jesus, but to no avail. His Name, in those instances, "didn't work," they say. However, in *every one of those cases*, when the minister asks the tormented person about their relationship with Jesus, they either say they a) had no relationship with Him at all and only dropped His Name as a desperate measure to relieve their agony, or b) believed Him to be something other than what the Bible says He is, such as the New Age, "Christ consciousness" idea that views us all as godlike beings who are merely struggling to tap into our own divinity and become one with Him, or something similar. Even the demons believe in Christ, we read in James 2:19, but they tremble at the thought of Him and are in no position to call on His Name for assistance, so it's not enough to simply believe He exists. History is replete with occasions when people have called out in earnest and received help from Him, even if they never had a relationship with Him prior, but that is God's own prerogative to answer those *He* deems are truly seeking in such a way that His intervention will be the beginning of someone's ongoing godly life. If we know and believe, yet wickedly follow our own way—or if our petition, once answered, has the potential to further confuse our understanding of who Jesus really is—we cannot assume Christ's Name will hold some kind of formulaic power that will drive everything out. That's especially true considering that God knows the heart of everyone and can foresee which of us will offer up a quick, superficial "thank you" when we're delivered from evil, just to go straight back to that evil the following day. God is not a tool, and if we act as though we consider Him to be nothing more than one, we can't expect true deliverance. In some cases, the "aliens" shrank back in fear, shook with anger, or prevented a person from uttering His Name again, but it wasn't until the abductee or tormented person truly gave their hearts to Christ that the "aliens" discontinued their appearances.)

Shaun Doyle of Creation Ministries International, in his article "Was Jesus an Alien?" also identifies some self-kingdom-sabotage innate in the theory he repeatedly calls "ludicrous."[28] He correctly acknowledges that Arthur C. Clarke's third rule ("Any sufficiently advanced technology is indistinguishable from magic," as quoted earlier in this book) is used as a huge support for "alien Jesus" theorists. In general, aliens are *so* intrinsically associated with advanced technology that "alien Jesus" theorists have little choice but to accept that their "kingdom" is highly scientific. Yes? Of course. Doyle then states Clarke's "rule" is:

> ....simply not true. Physics limits technology. Only supernatural beings can transcend physics. And only God can change physics itself. If the "alien Jesus" proponent wishes to say that physics can spontaneously change, then they've undercut their faith in science as the only reason for ruling out God as an explanation—science can't work if physics can spontaneously change...
>
> The "Jesus was an alien" idea...denies the obvious to establish the ludicrous.[29]

"Alien Jesus" theorists have no problem accepting the veracity of the miraculous events recorded in the New Testament. In that regard, they are similar to Christians in that they must place their faith in the supernatural in order to admit Christ walked on water, rose from the dead through no other power than His own, cast out demons, healed countless afflicted people, and carried out many other acts that defy the natural order of the universe and physics. So far, so good: They believe the Gospels. The (obvious) point where they differ from Christianity is in identifying Jesus as an extraterrestrial entity. In the conclusion of Doyle's article, he drives home the most glaring contradiction of them all, stating the act of reading the Gospels would be, for the "alien-Jesus" theorist, the "worst thing for their 'faith,'" because "they already trust the hardest-to-believe aspects of the Gospels, and Gospels don't allow for any other explanation for Jesus' miracles other than that He truly is God's unique Son."[30]

Either Jesus is the Son of God, or He's not, but the Son of God cannot be "of the same kingdom" as the one that carries out crude experiments on the bodies of people who have no choice about whether these terrifying creatures were invited into their home to supernaturally steal away their free will and render them helpless. And if the Name of Jesus is *truly* the Name that compels all of these malevolent beings to flee, then Jesus is either casting out Jesus—a theory that dissolves immediately when the implications behind His words about Satan being unable to cast out Satan are reviewed—or He is a hypocrite standing against His own teachings...which the New Testament descriptions of Him do not permit. The theory will never make sense once the pretty package is opened, allowing the looping, circular logic to vomit out from within.

Doyle is not alone in his assessment of the incompatibilities between God and aliens. Another group of scholars behind the radically popular book *The Kingdom of the Occult* have identified additional faults in any attempt to reconcile Jesus to an extraterrestrial nature. They explain what is commonly heard in alleged alien-abduction testimonies or telepathic communications from folks who emerge from their experience claiming to have found enlightenment of some sort. According to these conversations (telepathic or natural), aliens have stated they *do not* adhere to the following (which contradicts the Bible, as noted in the references): Jesus Christ is the only Savior or the only way to the Father (and He is; John 14:6); "the Bible alone is God's Word to the world" (and it is; 2 Timothy 3:16); eternal punishment exists (and it does; Matthew 25:46 and many other verses); bodily resurrection is a certainty (and it is; 1 Corinthians 15:35–58); and several other points of disbelief that put aliens at odds with God. On the contrary, the ET religion proposes reincarnation to be true (and it is *false*; Hebrews 9:27–28). To adherents of this religion, "reincarnation [means that] people evolve from planet to planet in order to reach perfection." Furthermore, "UFO religions are occultic because their spiritual information is obtained through occult methods...[such as] specialized visions, dreams, trances, [or] hypnotic regression."[31]

This team makes another fantastic point: Exodus 20:4–6 gets a lot of attention for prohibiting the assembling of idols and the worship of other gods, but rarely is it remembered that a portion of this passage provides locations apart from Earth's habitational surfaces: "anything that is in heaven above, or that is in the earth beneath, or that is in the water under the earth." In the context of this particular subject, the fact that we're told never to worship any gods, even from "heaven above" (space), is in itself a kingdom-cannot-stand self-sabotage if it relies on the occult to obtain said "spiritual information." If there is even the slightest doubt in a seeker's mind that Christ is *not* an alien, then choosing to participate in the belief systems or worship of a UFO cult or ET religion presents dangerous hypocrisy as a foregone conclusion with eternal consequences. One must therefore be absolutely and irrefutably *certain* Jesus is an alien in order to worship Him within that framework, or else they, too, belong to a satanic kingdom that contradicts and, therefore, crumbles, as *The Kingdom of the Occult* authors recognize:

> If UFO religions were truly the revelations of alien races, then it would be logical to expect some basic consistency from them…. The Bible is *consistent* in its creation; it had more than forty writers from different cultures, nations, continents, and ethnicity, who wrote for God over a period of fifteen hundred years, but their message testified to the same God and His story of redemption for mankind. The Bible is *coherent* in its logic; the things taught in God's Word make sense; it is *cohesive* in its truth—thoughts from the one true God support one another, they are not self-contradictory, but they, in fact, adhere to the law of noncontradiction. This is not so among UFO religions….
>
> It might just be that the UFO very real, but if it is real, it is working through the influence of Satan "with all power, signs, and lying wonders" (2 Thess. 2:9). If Satan is the god of this age, there is no reason that at the end of the age he cannot appear to be its savior. He has always wanted to be the object of worship.[32]

"ALIEN CHRIST": A THEOLOGICAL IMPOSSIBILITY! *By Donna Howell*

There *is* a great deception coming (a subject Derek and Allie both tackle later in this book), and one major argument will champion Jesus as an über-alien—thus, "alien-Jesus" theorists must accept that the Father and the Holy Spirit are aliens as well, since they are all "one" (see John 17, among countless other passages). A quick checklist or recap here may be a helpful reference for some, so remember the major points we've covered thus far:

1. What we call "aliens" or "extraterrestrials" are fallen angels, and since all angels—*before and after their fall*—are created beings, the eternal Jesus cannot be of the same substance, essence, or nature as they.

2. Neither Jesus nor the other members of the Trinity will ever: a) place people in a position wherein their free will is restricted; b) act out of character in regard to interactions with humanity; c) demand or force a free-will agent to worship against their will; or d) instill a *hostile* fear within those they appear to. Since this is congruent with modern abduction stories, no Person of the Trinity can be one of *them*.

3. And, perhaps most importantly, since a kingdom divided against itself cannot stand and Satan cannot cast out Satan, Jesus' authority as the Son of God *must be* different from what we believe aliens to be, since it is His Name that successfully casts them out.

How would the global population respond to an extraterrestrial event? Could a sophisticated being or race of beings visit Earth, claiming to be benevolent or even godlike beings, and bring the global population to its knees in submission? Has a historical precedent been laid over the centuries to groom the population for just such an appearance? It is precisely these questions Allie Anderson will tackle in the next chapter.

CHAPTER 6

GLOBAL RESPONSE
TO AN ET EVENT

By Allie Anderson

I magine, as crowds gather and watch in wonder, the night sky begins to light up with a thousand lights that appear from a distance and slowly approach Earth. Hundreds of sophisticated UFO craft begin to fill the space above our planet, and, as they near, a larger one emerges from amidst them and descends, seemingly self-identifying as the vehicle for the leadership for whatever new, alien race is preparing to land among humans. Once it has lowered, a nonhuman being steps out, assuring that the race has come in peace. Perhaps, as a gesture of goodwill, the being and its companions present Earth's leaders with long-sought-after cures for disease, clean-energy sourcing, highly advanced technology, or other much-desired solutions for human-kind's problems. Such beings would appear benevolent, kind, and advanced; they may even be regarded as the "higher power" humanity has always believed was supernatural. Perhaps their leader is revered as a god—an attitude that could quickly trickle into humanity's thinking if interactions between the two races are manipulated a certain way.

Now, imagine that this race presents a leader who, over time, positions himself as some sort of keeper of answers to all that ails the Earth's populace. However, his condition for rendering such assistance is that he is placed in a position of leadership within or even above the global governments. Would this being be elevated to a role as "world king" or even to a god-like status? How would the world's religious communities respond to such a scenario? In this chapter, we will explore this question.

Universal Ancient Phenomena?
Or Set-up for False Christ?

In Genesis 6:2–4, we read:

> That the sons of God saw the daughters of men that they were fair; and they took them wives of all which they chose. And the Lord said, My spirit shall not always strive with man, for that he also is flesh: yet his days shall be an hundred and twenty years. There were giants in the earth in those days; and also after that, when the sons of God came in unto the daughters of men, and they bare children to them, the same became mighty men which were of old, men of renown.

(A comprehensive analysis of this scenario, while potentially relevant to the outliers of our topic, would quickly become its own study and overtake the rest of this book. Because of this, a vastly truncated analysis is offered here, then we will move on with our discussion regarding the potential of extraterrestrial life. For this purpose, let's briefly explore who the "sons of God" might be. For more information, Defender Publishing offers a variety of books that cover this topic more exhaustively).

What we know from the above passage is that *some race of male beings* married/interbred with human women, and the resulting union was a race of giants: men of renown who were known for their super-human strength (6:4).

One popular interpretation for "sons of God" states these men were not necessarily unholy, but married these women because of physical lust. Based on the many verses in the Bible where believers are called "sons" or "daughters" of God, those subscribing to this belief assert this was a strictly human union; they offer little explanation for the reference to giants or men of great renown.[33]

Another popular interpretation asserts that "sons of God" refers to descendants of Seth (Sethites), and the "daughters of men" indicates Cainite women (descendants of Cain). By this logic, a great moral decline occurred as the result of intermarriage between the two groups.[34]

A more controversial interpretation states the "sons of God" were actually fallen angels, based on the same phrase referring to angels in Job 1:6. It is stated that these beings attempted to pollute human genetics with nonhuman DNA, producing a race of half-human, half-fallen-angel creatures known as the Nephilim. According to this theory, the injection of supernatural DNA into the human genome receives credit for the offsprings' status as giants or men of superhuman strength. Based on passages from the extrabiblical Book of Enoch, many scholars conclude that what we refer to in the modern day as "demons" are actually the evil and unsettled, roaming spirits of these giants, or Nephilim, which were disembodied when their physical bodies were killed. The purpose for mentioning this is to say that some who have asserted Nephilim souls as demons have also stated aliens could be the most recent manifestation of these beings. If this is true, then the appearance of ET life could be a disguise for a sinister agenda.

Historical Precedent for a Future Alien Religion: Groundwork Has Been Laid

A disclaimer: We authors are Bible-believing Christians. At times throughout this book, we refer to arguments made by folks in the secular world. This is to show ways a coming deception could align with certain secular narratives already circulating in society; we in no way suggest these secular stances are our personal beliefs.

Christians often argue that evil forces have a way of mimicking every miracle, event, or other phenomenon carried out by the Lord God Almighty. For example, when Moses stood in front of Pharaoh and cast his rod to the ground, the wood became a snake; this miracle was intended to show Pharaoh the Lord's power. However, Pharaoh called in his own wise men and sorcerers, who replicated the wonder (Exodus 7:10–11). God is present in the Holy Trinity of the Father, the Son, and the Holy Spirit, while Satan will establish his kingdom during the end times by appearing in a triune system that includes Satan, the Antichrist, and the False Prophet. The Bible offers other examples of these bogus imitations throughout.

In contrast to the Genesis 6 account of *fallen* angels visiting human-kind, many biblical accounts record visits from God-sent angels. During many of these encounters, similar exchanges are made between the holy messengers and the humans. We often see the following:

- An angelic being visits a human, often one who has been unable to have a child (due to barrenness, old age, or lack of pro-creative activity).
- The angel foretells the arrival of a baby, often providing the parents with the name of the prophesied offspring and other instructions regarding how to raise the child.
- This child is born and grows to fulfill all that was foretold. The child is typically some type of historical figure or other "game-changer" for the people he is born into.
- The child is always born, never miscarried or stillborn, and is always somehow "special," as foretold.
- Importantly, within the secular world, one argument regarding these visitations and subsequent births are based on the notion that, in these circumstances, a sexual inter-action is not noted as following these predictions (more on this in a bit).

76

Examples of these visitations and births in the Bible include Samson (Judges 13), Isaac (Genesis 18), and even Jesus and John the Baptist (Luke 1:27), to name a few. Each case includes the above criteria: the parents are told there will be a child, are informed about what that promised descendant should be named, and are given special instructions regarding the child's upbringing (for example, Samson's mother was told never to cut her son's hair; see Judges 13:5). In every instance, the parents would have otherwise been unable to conceive, but a special child is indeed born and fulfills a promise to humanity.

One important note regarding the final point of the bullet list above is that in these and similar biblical accounts, people are promised a child and the child is subsequently born...without mention of sexual intercourse. This is in contrast to narratives such as Genesis 4:1, which states Adam laid with his wife and she conceived Cain, and Genesis 16:4, which states Abraham had intercourse with Hagar, impregnating her with Ishmael. The distinct omission of information about the act of procreating is used in some secular spheres to make the argument that the promised birth was *not* the result of sexual intercourse between two human beings at all. In other words, if Samson were the product of physical relations between his earthly mother and father, then Scripture would have stated it as it does in accounts such as those about Cain and Ishmael. This distinction *then* becomes a platform for the argument that the prophesied child was, on the other hand, the product of sexual activity or other means of impregnation that would have taken place between the visiting angel and the woman receiving the message. This would have made the offspring no regular human being; rather, it would be a hybrid creature: half angel and half human. The argument then points to other "hybrid" (half-human, half-god) figures throughout history or mythology, such as Hercules, Perseus, or Theseus.

From here, the narrative begins to drift into one of several directions, depending on one's belief system. The first possible conclusion is that it is all ancient mythological fiction, meaning some people don't subscribe to any of it as being grounded in reality. The second is that, within the secular world, the aforementioned biblical accounts are sometimes referred to as having been hand-picked for inclusion in the Bible, but are said to compare to other, nonbiblical accounts of key figures in the ancient record such as those just noted. On that note, some believe all of the accounts are—on some level—true, but are irrelevant today, and the differences between the reporting sources are attributed to variations in oral tradition, who initially recorded them, and how they were filtered through the worldview of those passing down the story. The third potential conclusion would be to say that for every pure and beautiful gift God gives humanity, Satan provides a counterfeit or finds a way to corrupt the narrative. And, the fourth potential conclusion would be to say there are members of a race of higher, otherworldly intelligence who have been visiting our planet since the beginning of humankind and have been working on a hybridization plan over the centuries to—for whatever reason—alter the human genome by inserting something foreign into it. Further, when these otherworldly entities do so, they like to make their presence known by announcing the special child's arrival, leaving instructions, and endowing said human half-breed with the ability to do miracles and the possession of superhuman strength, or with the capability of otherwise fulfilling a role that humanity greatly needs to be filled.

The issue with believing these intelligent beings to be part of legend, for a Bible-believing Christian, is to bundle Jesus into the same fictional category as a mythological figure. This is to deny Jesus' deity, or, quite frankly, His existence. The problem with the second response is that by perceiving biblical accounts to have been hand-picked as the only ones recorded and preserved with bias from the biblical worldview of Old Testament authors, the default seems to acquiesce that Old Testament authors manipulated Scripture by writing a narrative that suited their own agenda rather than recording what God told them to record. It also dismisses any modern relevance the stories may offer. Regarding the third response, this would seem a stance for many Christians who would be content to leave the argument at that. But, taking the issue one step further and entertaining the fourth possible reply could present its own dangers. On one hand, perceiving prominent biblical figures as hybridizations of visiting aliens could create the perception that our entire religion is invalid—or, worse, that God never even existed, crediting instead otherworldly visitors for anything that, until now, appeared miraculous or supernatural. For this reason, these authors are careful not to clump our Old Testament figures into the narrative of hybridization that circulates in secular spheres. Conversely, this argument could become a compelling deception for a fallen world of folks seeking a nonbiblical explanation for such manifestations as the miraculous or supernatural.

However, the notion of hybridization in some cases is a reasonable theory for those who believe the Genesis 6 narrative is referring to fallen angels who, in attempt to pollute the human genome, had intercourse with human women and impregnated them with a race of giants. What would be their motivation? Some argue this would have occurred to corrupt the Messiah's lineage. Others would say the destruction of humanity—made in the image of God—has always been Satan's goal. Still others might say it is a plot that will play into future, prophetic events.

The concept, however, of human beings who are half-human, half-god, as mentioned before, exists throughout various ancient religions. Some biblical scholars state these hybrids are found in the Bible as well under the name "Nephilim." Some believe Goliath was one, based on his lineage from Anak (1 Samuel 17), and Nimrod was believed to be one also, as Genesis 10:9 indicates he was a mighty figure who was hostile toward the Lord.

To take the cultural and historical commonality of hybridization among many ancient religions one step further, a study of nonbiblical ancient belief systems also produces accounts of crossbreeding between animals and humans, resulting in creatures such as the Minotaur, centaur, mermaid, and satyr. However, these aren't found in biblical accounts. Rather, God notes that it is good when animals reproduce after their own kind (Genesis 1); further, bestiality is condemned, including a mandate to kill the violated animal (Exodus 22:19, Leviticus 18:23, Deuteronomy 27:21).

The inclusion of hybrid human/animal chimeras throughout so many ancient religions begs the question: Are these mythological recordings a documentation of things the ancient world was encountering? Perhaps, if there *were* a hybridization of humanity in the ancient world, the only way for God to clean up the resulting mess would be to search out some genetically clean samples of His creation, place them in a safe container, and wipe out the rest in order to start fresh. Some biblical scholars believe this is what prompted the Flood of Noah, *and* it is noteworthy that it occurred immediately following the scriptural account of the giants in Genesis 6:1–4. Let's look at the evidence that this could actually be the case:

- We know *something* bad happened when the "daughters of men" and the mysterious "sons of God" interbred, resulting in a race of giants (verses 2–4).
- Humankind became only evil continually, and it grieved God that He had created them (verses 5–6).
- God decided to destroy not only the people, but also the animals (verse 7).
- Noah was deemed "perfect," which some scholars say means he was genetically untampered with (verse 9).
- It was pointed out that all flesh had been corrupted, to which God stated the end of all flesh must come (verse 12).
- God instructed Noah to build an ark and made a plan of safety for Noah, his family, and enough animal life to repopulate human and animal life on Earth (verses 14–22).

Considering all these events in conjunction, we must assume something irreparable occurred at this moment in history. After all, God was destroying the creation He had once deemed as "good." (Genesis 1:31). Recall for a moment the account of Cain and Abel, the first Earth-born brothers (Genesis 4). Cain ruthlessly, without just provocation, murdered his brother, and when God asked him about it, Cain arrogantly reminded Him that he was not his brother's babysitter

(Genesis 4:9). Yet, God didn't wipe him out as he would later do to the individuals on the Earth during the Flood. In fact, God marked Cain to protect him from anyone recognizing him and harming him as vengeance for Abel's blood (Genesis 4:15). In this way, the concept of human evil in Genesis 6:5 points to something much more sinister than just being a mere, "average" amount of "sinful." A modern paraphrase of the ancient Hebrew phrase "every imagination of the thoughts of his heart was only evil continually" might sound something like "the very framework of everyone's mind was only malignant and evil without a break, day or night."[35] Consider that for a moment. When we think about some of the evilest people alive today, do we really know someone who is purely and exclusively evil 100 percent of the time? Surely even the most wicked have some portion of good in their hearts. But these men and women described in Genesis 6:5 had been reduced to such evil that the very framework of their minds was unable to produce any good whatsoever, which might suggest perhaps humanity had become something that was no longer made in the image of God.

We *do* know, however, three important things about Noah: 1) he found grace in the eyes of the Lord, indicating an important and redeemable contrast between Noah and his peers; 2) he walked with the Lord, indicating his choice to live in holiness despite the corruption of the society around him; and 3) he had three sons. Presumably, these sons set the tone for their households, so we can assume the Lord's favor extended to their families as well. Such a scenario would completely change the signs we're watching for when awaiting the end times. For example, consider Matthew 24:37–39:

> But as the days of Noah were, so shall also the coming of the Son of man be. For as in the days that were before the flood they were eating and drinking, marrying and giving in marriage, until the day that Noe entered into the ark, and knew not until the flood came, and took them all away; so shall also the coming of the Son of man be.

Many people perceive talk about the "days of Noah" to mean that when sin is rampant and society has taken an irreparably hedonistic turn, God will rapture the Church and the Tribulation will begin. But if all we're watching for is sinfulness that's completely off the rails, then wouldn't we consider previous times in history as being so sinful? For example, *Top Tens* lists the most terrible events in world history as: 1) the Holocaust, 2) World War 2, 3) the Black Plague, 4) 9/11 World Trade Center attacks, 5) trans-Atlantic slave trade, 6) atomic bombs on Hiroshima and Nagasaki, 7) World War 1, 8) the sinking of the Titanic, 9) the Pearl Harbor attack, and 10) the Crucifixion of Jesus Christ.[36] To be fair, a few of these events, such as the Black Plague, weren't the results of an overt act of evil, but if the presence and practice of evil were our only qualifier for extreme, world-destroying levels of God's wrath, then you'd think it could have happened already. *Something* in Genesis 6 occurred that made God say the end of all flesh must come, despite the fact that carrying out that judgment brought Him sadness. Perhaps something more than regular human sinfulness is the trigger point here; maybe it is when our very makeup (such as the mind's framework?) has become so corrupted we are no longer Image-bearers whose intellectual processes have a capacity for morality.

Perhaps the sign of the times of Noah will take place when the ultimate hybridization begins to happen. It might not be completely physical; possibly it will be when a new religion proliferates around the world, one that explains away God; His miracles; His angelic, holy messengers and their visitations; the seeds of deliverance both promised and delivered through the accounts of the Old and New Testaments; and every other supernatural event that has people believe there is a higher power—a God in heaven—who loves them and has the power to forgive their sins.

What if a sophisticated, intelligent race of beings made contact with humankind and, in their presence, empirical data were to surface rendering religion completely obsolete? They might bring with them advanced technology that solves humanity's problems of disease, provision, energy sourcing, justice and equality, and myriad other historical issues mere earthlings struggle with. Further, if these entities possessed advanced technology allowing humanity to convert their genome into anything they desired, they could bring back hybrid chimeras of ancient times (if these indeed existed).

Abduction Phenomenon

Such is the substance for those who state hybridization is the motivation for alien encounters and abductions. Some of those who say fallen angels are responsible for the giants occurring as a result of the Genesis 6 encounter assert that modern-day alien abductions are merely a rebranding of a similar phenomenon. If this is true, these same individuals claim the motivation behind this tampering is the search for a new way of corrupting the human genome. Let's take a brief look at some commonalities regarding abduction-experience claims:

- Abductions often occur in secluded places such as on a rural road far from civilization or in a bedroom, where a single or very few family members are isolated.
- Abductees usually first see a bright light or many lights at the onset of the incident.
- Victims often feel overpowered and are even restrained by unseen mechanisms, as though by some sort of telepathic power that keeps them from moving.
- Many report multiple entities, usually described as "greys," surrounding them; one reptilian leader is often observed.
- Those who have experienced alien abductions state they were communicated with telepathically. Often, their questions are answered, but responses to their queries are met with cold, clinical replies that lack empathy.
- Many abductees experience what they describe as "time travel" or a "time lapse," or they otherwise report missing time episodes.

- Some find themselves subjected to a variety of medical or laboratory experiments. They often describe feeling as though they were regarded as a mere specimen. Reports include people having objects implanted within their bodies and subsequently removed during a later abduction; having fetuses implanted into and/or stolen from their body; having samples taken from their bodies; sensing a metallic taste; or undergoing other sensations. Some have described seeing laboratory-type rooms filled with containers of human bodies, embryos, or fetuses. They report experiencing fear, pain, violence, and discomfort, while captors show a lack of respect for their captives' physical or mental comfort, life's sanctity, or dignity.
- When the incident is finally over, abductees often note unsettling details related to the perceived time lapse. For example, they're often moved to an area near where they were taken, although they sometimes resurface in places strangely far—impossibly far, even—from where they had been. In some instances, they feel as though hours have passed, just to note the time is strangely close to the when the event began. In others, it seems a short time has gone by, but in reality a disproportionately extended time has lapsed.
- While much about these occurrences seems difficult to believe, keep in mind that on many occasions, multiple people have shared the experience and have even interacted with one another during the incident. This adds credibility to the accounts and diminishes the notion it's all the product of delusion.
- It is nearly universal that these experiences leave victims carrying a lifetime of psychological scarring and trauma that are a struggle to heal from.

The correlation between what may be genetic experiments on human specimens and a previous (Genesis 6) attempt to corrupt human genetics makes one wonder if there is credibility to this account. The concept of hybridization in ancient times makes more sense to the topic of extraterrestrial life when considering that a high percentage of abductees recall having been experimented on in ways that tampered with their reproductive systems. While abduction claims are relatively rare—about 6 percent of Americans have reported these experiences[37]—they almost always cite these types of procedures.

However, while there are others, including scholars and scientists, willing to acquiesce that these abductions are occurring, they also assert it's being done by a race of intelligent lifeforms looking to help the human race. For example, a University of Oxford instructor not only believes the phenomenon is going on, but interprets these beings' motivation as being to help humanity physically survive global changes—in other words, creating "alien-human hybrids as a hedge against climate change."[38] Regardless of why alien beings tamper with humanity, the activity is widespread enough to the gain attention of and draw hypotheses from scientists, and it is the object of research resources.

One Must Ask

By now, you may feel tempted to throw this book out at the notion that we authors would entertain the concept of the hybridization of humanity. Please note that, while we consider the more sensationalistic aspects of this narrative to be one plausible strategy for a coming deception, it isn't necessarily the only explanation for the actual phenomenon. However, when we look at such possibilities in light of repeated patterns over history—such as the implications of the ancient Flood event and the potentially similar repercussions of today's abduction phenomenon—the connection could hold some merit. Even so, ultimately, we don't need to be asking one single question, but two: 1) *Is* intelligent life out there? and 2) if there is a sophisticated, otherworldly race, is it simply another intelligent lifeform or is it indeed evil fallen angels who have returned in disguise in another attempt to corrupt the human genome?

If we're talking about the second question, then it seems apparent that this otherworldly race is up to no good, and humanity must be wary. It would certainly explain why the beings show no regard for the fear, pain, and lack of dignity they impose upon their victims. It seems they aren't capable of compassion or empathy. Since they communicate with their captives telepathically, then *why* wouldn't they offer some simple thought of comfort or an explanation of the terror their abductees are experiencing? Consider this: An alien abduction story would be an entirely different narrative if the experiencer could say something like, "They took me into a big, sterile room where they explained to me that they were going to remove some samples from my body because they're trying to help humanity find a cure for cancer and need my cells for their research. They told me that I would be okay, that they would cause as little harm as possible, and that I would be back in my bed, safe and sound, before the night was over." Yet victims report having received no such comfort. Worse, they are regarded as specimens, nothing more than laboratory animals. This supports the idea that these beings are innately evil and have no capacity for regarding the sanctity of human life.

On the other hand, if these entities are just another species curious about humans and wanting to study us, what would be their motives? What are they leaving behind, and what could they possibly gain? If visitations are not for some overtly evil purpose, such as to deceive, experiment on, or torment humanity, then why? We authors have the following reservations when considering the following possible answers for this question:

1. **Knowledge:** We believe if these creatures know about Earth and humanity and have been visiting over a period of ages, then they likely would have already observed the criteria that initiated visitations. Because of the redundancy of and similarity among UFO and abductee accounts, it would seem that, by now, they would have collected their data and moved on. Further, since the implications of a nonhuman race hint at

technology and knowledge advanced beyond what earthlings currently possess, then it seems unlikely that we have knowledge to offer them.

2. **Benevolence:** With the entire globe constantly thwarted by painful and tragic events, if these entities were looking to act benevolently, we believe they would have intervened already, offering some new type of special skill, technology, or information to relieve the problem. If their skills and resources are advanced, surely they would have intervened during the COVID-19 pandemic or other recent plights of humanity. Further, when considering the physical (which can or cannot be qualified or proven), emotional, and psychological harm inflicted on abductees, we must scrutinize the *nature* of such entities. They operate without fear, restraining or intimidating their victims as they conduct sterile and clinical operations, and they never bother to seek consent from their captives. Abductees have reported being intimidated and repeatedly tormented, and they carry a lifetime of trauma at the hands of these beings; the victims often suffer PTSD (post-traumatic stress disorder) following their ordeal. It would seem any being that regarded the sanctity of human life would have an ethical infrastructure that would prohibit this inhumane treatment. To be fair, some argue that the beings conduct themselves in this way for the *betterment* of humanity, stating the results will *still* one day be used to benefit humankind. In other words, some say these entities have people's best interests at heart, so the end will justify the means. However, abductees also often describe being spoken to telepathically. If the nonhuman beings have this ability, why wouldn't they communicate their motives to abductees? Why wouldn't they at least send a message of comfort or peace to ease the human's terror?

3. **Sharing of technology:** If these creatures were to share their technology with humankind, it seems such an action would mirror the fallen angels' activity as recorded in historical

documents such as the Book of Enoch. Further, what technology they *do* have seems to have been used to experiment on human beings and it evades our understanding, which contradicts the notion that they're sharing their technology or revealing helpful solutions to planet Earth. While some may argue the extraterrestrials are still studying earthlings so they can *eventually* help us, we authors again defer to the previous point that these beings have done nothing to comfort or soothe their subjects.

4. **Timing of manifestation:** Perhaps these beings—whoever they are, if they even exist—are waiting for just the right moment to come to Earth and finally present humanity with some sort of technology, disease cure, or other benefit to improve the course of humanity's plight. As stated, when considering all the earthly disasters such a race will have seen before they finally intervene, one would have to wonder what's taken them so long to help us. Further, we also have to ask, while these beings had been *observing* Earth, were they indeed *intervening* after all? In other words, perhaps they have had a hand in the events on our little globe—maybe they've even contributed to the troubling events—to orchestrate a situation wherein they could step in, answers in hand, to win the trust of our planet's entire population with one grand gesture. If this were to happen, humanity's reception of such a race would be handled from a place of gratefulness. The need for people to take a defensive posture would be replaced by a sense of indebtedness; humankind would likely esteem the "benevolent helpers" and might even yield to their authority in recognition of their sophisticated and advanced resources.

Empirical Data

Empirical data is defined as "originating in or based on observation or experience/capable of being verified or disproved by observation or experiment."[39] It often refers to the results of a study, research project, or experiment. In the clinical and scientific world, empirical data has the power to give—or detract from—the credibility of a theory or hypothesis. For example, when an article in a science journal states an idea has been backed by empirical data, it means credible scientific or clinical research has been done, with the results having been peer reviewed (checked closely by qualified professionals in the same field) to ensure that the findings are credible. The point at which extraterrestrial life were to actually appear to Earth-dwellers, making contact with humanity, is the time when the theories of their existence would cease to be theories; their existence would become a known, *empirical* fact that might be the first element in a series of dominoes falling… possibly causing people of all religions to lose their faith.

Those who look to empirical data for explanations of miracles or the supernatural will see the visible, tangible signs and wonders of these beings in real time as they interact with humankind, providing an empirical explanation for what was previously called a matter of faith. It might be hard for those who previously had faith in God (or any higher power, for that matter) not to attribute this newly discovered "natural explanation" as being at the center of what was previously described as an act of God.

For example, the Old Testament's account of Elijah being drawn up into the sky, on a chariot of fire, reads as follows:

And it came to pass, when they were gone over, that Elijah said unto Elisha, Ask what I shall do for thee, before I be taken away from thee. And Elisha said, I pray thee, let a double portion of thy spirit be upon me. And he said, Thou hast asked a hard thing: nevertheless, if thou see me when I am taken from thee, it shall be so unto thee; but if not, it shall not be so. And it came to pass, as they still went on, and talked, that, behold, there appeared a chariot of fire, and horses of fire, and parted them both asunder; and Elijah went up by a whirlwind into heaven. And Elisha saw it, and he cried, My father, my father, the chariot of Israel, and the horsemen thereof. And he saw him no more: and he took hold of his own clothes, and rent them in two pieces. (2 Kings 2:9–12)

Depending on one's belief—or lack of—in the Bible, some people believe this account on faith in the supernatural, while others do not. Still others might believe that, while the text isn't an outright or intentional *lie*, there surely must be another explanation. Those in the latter group would likely give the benefit of the doubt to the author, trusting that he was stating what happened to the best of his abilities in the challenging situation of having to describe events that didn't fit the template of experiences he or his audience would have had.

Let's explore what members of each of these three groups might say about this passage after an ET event. The first group—people who believe in blind faith that God raptured Elijah into heaven—might become divided, as some feel the empirical confirmation of a natural explanation discredits the account's supernatural nature. The second group—people who have never believed this passage to be true in the first place—might see alien contact as evidence supporting their disbelief in the supernatural. The third group—those giving the writer the benefit of the doubt in the face of having to describe unfamiliar events—will likely consider the ET encounter as the very occurrence the writer of the Second Kings passage was trying to describe; they might state that the missing piece to the puzzle has finally, many centuries later, been found. And everyone who loses faith in the God of the Bible will have what *appears* to be solid, empirical evidence on their side.

We see a similar reaction to the interpretation of the Second Kings passage in the account of the wheel described in Ezekiel 10. Across the decades, many have come up with a variety of theories regarding just what Ezekiel was describing when he looked upward. At one point, German engineer Josef Blumrich explored whether the prophet had actually seen a spacecraft and offered a rendering of what he believed the craft to be. Separately and later, another engineer, Hans Herbert

Beier, sketched out what he perceived to be the measurements detailed in the second half of Ezekiel to indicate. As researchers put these two concepts together, many connected the craft produced by Blumrich with a perceived "landing pad" for the UFO depicted in Beier's work. To many, this connection proved Ezekiel's wheel was indeed a spaceship. While these authors don't necessarily share this opinion, it's interesting to note the responses of many scholars in related circles upon seeing this "evidence." For example, Giorgio A. Tsoukalos of *Legendary Times Magazine* put it this way:

> Whatever was described in the Old Testament wasn't God, it was a misunderstood, flesh-and-blood extraterrestrial whom our ancestors misinterpreted as being divine and supernatural. Any why? Because of misunderstood technology.
>
> Our concern is that similar disillusionment could generalize out to many—or even all—other supernatural or miraculous events recorded in the Bible—for example, Jacob's ladder (Genesis 28:10–17); the Transfiguration of Christ (Matthew 17:1–13; Mark 9:2–13; Luke 9:28–36); and even the return of Christ (Revelation 19:11–16) could one day be stripped of their spiritual gravitas, falling into a category of "archaic beliefs that empirical data has now disproved." As 1700s philosopher David Hume reportedly argued, "We shouldn't accept stories about miracles since…there will always be a more likely, non-miraculous explanation for any extraordinary event. Our interpretation depends on our assumptions;" Humes' assumptions, it was stated, "did not stretch far in the direction of God."[40]

Along this line, we Christians need to have our faith secure so we'll be ready to address future discoveries with a balanced and practical view. It will be vital to understand how to accept puzzling new developments without displacing or distorting our faith. Many folks will be content to allow emerging discovery to replace phenomena previously revered as supernatural, especially if sophisticated, otherworldly life is revealed. They may say it has merely been "them" visiting us all along, and that humanity has simply inserted the concept of a deity into the explanation of these misunderstood occurrences, for lack of a better explanation. As this "new revelation" is propagated throughout the global populace, old-time religion could become obsolete as humankind basks in this freshly evolved knowledge. From this point, the masses could potentially decide there is no God, or they might elevate such visitors to godly status, while viewing Christianity as the archaic ramblings of a society that refuses to accept updated empirical facts.

The Need to Worship Something

The idea of people stationing a person, entity, or other element in a place of worship isn't new. In fact, a common characteristic among most civilizations in history is the tendency for each society to adopt or instigate their own religious system. People have always expressed the need to connect with a higher power. Taking that concept further, note that even in our modern, secularized world where many claim to not believe in God, many still acquiesce to the existence of a "higher power" or engage in activities that mimic religious sacraments. We'll look more closely at this latter concept later in the chapter, but for now let's talk about the historical need for humankind to connect with a deity.

Vast proof of this compulsion toward a higher spiritual power can be seen when we analyze where much of ancient religion originates. For example, various isolated groups have typically created their own theistic systems or pantheons based on elements of nature, celestial bodies, seasons, or geographical formations. Without digressing into a full-blown analysis of every ancient belief system, we can simply state that most had a god for the sun, the moon, and other prominent cosmic bodies—usually those that impacted the human lifestyle in some way, such as the ones "in charge of" facilitating light and dark or day and night. There was usually some sort of entity as well for the oceans, rivers, streams, and other bodies of water. Further, fertility gods were petitioned on behalf of the crops, animals, or human beings. Some gods were responsible for matters of giving and taking life, and some needed appeasing so they would allow worshippers to enter the after-life. Other assigned deities were responsible for natural processes such as rain for crops. When the gods were angry—be it at one another or at humanity—they would manifest their wrath in the form of natural disasters like earthquakes, hurricanes, tsunamis, floods, or droughts.

Anthropologists estimate that at least eighteen thousand different gods, goddesses, and various animals or objects have been worshipped by humans since our species first appeared. Today, it is estimated that more than 80 percent of the global population considers themselves religious or spiritual in some form.[41]

Despite the majority of people claiming to be spiritually minded, many who acquiesce to a spiritual worldview do not subscribe to organized religion. As mentioned, older belief systems assigned gods to natural elements that—at the time—civilizations were otherwise unable to understand. As science progresses and humanity learns more about these natural elements, the need to apply a personality to an entity fades—and is replaced by scientific explanation. Thus, for many in the current secular sphere, previously held beliefs such as the existence of a rain god who sends drought as punishment for lack of being appeased or an angry oceanic entity who is responsible for unleashing a tsunami have been long abandoned as the religious concepts of a less-scientifically-educated civilization. The point here is two-fold: 1) The consistency of such religious constructs throughout history supports the tendency humankind has always had to seek a higher power to believe in, serve, fear, or even commune with on some level; 2) In the same way scientific discovery has rendered some ancient religions no longer valid, a future revelation of sophisticated, powerful, knowledgeable extraterrestrial beings may cause some within secular communities to discredit Christianity or the existence of God as well, stating His sovereignty over the course of Earth's history is now explained by other discovery.

God-seeking Gene?

In 1979, some researchers became curious about the correlation between religious compulsion and genetics. In other words, they were wondering if a person's religious devotion derived more from nature or upbringing. They polled fifty-three pairs of identical twins and thirty-one pairs of fraternal (not identical) twins who spent their childhoods completely separated from one another. Ironically, the researchers found that each set of twins shared many eccentricities (such as flushing the toilet both before and after use and biting their fingernails, just to name a couple), despite having been raised apart. Impressively, there was no significant correlation between how or whether each twin participated in religious practices or customs; however, they did show a correlation in their *spiritual disposition*. Identical twins were more than twice as likely as fraternal twins to mirror one another's spiritual disposition. In simpler words, the religious *customs themselves* were likely influenced by lifestyle or culture, but "whether we're drawn to God in the first place is hardwired into our genes."[42]

Many anthropologists and other researchers have studied the fundamental tendency of humans to look toward a higher power, and this research has followed a number of other similar questions and presented countless related hypotheses over the centuries. Some observers have connected this internal desire to the human drive toward activism and the desire for community with one another through gatherings such as clubs and organizations; they even attribute this disposition to people's willingness to go to extremes to "belong," such as enduring hazing or initiations for gangs, fraternities, and even cults, and their readiness to sacrifice joy in this life in the hopes of some sort of payoff in the next.[43] One secular author observes:

> Humans seem to know that there is something that they are supposed to be adoring, [and] worshipping, but what that thing or being consists of is fraught with confusion. In their

eagerness to worship something, people may choose the wrong idea/person/thing and as a result, waste their adoration on something unworthy. Perhaps part of our human quest is searching for what is worthy of our utmost devotion.[44]

Other commentators have pointed out links between what people recognize themselves to be (or not to be) and what they perceive as worthy of adoration in attempt to pinpoint what drives the inward tendency to worship. For example, one blogger notes that those who feel unlovely might elevate the beautiful; those who feel weak may adore those who show strength. Those who are lonely may revere symbols of fame or status. The vulnerable often long after the ones who are in control or have power.[45] In a nutshell, when someone perceives a personal shortcoming, he or she is drawn—and may even submit to—a being of higher status that portrays these attributes.

Interestingly, organizations known as "secular churches" have been springing up throughout the nation. The groups assert their values as being "good without a God," and their meetings are similar to conventional religious church gatherings—without any type of dogmatic teaching.[46] At secular churches, attendees may sing inspirational songs, share testimonials or words of wisdom, and collect donations for the needy within their churches or communities. The meetings often feature one central lecture by a guest or group member.[47] In contrast to Christianity, these churches even hold "de-baptism" ceremonies, giving participants the opportunity to publicly denounce a former religion.[48] The mission statements of these kinds of groups generally indicate that humans have needs regarding their community, their personal mission, and their purpose, and that the church can help members met those needs, despite the aversion of many to institutionalized religion. It provides an opportunity to gather with peers, celebrate their lives and accomplishments, inspire one another, and connect with a meaning and purpose—which, in these authors' opinions, is an attempt to fulfill a spiritual need—while escaping any obligation to a "god-type" entity or said being's rules or commandments.

The more we explore what drives us spiritually, the more we're drawn to a parallel conclusion. What we mean is, when we scrutinize what people are drawn toward or opposed to concerning religion, many common factors seem to surface. Those who are compelled toward religion are often drawn by the sense of multiple types of safety, a sense of belonging and community, the ability to live with a mission and purpose, and all of the things that feed a deeper sense of joy in their lives. What seems to repel many people from religion seems most often related to two matters: 1) religion that offers a god they feel is impersonal, uncaring, distant, or worse—one who is waiting for a chance to smack people down at the first sign of wrongdoing, if they believe such a being exists at all; 2)religious people who are hypocritical or have portrayed religion to be a cold, cliquish setting wherein only certain people are accepted, money is wasted or misappropriated, or the rules/commandments are used as a means of control.

So, in a book exploring the potential for extraterrestrial life, why are we delving so deeply into a conversation about what drives people to or from religion? Because we must consider this: What would happen if a more palatable—and believable—model for religion surfaced? If an ET race suddenly appeared on the Earth, they might claim responsibility for matters that have always been left to faith to explain—much as the deities in ancient civilizations' pantheons are now replaced by modern science. They may receive credit for historic angelic visits, their technology might be credited for miracles or unexplained phenomena recorded in the Bible or historic documents, and their superiority may cause many to believe there never was a god, but rather, we've never been without alien company. The narrative could even include a component asserting that, as "primitive" humans, we haven't been capable of comprehending the full interaction of ET involvement until now, and that's why they will have waited to reveal themselves. If such a "revelation" were presented to humanity, the potential spiritual deception could have worldwide reach, extending even beyond the possible deception we've already mentioned. Those who may have thought the concept of a god or higher power simply wasn't believable may say their suspicions have been confirmed. Many people within religious circles could lose their faith when the mystical components of their beliefs now have a seemingly plausible explanation. As people with diverse worldviews respond differently, it is likely that one commonality will surface amongst them: The manifestation of a sophisticated, "superior" race will likely cause millions to abandon their old belief system.

In an attempt to analyze how the masses might respond to an ET event, one might think our first line of defense against deception might be our most skeptical crowd: those who deny faith in or the existence of God. After all, if a person has denounced being involved in a faith, then they would need to obtain it—faith—before it could be driven askew, correct? Let's continue this discussion as we consider those whose outlook is the least "religious" and how this guarded crowd might respond to the concept of an ET religion.

Agnostic and Atheist

Many use the terms "agnostic" and "atheist" interchangeably, but they are actually very different terms. First, "agnostic" doesn't only refer to someone's belief about *spiritual* issues. It simply describes someone who doesn't perceive answers to be knowable or understandable—*whatever the context or topic*.[49] Being "agnostic" doesn't necessarily mean religious or spiritual matters hold no importance. Rather, it asserts the perception that "the answers to the basic questions of existence, such as the nature of the ultimate cause and whether or not there is a supreme being, are unknown or unknowable."[50] In this regard, we must wonder if this stance would unravel quickly at the arrival of an ET race. It would seem that if a convincing, perceptibly religious, or spiritual event occurred in front of agnostics' eyes, they would be unable to remain agnostic. Asked what is beyond an unopened door, they might say there is no way to know—making them "agnostic" about that issue. However, if someone opened the door, their agnostic position would shift. So, it could be that those who currently label themselves as "agnostic" would become believers very quickly…if the right event were to occur.

An "atheist" is defined by Merriam-Webster as "a person who does not believe in the existence of a god or any gods,"[51] yet, Pew Research Center reports that 23 percent of self-proclaimed atheists believe in a higher power of some kind.[52] As we will explore, this conflicting information indicates that some who claim the atheist worldview might actually be opposed to religion, but not to the concept of a higher power. This is an important distinction to make when we're considering the potential of a superior race visiting the Earth and taking steps to convince humanity they are some form of divinity.

When we analyze the group of people who are set against the notion of religion, it becomes necessary to ask: What, *specifically*, is it about a religious belief system they are opposed to? Here are a couple of interesting points that offer a clue as to where some stand on the matter. First, 94 percent of atheists say "religion causes division and intolerance," while 91 percent agree with the statement, "Religion encourages superstition and illogical thinking."[53] Obviously, some atheists absolutely believe there is no higher power and no god or gods. But what these authors find telling is that 73 percent of these skeptics in the US claim "religion does more harm than good in American society."[54]

So, is the problem atheists have with religion *really* found in believing in a higher power? Or, could it be that institutionally religious inefficacy, perceived bigotry, abuse, or other bad behavior carried out by the Church has sent them into a mindset that believing in God means subscribing to a religion, and *religion itself* is intolerable? In a world where each person is free to operate autonomously (free will), perhaps many are off-put by the "rules" of religion—especially when they see that those who assert the rules often don't follow them, themselves. But, we digress…

The point here is not to pick on atheists for their beliefs or for the fact that they don't subscribe to a belief system that aligns with ours. This conversation is directed toward exploring whether our modern population could fall prey to a new "religion" that might sweep the nation. And what better way to assess this possibility than to evaluate those who fall in the demographic group who would likely be the most unbelieving critics?

Perhaps you've never heard of culturally religious atheists who practice religion, observe religious rites, or embrace religious values... but don't believe in the actual existence of a God (such as those attending the secular churches mentioned earlier). They may do this because their children attend a religious school, because they are married to a religious person, or because other lifestyle elements compel them to practice despite their unbelief.

Another category of atheists is known as spiritual atheists. They sometimes iterate notions of right and wrong or other questions of morality through an internal construct that denies actual religious elements but focuses on the "awe and wonder provoked through the scientific understanding of the world...[and] such constructions of spirituality are consequential for secular spiritual practices."[55] In other words, the religious construct is a useful tool if a person is looking for a healthy moral filter based on reverence and respect for all living and nonliving things, but without the need for bringing a "higher power" into the picture.

The point is, for many atheists, the right event may trigger a new worldview they would be willing to adopt. If that event involved the "superior" race discussed throughout this chapter, many atheists may convert to the new religion these beings brings.

Further, 79 percent of American atheists say they "feel a deep sense of wonder about the universe at least several times a year."[56] So, if even a percentage of atheists—our toughest crowd when it comes to convincing them there is a higher power—finds themselves being in awe at the universe and believing in a higher power, then even our hardest skeptics could be convinced to engage in an alien religion... if the package were compelling enough. J. Kluger, in an article for *Time* magazine, said: "Ask true believers of any faith to describe the most important thing that drives their devotion, and they'll tell you it's not a thing at all but a sense—a feeling of a higher power far beyond us."[57] Making believers out of any part of the population and bringing them into a certain "faith" might only require an undeniable "spiritual" experience.

The Benefit of Acknowledging a Higher Power

Many people believe in the concept of a higher power, but not in an actual god. For some, "higher power options include elements such as the 'laws of nature,' 'laws of science,' 'love,' 'the flow of the universe,' 'music and the arts,' and 'humanity'" (meaning the community of others).[58] Considering that even humans who have rejected the God of the Bible often are willing to accept the notion of a higher power, it seems that an emergent, sophisticated intelligence who asserts himself as God could be given this regard when his deeds perceivably match his claims.

Christians' Response to Discoveries

Groups whose worldview recognizes humans as more than physical beings but do not acquiesce to the God of the Bible may be particularly open to such a concept. They will likely welcome new evidence as a logical explanation for mysteries that have previously divided religious from nonreligious people. Further, they may even regard the evidence as a long-overdue solution to the ongoing debate between religion and science.

However, those who have previously held their faith dear may see such a new wave of empirical knowledge as the ultimate threat. Faith in *God* could be mistakenly thrown out when bundled with emergent scientific data or proven experience. Vital for believers will be to realize that God *is* still God, regardless of what occurs in the natural world. Any new science or discovery that emerges poses no threat to Him; He is still above it, as He is the Creator of all (Colossians 1:16), and nothing surprises Him (Ecclesiastes 1:9).

The clash between science and religion causing people to lose faith has occurred throughout history. For example, in the 1600s, Galileo Galilei designed a telescope that allowed him to observe formations on the moon, sunspots, satellites revolving around other planets, and even rings around Saturn.[59] Today, this Galileo is accredited with endowing humankind with vast, valuable knowledge about conditions beyond planet Earth. However, in his own day, his contribution was less appreciated, as it was a time when "the church increasingly demanded obedience to its views."[60] Before Galileo's telescope, Nicolaus Copernicus had advocated for the theory that the *geocentric* model of the solar system—meaning Earth was at the center—was inaccurate. Rather, he asserted a *heliocentric* model, placing the sun at the center of the rotating planets. This had been, after heated controversial debate, a theory declared by the Catholic Church to be heretical and its teaching was forbidden.

The reason for this prohibition is complex and outside the scope of this book, as it quickly begins to drift into arenas that, to fully explain, would require an assessment of the Church's theocratic control during that era. However, the key point the Church argued was that the heliocentric concept directly contradicted teachings found in Scripture, such as:

- "Fear before him, all the earth: the world also shall be stable, that it be not moved" (1 Chronicles 16:30).
- "The Lord reigneth, he is clothed with majesty; the Lord is clothed with strength, wherewith he hath girded himself: the world also is stablished, that it cannot be moved" (Psalm 93:1).
- "From the rising of the sun unto the going down of the same the Lord's name is to be praised" (Psalm 113:3).

Those who interpreted these passages literally thus believed that the Earth *never* moved and the sun is what "comes up" and "goes down." Of course, in current times, we accept that these verses poetically indicate that God has firmly established His authority over creation, and that He is to be praised while we're awake and able to do so. But, the Church of Galileo's time didn't appreciate it when, after using his advanced telescope, he published confirmation that Copernicus had been accurate in asserting a heliocentric model for the Earth's track.

In fact, Church officials were so off-put by this confirmation that Galileo was taken to court, accused for:

> Having believed and held the doctrine—which is false and contrary to the sacred and divine Scriptures—that the Sun is the center of the world and does not move from east to west and that the Earth moves and is not the center of the world; and that...opinion...has been declared and defined to be contrary to the Holy Scripture."[61]

Sadly, the same Church and court required Galileo to live out the rest of his life under house arrest, and when he died, he was forbidden a burial on consecrated ground. Not until a century later, when the heliocentric theory finally gained some ground in scientific and religious realms, were his remains moved and reburied in a proper plot.[62] My point in bringing this up is that, as human beings, there is much we simply do not know. If our very faith is threatened by scientific discovery to the point that discoverers are called heretical and emergent knowledge must be completely censored in order to preserve our ability to feel religiously secure, then we have a deeper problem than the discovery itself. It is easy, in hindsight, to perceive that heliocentrism and faith in God can be completely separate and mutually true, neither threatening the other. However, it took more than a century for those ancient folks to figure how to accept both facts without it seeming heretical.

Similar guardedness occurs today between religious and scientific factions. In 2014, when NASA offered a $1.1 million grant to the Center for Theological Inquiry, many were suspicious of their motivations. Members of the Freedom from Religion Foundation were outraged, asserting that separation of church and state had been violated by the government granting funds to research matters properly handled within the religious sphere. NASA's response was to explain that if or when an ET encounter should happen, many of the philosophical questions we take for granted as being moral or ethical (such as "what is life?") may need to be revisited when our understanding of life within the universe necessarily shifts.[63]

We authors are also aware that, these days, scientific "facts" aren't always reported truthfully, news is often skewed or slanted, and generally consuming any information asserted by the media falls under a "buyer beware" umbrella. This means that, should there be a discovery of ET life or other groundbreaking explorations, we must all carefully filter what we receive as truth. In fact, *for this reason,* our faith must be hinged solidly to God alone, regardless of what info is being generated by the media.

Does new scientific discovery necessarily have to threaten us? Not to some Christians, who readily assert that, indeed, there is much to be gained the more we find. For example, American astronomer Carl Sagan, though many believed him to be agnostic, observed:

> How is it that hardly any major religion has looked at science and concluded, "This is better than we thought! The Universe is much bigger than our prophets said, grander, more subtle, more elegant. God must be even greater than we dreamed"? Instead they say, "No, no, no! My god is a little god, and I want him to stay that way." A religion, old or new, that stressed the magnificence of the Universe as revealed by modern science might be able to draw forth reserves of reverence and awe hardly tapped by the conventional faiths.[64]

As for an ET experience, our ability to rejoice as heartily as the above excerpt suggests may depend on whether the beings appear to be evil entities, fallen angels, or merely other created lifeforms. Some religious leaders have made such statements as, "Life on other worlds may actually stir our Christian faith," noting the added discovery of intelligent life would only add to the magnificence of God's repertoire of miraculous works and majestic creation.[65]

The late Christian evangelist Billy Graham indicated he wasn't at all threatened by the notion of extraterrestrial life. He stated:

> If there is life on other planets, then God created that life, for God created everything. As the Bible says, "In the beginning God created the heavens and the earth.... Thus the heavens and the earth were completed in all their vast array" (Genesis 1:1; 2:1). Furthermore, if there are beings on other planets that have souls and can know God, then God created them in His image, just as He did us. And you can be sure that He has somehow made it possible for them to know Him.[66]

Graham follows up the words quoted above by reminding contemporary Christians to focus on their own faith and remember that God is most interested in what *we* do in the *here and now*.

Image-Bearers

You are an Image-bearer. This is an endowment to you—to each of us—by God Himself. It is an attribute we don't earn, nor must we jump over any hurdles—religious or otherwise—to keep it. If hybridization theories discussed earlier in the chapter are true, then this "image-bearing" attribute is apparently a threat to the enemies of God. But what does it mean to be an Image-bearer? The obvious answer is that God has made us in His image, as indicated in Genesis 1:26–27:

> And God said, Let us make man in our image, after our likeness: and let them have dominion over the fish of the sea, and over the fowl of the air, and over the cattle, and over all the earth, and over every creeping thing that creepeth upon the earth. So God created mankind in his own image, in the image of God he created them; male and female he created them.

It's important to note in the account of humanity's creation how God went about the process, and how that process differed from the creation of the other creatures and wonders until that point. Until He created humans, God had simply *spoken* everything into existence: "Let there be light," (Genesis 1:3); "Let there be a firmament in the midst of the waters [which is the sky]," (verse 6); "Let the earth bring forth grass, the herb yielding seed, and the fruit tree," (verse 11); and so on.

But then God stopped *speaking* the world and its elements into existence and started *doing*: He took dust from the ground and formed a man from it, breathing into it life:

And the Lord God formed man of the dust of the ground, and breathed into his nostrils the breath of life; and man became a living soul. (Genesis 2:7)

Consider what commentator James Murphy says regarding this passage:

There his creation as an integral whole is recorded with special reference to his higher nature, by which he was fitted to hold communion with his Maker, and exercise dominion over the inferior creation.... He is a compound of matter and mind. His material part is dust from the soil, out of which he is *formed* as the potter moulds the vessel out of the clay.... The "breath of life" is peculiar to this passage. It expresses the spiritual and principal element in man, which is not formed, but breathed by the Creator into the bodily form of man. This rational part is that in which he bears the image of God, and is fitted to be his vicegerent here on earth.[67]

The word "vicegerent" is defined as "an administrative deputy of a king or magistrate."[68] In other words, God placed humans on Earth to be His representatives on this planet: to compassionately rule over subordinate beings, to care for and maintain creation using His gentle authority, and to occupy while representing and communing with Him.

We see this wondrous attribute elaborated upon in the account of God making Eve:

> And the Lord God said, It is not good that the man should be alone; I will make him an help meet for him.... And the Lord God caused a deep sleep to fall upon Adam, and he slept: and he took one of his ribs, and closed up the flesh instead thereof; And the rib, which the Lord God had taken from man, made he a woman, and brought her unto the man. And Adam said, This is now bone of my bones, and flesh of my flesh: she shall be called Woman, because she was taken out of Man. (Genesis 2:18, 21–23).

Murphy illuminates this passage for us as well:

> [Adam] had met with his superior in his Creator, his inferiors in the animals, and he was now to meet his equal in the woman...by the divine command his moral sense had been brought into play, the theory of moral obligation had been revealed to his mind, and he was therefore prepared to deal with a moral being like himself, to understand and respect the rights of another, to do unto another as he would have another do to him.[69]

Recall that Genesis 1:27 specifically states man and woman were both made in the image of God. Amongst all the other created elements God simply spoke into existence, Adam and Eve were the two God completely stopped and handcrafted to be in His image.

Consider the kings of ancient times and even rulers of today. Since leaders can't be everywhere in the territories they rule, they place markers of their authority throughout their jurisdiction. Ancient kings would station images or likenesses in various places, while modern governments post their seal, flag, or other icons across their dominions. While God isn't limited, as are human beings, and He *is* everywhere all at once (Jeremiah 23:23–24), His stationed likenesses across Earth are human beings. We are His representatives who bear His image, His workmanship (Ephesians 2:10), and we carry His authority on earthly realms. Bearing His image is an innately human attribute. If enemies of God are threatened by our ability to carry His image, then corrupting that image may be their reason to target humans as enemies as well.

Will *Christians* Fall for a Coming Deception?

Whether Christians *fall* for a coming deception has a direct correlation to how well their faith is grounded and if they have worked through their belief system using and knowing Scripture. We can add to this query whether the existence of otherworldly lifeforms would cause Christians to *lose* their religion altogether, whether the entities aim to deceive humankind or not. Certainly, there are instances throughout religious history wherein the Church fathers have noted being open to the concept that other intelligent lifeforms may be out there. For example, in a *Christianity Today* article, author Andrew Davison discusses several of these figures who became outspoken on the matter as cosmological knowledge began to expand, challenging the faith of some:

> In the 15th century, we have a Franciscan friar, Guillaume de Vaurouillon, and Nicholas of Cusa, perhaps the greatest theologian of his age. In the 17th, there's the Dominican Tommaso Campanella (writing in defense of Galileo). We could add English Puritan theologian Richard Baxter and Anglican John Ray, who wrote of the possibility of other solar systems with planets that were "in all likelihood furnished with as great variety of corporeal creatures, animate and inanimate, as the earth is, and all as different in nature as they are in place from the terrestrial, and from each other."[70]

Or, consider the words of notable nineteenth-century "prince of preachers," Charles Spurgeon:

> He is the Governor of all worlds, and must maintain his government. There may be tens of thousands of races of creatures all subject to him, and governed by the same law of immutable right and justice, and if it were whispered throughout the universe that on so much as one solitary occasion the Judge of all the earth had winked at sin, and exercised his sovereignty to suspend his moral law, and to deny justice its due, it would not matter how obscure an object the tolerated sinner might be, he would be quoted in every world and mentioned by every race of creatures, as a proof that divine justice was not invariable and without respect of persons.[71]

Before moving on, we will offer the musings of one more renowned figure—C. S. Lewis, a British writer and scholar who boldly considered the "possibility that Jesus could have 'been incarnate in other worlds than earth and so saved other races than ours.'"[72]

While some remain open to the notion that other created life could be in outer space, some carefully remind us that, since Scripture only discusses the image of God being imbued into humanity, if there are other intelligent beings, they would not bear this "image of God" attribute. Others simply but firmly state there is no other intelligent life—and entertaining such concepts is to indulge in fantasies.

However, for those who genuinely believe extraterrestrial life is a possibility and struggle to rectify the Bible's seeming omission of such topics, Alvin Platinga, a twentieth-century philosopher, offers some helpful insight:

> You may be wondering why the Bible doesn't have more to say, then, about God's activities outside of the Earth. But, if you consider the approach of the Bible, it is consistent. The majority of the Bible is spent telling a story from the vantage point

of one family—Abraham's. But, nowhere does the Bible say that the nation of Israel (Abraham's family) is the only country or the only country that God cares about. The absence of alien life found in the Bible does not mean that the Bible necessarily rejects aliens.[73]

The Apostle Paul, in Philippians 2:12–13, instructs us:

Wherefore, my beloved, as ye have always obeyed, not as in my presence only, but now much more in my absence, work out your own salvation with fear and trembling. For it is God which worketh in you both to will and to do of his good pleasure.

With that passage in mind, one final red flag I want to point out before moving on is the danger of Christians who exist merely to congregate in churches on Sunday, but who don't know what the Bible itself says about matters important to life, and who can't articulate *why* they believe what they do. In the moment that—whether by the discovery of extraterrestrial life or some, much simpler, happenstance—their faith is tried, they may be at risk of "losing their religion" because of their lack of the ability to defend their faith.

Currently, many who observe trends within Christianity have already noted a great chasm between God and many of His self-proclaimed followers. Some have even stated we are witnessing the beginning of the prophetic "falling away" spoken of in 2 Thessalonians 2:3, which describes the spiritual climate of the Antichrist's introduction to society. Perhaps the real threat to Earth does not come from *outside* of it, but from the godlessness *within* it. Those who consider ourselves ambassadors for Christ must, as an urgent matter, equip ourselves with the armor of God: truth, righteousness, a readiness to share the Gospel message, faith, salvation, and the Word of God, as described in Ephesians 6:10–18.

Unfortunately, however, many have grown not only complacent, but remain uneducated as to what the Bible says, they don't follow

His commandments. Over the past forty-five years, numbers of those claiming to read the Word have declined dramatically, especially during and after the COVID-19 event, which rendered the following horrific effects on our Bible-reading society, according to a study conducted by the American Bible Society for its State of the Bible project:

> In every study since 2018, Bible users have accounted for between 47 and 49 percent of American adults; however, the 2022 data showed a 10-percent decrease from the same time in 2021. That means nearly 26 million Americans reduced or stopped their interaction with Scripture in the past year.[74]

Other polls find sharp deviances between the numbers of people who claim to be Christian, but who are aware of its creeds. In our book *Dark Covenant*, Donna Howell and I discussed the deplorable negligence of the modern Church regarding this and other relevant practices for maintaining a healthy relationship with God. The following is an excerpt from this work:

> When ruminating about the disease of the Protestant Church, truly "being" followers of Christ and not just "looking like" followers of Christ is by far the most important consideration, since any other position is a cultic counterfeit.
> The creed of the Church says, "I follow Christ."
> The deeds of the Church say, "I don't follow His tenets or believe what the Word says about Him."
> For instance: The Christian statistics research group, Barna Group, in its definition of the term "biblical worldview," identifies six universal nonnegotiables within Christianity as a belief system, based on interdenominational tracking of central Christian tenets compiled since 1995. These essentials, which apply to all Protestant denominations, are:

1. "Absolute moral truth exists."
2. The Bible is wholly reliable and accurate.
3. Satan is a real being, not merely a symbol of sin.
4. Simply being a good person does not send one to heaven.
5. Jesus came to Earth and was sinless.
6. "God is the all-knowing, all-powerful creator of the world who still rules the universe today."

These authors (and everyone in the SkyWatch TV and Defender Publishing circle) concur with every item on this list. Though we would likely add several things, we certainly wouldn't take anything away from these rudimentary, fundamental components of Christian belief. However, Barna reports, only a staggering 17 percent of practicing Christians in the US have a "biblical worldview" based upon belief in these six things.

That may come as a shock (it certainly did to us!), but it's a believable statistic when we really dig to see what today's Western Christians actually believe: One study reports that 45 percent of American Christians admit that "certainty about [Christ] is impossible," and only 34 percent believe He is "involved in their life," whereas another study states that 46 percent of born-again Christians believe that Jesus sinned while He was on earth. One report shows that only 41 percent of self-identified US Christian adults in the Baby Boomer generation believe that Scripture is "totally accurate in all of its teachings," and this staggeringly low number only jumps to 43 percent for the same category of believers in the Millennials, Gen-X, and Elders generations. Between 1993 and 2018, Christians declined from 89 percent to 64 percent in their belief that witnessing to the lost is a duty of their faith, whereas 47 percent of Millennial-aged, practicing Christians actually think evangelism is morally wrong, as it may pressure someone to change faiths! These authors don't know what's worse: the fact that so many Christians don't think the Great Commission is a responsibility of theirs—or the fact that, out of 1,004 regular Christian church attenders in the US who were asked about the Great Commission in 2017, 25 percent couldn't remember what it was and 51 percent had never even heard the term in their lives! This means at least 76 percent of Christians are ineffective in spreading the Gospel. Maybe the numbers would be more impressive if we knew how to pray with people, but as it currently stands, only 2 percent of praying Americans do so with another person present.

As of October 2020, the latest large-scale research and statistics report reflects that 58 percent of evangelicals have "demoted the Holy Spirit to symbolic status," denying His role as a true Person of the Trinity. A lie is no longer a sin, according to 40 percent, so long as "it advances personal interests or protect one's reputation," and premarital sex is agreeable to half of all evangelicals. Salvation can be earned by doing good, 48 percent say. Abortion is morally acceptable to 34 percent, which makes sense when 44 percent don't think the Bible's teaching on the subject is clear and 40 percent don't believe human life is even sacred. This is probably why 39 percent don't respect anyone who holds to a different faith (which is ironic, since the entire faith system being described here isn't orthodoxically any religion). Pentecostals/charismatics aren't any more impressive, however: 69 percent reject absolute moral truth; 54 percent disagree that human life is sacred; 50 percent claim the Bible is ambiguous about abortion; and 45 percent are not born again! But of all groups, mainline Protestants take the lead for syncretizing their Christianity with the secularized culture of the West: 63 percent say God is not the provider of truth and the Bible cannot be trusted to fully represent God-given principles; a shocking 81 percent believe that people can be their own moral compass because humans are essentially good; only 33 percent make it a habit to confess sins and seek forgiveness from God, and a meager 13 percent read their Bibles regularly. The summary provided by the study states: "Sixty percent (60%) of mainline Protestants' beliefs directly conflict with biblical teaching."

When our creeds don't match our deeds, that's called "hypocrisy." Keep that in mind.

It's not all about what data the veteran research group Barna collects, though.

Ligonier Ministries conducts up-to-date surveys about the state of the Church, and researchers there have dedicated themselves to reporting every two years about how Protestant churchgoers in the West feel regarding the central doctrines of Christianity. The most recent survey, conducted in partnership with LifeWay Research, was released in September of 2020. The findings were appalling. Thousands of people of all faiths, as well as atheists and those with undisclosed or undecided positions, weighed in. In total, 48 percent agreed that the Bible was merely one of our world's historic "sacred writings" that record "ancient myths," but that it does not contain any truth, and 52 percent denied the divinity of Christ. This is sad for the public, surely, but far, far worse were the numbers reported specifically about the belief of evangelical Christians in the West, which start off bad and only get worse:

- 26 percent think that church ministries cannot be effective to the world unless their worship services are "entertaining."
- 39 percent agree that "material blessings" are a guaranteed reward of faith (that evil prosperity gospel of recent decades is still clinging on...).
- 46 percent take a relaxed position on sin, agreeing that people are generally "good by nature."
- 65 percent believe that Jesus is a being whom God created (as opposed to belief in the Incarnation of God, the Word

made flesh, aka the way through which salvation is even possible—cf. John 1:1, 8:58; Romans 9:5; Hebrews 1:1–4).

- 30 percent agree with the statement that "Jesus was a great teacher, but he was not God" (an outright denial of Christ's divinity).
- 18 percent answered that the Holy Spirit can tell a Christian to do something that the Bible expressly forbids (folks, 18 percent may look like a small and encouraging number, but remember that it represents almost one-fifth of all evangelicals, which is alarmingly high considering how blasphemous it is to suggest that the Spirit of God would lead us in the opposite direction of His own Word!); but the most demoralizing statistic of all is that:
- 42 percent (almost half!) of all evangelicals embrace the blatantly syncretistic/idolatrous heresy that "God accepts the worship of all religions."

President and CEO of Ligonier Ministries, Chris Larson, is correct in his rebuke when he writes, "people inside the church need clear Bible teaching just as much as those outside the church." Elsewhere, the ministry's chief academic officer Stephen Nichols, who also sits as president of Reformation Bible College, offered his opinion after seeing the crushing blow of the survey: "As the culture around us increasingly abandons its moral compass, professing evangelicals are sadly drifting away from God's absolute standard in Scripture.... This is a time for Christians to study Scripture diligently."

No, Stephen, that time was yesterday. Today, we are late...

———————

So, what is the true Body of Christ to do if we're looking at an overwhelming battle, and we're already running late?

We encourage readers to truly *study* their Bible, learning how to defend their faith at apologetic and logistic levels. ("Christian apologetics" means understanding how to defend the faith). Start now—today! Learn all the nuances of the Bible's message you possibly can. As you do so, your own faith will become tempered within your soul, making it unwavering in the face of adversity, anti-Christianism, and even deception. Have conversations with those who don't share your beliefs, and when you do, engage with others in humility and love. Don't be afraid to tell others you simply don't know the answer; research it, and even be willing to accept that fact that—once you've done your due diligence through research, prayer, and study—there are simply some things we don't know in this life. A Christian who pretends to have all the answers appears arrogant and has the power to frustrate both unbelievers and other Christians when tough questions are posed and their answers are either inadequate or nonexistent. Recall that John 13:35 states, "By this shall all men know that ye are my disciples, if ye have love one to another." Further, Jesus' own words warn us of the hypocrisy of claiming what we do not practice:

Ye hypocrites, well did Esaias prophesy of you, saying, this people draweth nigh unto me with their mouth, and honoureth me with their lips; but their heart is far from me. But in vain they do worship me, teaching for doctrines the commandments of men. (Matthew 15:7–9).

It may seem as though we've spent many pages discussing a controversial, fantastical, even world-threatening topic, simply to leap into left field, quoting clichés and oversimplifying matters rather suddenly. We don't mean to do that at all! In fact, we authors recognize that the Earth is—with or without an alien event—facing extremely difficult and ominous situations that will eventually escalate into end-times events. We do not take this lightly. However, the best preparation for saving humanity in all ways—physically, emotionally, spiritually, materially, etc.,—is for believers to step up, empowered as the Body of Christ to become an effective force for good in the world. We assert that this Body can be made strongest is by each of us strengthening ourselves our own faith, prepared for spiritual warfare, since that's the source of all other problems (Ephesians 6:12). In other words, we must know God's Word, while remaining approachable, humble, loving, kind, generous, and respectful of those with other beliefs; we should also practice what we preach. If each of us were to embody these principles while devoutly seeking God, we would become the source the world will look to for help when crises of any kind occur on Earth.

A Coming Deception?

> But as the days of Noah were, so shall also the coming of the Son of man be. (Matthew 24:37)

What will the future "days of Noah" look like? It could be that nearly the entire population of Earth will become sinful and fall away from God. Or, intelligent life could come to Earth, providing a "natural" explanation for all that was once considered supernatural, causing many to cancel religion and deny the existence of a higher power. It might even occur in the form of extraterrestrial beings that deceive humankind by asserting themselves to be gods, assuming credit for all supernatural deeds recorded in the Bible or claimed by any other religions. Perhaps this could be the great one-world religion prophesied in Revelation 17. In fact, it could even be that some nonhuman entities will attempt to hybridize humanity by altering the genomes of the Image-bearers. Of all these potential atrocities and others not brought up in this work, we don't know whether or how such disasters may manifest. The range of possibilities and concepts is broad. But, regardless of whatever comes to pass for planet Earth, we authors once again emphasize that the best thing we can do to prepare is to fortify our faith, know God and His Word, and be ready to defend our faith—even using apologetics and logical conversation that can hold its own when brought under scrutiny.

At the beginning of this chapter, I asked readers to imagine looking to the sky as a potentially alien ship descends to Earth. As the people in the world around you begin to ask questions, you feel a palpable panic surging in the confused crowd. Perhaps a person to your left shouts, in fear, a prediction that "everyone is about to die!" In response, someone on your right retorts that there is no threat, but that humanity is about to witness the hand of the divine, certain that a race of deities has arrived. Yet others turn to one another posing urgent questions.

Imagine, in that moment, being armed with knowledge—maybe not an all-inclusive knowledge regarding precisely *who* or *what* these beings about to land on Earth's soil are, but more like a certainty about your own faith. Picture, in that minute, having a firm and confident knowledge about who God is, who holds the future, and where your help comes from (Psalm 121:1–2).

In that moment, facing the completely unknown within that circumstance, you are ready.

This is what we urge readers to become—*ready*. By learning who God is and knowing His Word, believers will be aware of the signs to watch for in order to maintain vigilance in uncertain times or to identify prophetic events, to exude a peace that will draw others to place confidence in the One who holds your own assurance and will provide wisdom in dangerous situations. In the hypothetical scenario I opened this chapter with, visualize yourself watching these enigmatic alien craft, covered in lights, descend toward Earth. You are prepared and unafraid, grounded in your faith to the point that even in the most tentative circumstances, there is no doubt that you *know* who God is. Regardless of new revelations about to unfold about the otherworld, you are ready to stand solid. Picture yourself, even in the face of incoming false religion or spiritual warfare, knowing that, by His power, you are ready (Zechariah 4:1).

Begin now. Prepare yourself for that moment.

CHAPTER 7

MYSTICAL SCIENTISM

By Derek Gilbert

H ow has the creation of a modern mythology around the UFO/ UAP phenomenon developed into a thriving cottage industry from so little physical evidence? It says more about America's religious beliefs than it does about the number of times strange lights in the sky have been seen by credible witnesses.

Humans have wondered about the stars since forever. That's understandable; they're beautiful and mysterious, as out of reach as mountain peaks. And, perhaps for the same reasons, the earliest speculation about the stars revolved around gods, not extraterrestrials.

As with mountains, humans have associated stars with deities since the beginning of human history. Three of the most important gods in the ancient Near East, from Sumer to Israel and its neighbors, were the sun, moon, and the planet Venus. To the Sumerians they were the deities Utu, Nanna, and the goddess Inanna; later, in Babylon, they were Shamash, Sîn, and Ishtar. The Amorites worshipped Sapash, Yarikh, and Astarte (who was also the god Attar when Venus was the morning star—and here you thought gender fluidity was new).

God not only recognized that the nations worshipped these small-g gods, He allotted the nations to them as their inheritance—punishment for the Tower of Babel incident.

When the Most High gave to the nations their inheritance, when he divided mankind, he fixed the borders of the peoples according to the number of the sons of God. (Deuteronomy 32:8, ESV)

And beware lest you raise your eyes to heaven, and when you see the sun and the moon and the stars, all the host of heaven, you be drawn away and bow down to them and serve them, things that the Lord your God has allotted to all the peoples under the whole heaven. (Deuteronomy 4:19, ESV)

In other words, God placed the nations of the world under small-g "gods" represented by the sun, moon, and stars, but He reserved Israel for Himself. The descendants of Abraham, Isaac, and Jacob were to remain faithful to *YHWH* alone, and through Israel He would bring forth a Savior. But the gods *YHWH* allotted to the nations went rogue. That earned them a death sentence.

God has taken his place in the divine council;
in the midst of the gods he holds judgment:
"How long will you judge unjustly
and show partiality to the wicked?" *Selah*...
I said, "You are gods,
sons of the Most High, all of you;
nevertheless, like men you shall die,
and fall like any prince." (Psalm 82:1–2, 6–7, ESV)

To be absolutely clear: Those small-g gods are not to be confused with the capital-G God, *YHWH*, Creator of all things including those "sons of the Most High." We know the consensus view among Christians is to treat the gods of Psalm 82 as humans, usually described as corrupt Israelite kings or judges. With all due respect to the scholars who hold that view, they're wrong. Besides the fact that the Hebrew word *elohim* always refers to spirit beings, not humans, Psalm 82:7 ("nevertheless, like men you shall die") makes no sense if God was addressing a human audience.

No. When the Bible says "gods," it means gods.

There are other, more technical reasons to view the divine council as a heavenly royal court. We direct you to Dr. Michael S. Heiser's excellent website TheDivineCouncil.com for accessible, scholarly, biblical support for this view.

The divine council view is critical to understanding what's going on with the UFO phenomenon (and why the world is still such a mess, for that matter). Supernatural beings have exercised the free will they were created with to rebel against their Creator. As Christians, this should be our default view. After all, Paul spelled it out:

> For we do not wrestle against flesh and blood, but against the rulers, against the authorities, against the cosmic powers over this present darkness, against the spiritual forces of evil in the heavenly places. (Ephesians 6:12, ESV)

Rulers, authorities, cosmic powers, spiritual forces of evil: Those aren't concepts, ideas, or random acts of misfortune. Paul was warning about supernatural evil intelligences who want to destroy us. And at least some of them are "in the heavenly places."

Why this detour though the Bible? Two reasons. First, to document that humanity has looked to the stars as gods for at least the last five thousand years, as far as Babel and probably beyond. And second, to set the stage for what we believe official disclosure is really about— the return of the old gods.

You see, the Enemy has been playing a very long game. Once upon a time, Western civilization—Christendom, if you will—generally held a biblical worldview. While the influence of the spirit realm on our lives wasn't perfectly understood, at least it was acknowledged. And while the Church of Rome can be fairly criticized for keeping the Bible out of the hands of laypeople for nearly a thousand years, at least the learned scholars and theologians made a decent effort to interpret their world through a biblical filter.

Admittedly, this is speculation, but it seems consistent with history: It appears the principalities and powers have nudged and prodded humanity through the Enlightenment, then Modernism, and into Postmodernism to move modern humanity from a supernatural worldview to one that could believe in an external creator—ancient aliens—while denying the existence of a *supernatural* Creator.

In other words, to accept our ET creator/ancestors, we first had to reject the biblical God. In 1973, British science fiction author Arthur C. Clarke wrote, "Any sufficiently advanced technology is indistinguishable from magic." By substituting advanced science for the supernatural, ancient alien evangelists are spreading a sci-fi religion for the twenty-first century. It offers mystery, transcendence, and answers to those nagging Big Questions. And best of all, ETI (extraterrestrial intelligence) believers don't need to change the way they think or act.

This view found fertile intellectual soil in areas influenced by Greek philosophy. The rise and spread of Greek thought has run parallel with the belief in life among the stars.

The idea that there are more inhabited worlds in the universe than just our own isn't new. Around the time Nebuchadnezzar led the army of Babylon across the ancient Near East to conquer, among other nations, the kingdom of Judah, a Greek philosopher, mathematician, and engineer named Thales of Miletus (ca. 620 BC—546 BC) is credited with developing the basics of the scientific method. According to later philosophers, Thales was the first to reject religious cosmology in favor of a naturalistic approach to understanding the world. Among his theories was the belief that the stars in the night sky were other planets, some of which were inhabited.

The influence of Thales is felt even today. While there are benefits to searching for the natural causes of, say, earthquakes rather than attributing them to the temper of Poseidon, denying the influence of the supernatural altogether has blinded scientists in many fields of inquiry. For example, researchers into the effects of prayer tend to focus on the physiological benefits. It reduces stress and makes you "nicer."[75] Well and good, but since prayer is a hotline to the Creator of all things, could there be more to the benefits of prayer than just sitting quietly? Is it possible that people who pray are nicer and more relaxed because they've tapped into what the Apostle Paul called "the peace of God, which surpasses all understanding" (Philippians 4:7, ESV)?

To a scientist with a naturalist bias, the answer is, "Of course not." Since God can't be observed and quantified, He must not exist. And so extra "niceness" is a result of what *can* be observed—the physical act of talking to (in their minds) an imaginary God.

The intellectual descendants of Thales included influential thinkers such as Pythagorus, who in turn influenced Plato, as well as Democritus and Leucippus, who developed the theory that everything is composed of atoms. Epicurus, building on the teaching of Democritus, proposed that atoms moved under their own power, and that they, through random chance, clumped together to form, well, everything—matter, consciousness, and even the gods themselves, whom Epicurus believed were neutral parties who didn't interfere in the lives of humans—which, sadly, is a view of God held by too many Christians.

Interestingly, about three hundred years after the death of Epicurus, Paul encountered some Epicureans (and their philosophical rivals, the Stoics) on Mars Hill in Athens. Epicurus, cited by the early Christian author Lactantius, is credited with posing what's called "the problem of evil":

"God," he says, "either wants to eliminate bad things and cannot, or can but does not want to, or neither wishes to nor can, or both wants to and can. If he wants to and cannot, then he is weak—and this does not apply to God. If he can but does not want to, then he is spiteful—which is equally foreign to God's nature. If he neither wants to nor can, he is both weak and spiteful, and so not a god. If he wants to and can, which is the only thing fitting for a god, where then do bad things come from? Or why does he not eliminate them?"

I know that most of the philosophers who defend [divine] providence are commonly shaken by this argument and against their wills are almost driven to admit that God does not care, which is exactly what Epicurus is looking for.[76]

You can see why the Epicureans wanted to tangle with a preacher of the Gospel of Jesus Christ. They must have thought Paul would be an easy target. Ha!

Of course, this so-called problem is often presented as "proof" God doesn't exist. Epicurus' argument assumes there is only one god who must be responsible for everything, good and bad. In other words, to satisfy the Epicureans, free will would be eliminated for every being in creation except the Creator, because to keep bad things from happening requires eliminating the power of people who want to do them.

And yet the philosophy of Epicurus—that everything is the product of natural processes, even the supernatural—influences our world to this day, even though most people who hold it have never heard of Epicurus. For example, the work of the late Dr. Edgar Mitchell, Apollo astronaut, sixth man to walk on the moon, and cofounder of the Institute of Noetic Sciences, a parapsychological research group "dedicated to supporting individual and collective transformation,"[77] was consistent with the teachings of Epicurus.

It's no coincidence the influence of the Greek philosophers faded with the spread of Christianity. The materialistic bias of Greek thought was pushed back for a time by the supernatural power and message of the Gospel. To be blunt, when you follow materialist philosophy to its logical end, you're left with the worldview of Epicurus—the only goal in life is to pursue pleasure and avoid pain.

What's the point? How would Epicurus answer the Big Questions? In short, the Epicureans view of life is depressingly bleak: We come from nothing through random natural processes; our purpose in life is to avoid being hurt; and we go nowhere when we die because our souls cease to exist.

Nothing, nothing, and nothing. That's what a materialist worldview offers.

And yet it came storming back after more than a thousand years underground with the dawn of the so-called Age of Reason, the Enlightenment. Ironically, the emergence of Islam in the seventh century AD may be partly responsible for holding back the influence of Greek philosophy in the West. After the first great wave of Muslim expansion wiped out Christianity in northern Africa, travel from the Eastern Roman Empire to Western Europe became more difficult as travel across the Mediterranean was no longer safe. It was only after the fall of Constantinople in 1453 and the resulting wave of refugees bearing what copies they could carry of the works of ancient Greek thinkers that the Enlightenment took root. And those ideas are blooming now in the twenty-first century.

The materialist ideals of the Greeks manifested in the rejection of a supernatural source for the Bible. And if those books were not inspired, then the words in them were free to be reinterpreted or discarded based on human reason. Likewise, supernatural experiences were open to interpretation based on human wisdom, without being filtered through comparison to the Word of God. This resulted in the odd mix of science with spiritism that is the legacy of Emanuel Swedenborg, an eighteenth-century Swedish scientist, philosopher, and mystic. He was undoubtedly brilliant, but sometimes the brilliant are blinded by their own light.

Swedenborg's theology encompassed the following concepts:

- The Bible is the Word of God; however, its true meaning differs greatly from its obvious meaning. Furthermore, Swedenborg, and only he, via the help of Angels (capitalized in his work), was in the position to shed light upon the true meaning and message of the Scriptures.

- Swedenborg believed that the world of matter is a laboratory for the soul, where the material is used to "force-refine" the spiritual.
- In many ways, Swedenborg was quite universal in his concepts, for he believed that all religious systems have their divine duty and purpose and that this is not the sole virtue of Christianity.
- Swedenborg believed that the mission of the Church is absolutely necessary inasmuch as, left to his or her own devices, humanity simply cannot work out its relationship to God.
- He saw the real power of Christ's life in the example it gave to others and vehemently rejected the concept of Christian atonement and original sin.[78]

Swedenborg believed the angels who contacted him lived elsewhere in the solar system. To this day, the Swedenborg Foundation offers a modern translation of the mystic's 1758 work *Life on Other Planets*, a book that "details Swedenborg's conversations with spirits from Jupiter, Mars, Mercury, Saturn, Venus, and the moon, who discuss their lives on other planets and how their cultures differed from those of earthly life."[79] Swedenborg's teachings on spiritism and angelic ETIs are still around, although it's been rebranded "the New Church."

Of course, Swedenborg, who died in 1772, wasn't the last word in the rise of mystic scientism. Others with a belief in the link between humanity and life from the stars included Joseph Smith, who founded Mormonism about fifty years after Swedenborg's death. The cosmology developed by Smith included the existence of many worlds. God to Smith was flesh and blood,[80] formerly a mortal man who'd earned godhood and, apparently, the right to create multiple earths.

[29]And [Moses] beheld many lands; and each land was called earth, and there were inhabitants on the face thereof.

[30]And it came to pass that Moses called upon God, saying: Tell me, I pray thee, why these things are so, and by what thou madest them?

[31]And behold, the glory of the Lord was upon Moses, so that Moses stood in the presence of God, and talked with him face to face. And the Lord God said unto Moses: For mine own purpose have I made these things. Here is wisdom and it remaineth in me.

[32]And by the word of my power, have I created them, which is mine Only Begotten Son, who is full of grace and truth.

[33]And worlds without number have I created; and I also created them for mine own purpose; and by the Son I created them, which is mine Only Begotten.

[34]And the first man of all men have I called Adam, which is many.[81]

A full analysis of the Church of Latter-day Saints is more than we can tackle in this book, but consider: A two-hundred-year-old religion that claims more than seventeen million adherents,[82] one of whom—Mitt Romney—might have been elected president of the United States, officially teaches there are many inhabited earths scattered throughout the universe. And the Mormon church isn't the only one that blends its theology with a belief in extraterrestrial life.

Beginning with the Second Great Awakening in the 1790s, which was itself a reaction to the rationalism and deism of the Enlightenment, nineteenth-century America saw successive waves of spiritual movements roll across the United States, spreading from east to west like supernatural tsunamis. A series of revivals, cults, and camp meetings followed European settlers westward as the country grew and prospered. The raw, unspoiled nature of the frontier contributed to a desire to restore Christianity to a purer form, free from the formality and hierarchy of the churches of Europe.

The Second Great Awakening, which swelled the numbers of Baptists and Methodists especially, peaked by the middle of the nineteenth century, but other spiritual movements followed close behind. The spiritualist movement, which emerged from the same region of western New York state that produced Joseph Smith and the Church of Latter-day Saints, the so-called Burned-Over District, first appeared in the late 1840s. Sisters Kate and Margaret Fox, ages twelve and fifteen, claimed to communicate with spirits through coded knocks or "rappings." They either convinced their seventeen-year-old sister, Leah, or brought her in on the con, who took charge of the younger two and managed their careers for years.

The Fox sisters not only enjoyed long careers as mediums, they left a legacy that continues to this day in the work of television mediums like John Edward, Theresa Caputo, and Tyler Henry. In fact, as we'll discuss in a later chapter, communication from disembodied spirits is a much larger part of the modern UFO movement than serious researchers are comfortable with. And this was even though Margaret and Kate admitted in 1888 that they'd invented the whole thing:

> That I have been chiefly instrumental in perpetrating the fraud of Spiritualism upon a too-confiding public, most of you doubtless know. The greatest sorrow in my life has been that this is true, and though it has come late in my day, I am now prepared to tell the truth, the whole truth, and nothing but the truth, so help me God!... I am here tonight as one of the founders of Spiritualism to denounce it as an absolute falsehood from beginning to end, as the flimsiest of superstitions, the most wicked blasphemy known to the world.[83]

The Fox sisters used a variety of techniques to produce sounds that fooled gullible audiences into believing spirits answered their questions, one of which was simply cracking their toe joints.[84] But even after their confession was published by a New York City newspaper, the spiritualist movement never skipped a beat. To this day, "many accounts of the Fox sisters leave out their confession of fraud and present the rappings as genuine manifestations of the spirit world."[85]

In other words, the movement lives on even though its founders admitted their act was as real as professional wrestling.

Why were the people who flocked to stage shows featuring mediums and psychics so eager to believe? Scholars speculate that the Industrial Revolution led people to explore spiritual frontiers to find meaning in rapidly changing lives.[86] Its quick adoption by prominent Quakers in New York tied the Spiritualist movement to several radical religious causes, including the abolition of slavery and women's rights.

Whatever the cause of its popularity, the Spiritualist movement continued into the twentieth century and attracted some well-known believers. Sir Arthur Conan Doyle, the creator of Sherlock Holmes, was one; in fact, Doyle wrote *The History of Spiritualism* in 1926, and he pegged March 31, 1848—the very first time Kate and Margaret Fox claimed to hear from spirits—as the date the movement began.

By the fourth quarter of the nineteenth century, Spiritualism was joined on the supernatural scene by the new Theosophist movement, a blend of Eastern and Western mystical traditions that found fertile ground among urban elites. Following the lead of their founder, Theosophists saw Spiritualists as unsophisticated and provincial. For their part, "Spiritualists rejected Theosophy as unscientific occultism."[87]

The founder of Theosophy, Helena Petrovna Blavatsky, is an enigmatic character, partly because it's difficult to confirm much of what she said and wrote about herself. According to the official histories, she was the daughter of a Russian-German nobleman who traveled widely across Europe and Asia in the 1850s and 1860s. By cobbling together traditions cribbed from Eastern sources, Blavatsky laid the foundation for the modern UFO phenomenon and ET disclosure movement.

Blavatsky acknowledged the existence of Spiritualist phenomena, but denied that mediums were contacting spirits of the dead. She taught that God is a "Universal Divine Principle, the root of All, from which all proceeds, and within which all shall be absorbed at the end of the great cycle of Being."[88] If you catch the Eastern flavor of her teachings, you're right—Madame Blavatsky wove Hindu and Buddhist concepts into her philosophy, and it's claimed that she and Henry Steel Olcott, with whom she founded the Theosophical Society in New York City in 1875, were the first Western converts to Buddhism. The success of Theosophy in the United States and United Kingdom did much to spread Eastern mysticism in the West, and the New Age Movement owes a debt to Helena Blavatsky.

Through her most famous books, *Isis Unveiled*, published in 1877, and her magnum opus, *The Secret Doctrine*, published in 1888, Blavatsky attracted international attention to her society and its goal of uniting the world in brotherhood by blending the philosophies of East and West through the study of comparative religion, philosophy, and science.[89]

In *The Secret Doctrine*, which Blavatsky claimed was channeled from a prehistoric work called *The Book of Dzyan* (and which critics accused her of plagiarizing), she wrote:

> Lemuria was the homeland of humanity, the place of the first creation. Further, there were to be seven Root Races ruling the Earth in succession, of which humanity today was only the fifth. The fourth of these races were the Atlanteans, who were destroyed by black magic. Lemuria would rise and fall to spawn new races until the Seventh Root Race, perfect in every way, would take its rightful place as master of the world.[90]

Who, you ask, were the Atlanteans, and what is Lemuria? In the nineteenth century, this odd marriage of Spiritualism and Modernism gave rise to competing claims that the human race was either evolving or devolving. Spiritualists accepted Darwinian evolution because it supported their belief in the continued development of the spirit after death. Blavatsky and her followers, on the other hand, believed humanity had left behind a golden age that collapsed when Atlantis fell beneath the waves.

Lemuria, like Atlantis, was another lost continent believed to be submerged somewhere in the Pacific or Indian Oceans. It got its name in 1864 when zoologist Philip Sclater noticed that certain primate fossils existed in Madagascar and India, but not in Africa or the Middle East. Sclater postulated a lost continent that connected Madagascar and India to account for the lemur fossils—hence Lemuria. Seriously. No kidding.

While the possible existence of Lemuria was dropped by the scientific community when plate tectonics and continental drift caught on, the notion of the lost continent was kept alive by pseudo-scientists and spiritual leaders like Blavatsky.

Mysterious symbols, tragic history, and memories of a glorious, golden past transmitted by disembodied Masters of Ancient Wisdom via "astral clairvoyance" to Blavatsky and later Theosophists like C. W. Leadbeater apparently stirred something in the hearts of those who read *The Secret Doctrine*. With nothing but the force of her powerful will, Madame Blavatsky convinced thousands that the history they'd been taught was a lie, and that humanity's future was to return to the golden age that was lost with the destruction of Atlantis.

To put it simply, in Theosophy, Helena Blavatsky gave the world a religious faith in human evolution. The goal was perfection and conscious participation in the evolutionary process—self-directed evolution, a concept that spurred the eugenics movement of the late nineteenth and early twentieth centuries—and, although they don't admit it, the transhumanist movement today. Blavatsky taught that this process was overseen by the Masters of Ancient Wisdom, a hierarchy of spiritual beings who'd been guiding humanity's development for millennia.

From a Christian perspective, it's easy to recognize the deception embodied by the doctrines of Theosophy. While Blavatsky's critics accused her of inventing her faith out of whole cloth, a discerning follower of Jesus Christ can recognize some common lies: Humanity is the product of random evolutionary chance; we once enjoyed a golden age when we lived like gods; and our destiny is to regain that exalted status through proper spiritual discipline, ultimately to become one with God and the cosmos. This describes a common belief system that Dr. Peter Jones calls "one-ism."[91]

Obviously, this is fundamentally at odds with the Christian faith, which recognizes above all that we are most definitely not God. But the idea that we contain within us the spark of divinity is appealing. It's a good lie. In fact, it's literally the oldest lie in the Book: "Ye shall be as gods" (Genesis 3:5).

And, as this book continues, even though it may not be obvious now, we'll show how this old lie is at the heart of the modern ET disclosure movement.

CHAPTER 8

CROWLEY, ET, AND THE LORD OF CHAOS

By Derek Gilbert

H oward Phillips Lovecraft (1890–1937) is one of the giants of twentieth-century literature, although he wasn't recognized as such until after his death. And because he wrote horror fiction, he wasn't the kind of writer who got invited to fancy society parties. Lovecraft and his friends, most of whom he knew through volumes of letters (by one estimate, one hundred thousand of them),[92] wrote to entertain, usually by crafting terrifying tales and conjuring monstrous images of overpowering, inhuman evil.

H. P. Lovecraft was a sickly child who missed so much school in his youth that he was essentially self-educated. He never completed high school, giving up on his dream of becoming an astronomer, because of what he later called a "nervous breakdown." It's possible that Lovecraft's intellectual gifts came at the expense of social skills. It's also possible that he was tormented by the same demons, psychological

H. P. Lovecraft

or spiritual, that led both of his parents to spend the last years of their lives in an asylum. Lovecraft lived as isolated an existence as he could manage most of his life, and he admitted "most people only make me nervous…only by accident, and in extremely small quantities, would I ever be likely to come across people who wouldn't."[93]

As a child, Lovecraft was tormented by night terrors. Beginning at age six, young Howard was visited by what he called "night-gaunts"—faceless humanoids with black, rubbery skin, bat-like wings, and barbed tails—who carried off their victims to Dreamland. The nocturnal visitors were so terrifying Howard remembered trying desperately to stay awake every night during that period of his life. It's believed that these dreams, which haunted him for more than a year, had a powerful influence on his fiction.[94]

From a Christian perspective, it's a shame Lovecraft's mother, who raised Howard with his aunts after his father was committed to a psychiatric hospital when Howard was only three, failed to recognize the phenomenon for what it probably was—demonic oppression. But by the late nineteenth century, the technologically advanced West didn't have room in its scientific worldview for such things. In fact, Lovecraft claimed to be a staunch atheist throughout his life.

Ironically, despite his disbelief, the fiction of H. P. Lovecraft has been adapted and adopted by occultists around the world after his death. The man who died a pauper not only found an audience over the last eighty-plus years, but has inspired an army of authors who have preserved and expanded the nightmarish universe that sprang from his tortured dreams.[95]

Although Lovecraft claimed he didn't believe in the supernatural, he was more than happy to use the spirit realm as grist for his writing mill. Lovecraft apparently saw potential in the doctrines of Blavatsky for stories that would sell. They did, but mostly after his death. During his lifetime, Lovecraft was barely known outside the readership of pulp magazines, the type of publications that had been called "penny dreadfuls" a couple of generations earlier in England.

While Lovecraft may have rejected the idea of a lost continent as the now-forgotten motherland of humanity, the concept served him well as an author. The notion that certain humans gifted (or cursed) with the ability to see beyond the veil communicated with intelligences vastly greater than our own also made for compelling horror. Lovecraft viewed the universe as a cold, unfeeling place, so in his fiction, those beings, unlike the kindly Ascended Masters of Blavatsky's world, had no use for humanity—except perhaps as sacrifices, slaves, or snacks. The horror of discovering oneself at the mercy of immense, ancient entities incapable of mercy is a common theme in Lovecraft's tales, and he gave those ideas flesh and bone with carefully crafted prose that infused them with a sense of dread not easily or often distilled onto the printed page.

It's fair to say Lovecraft's style of gothic horror has had a powerful influence on horror fiction and film over the last seventy-five years. Stephen King, Roger Corman, John Carpenter, and Ridley Scott, among others, drew on Lovecraft's style if not his Cthulhu mythos directly. Maybe that's not the kind of legacy left by Ernest Hemingway or F. Scott Fitzgerald, but compare the number of people who have seen *The Thing*, *Alien*, or any movie based on a King novel (*The Shining*, *The Stand*, *It*, etc.) to the number of people who've read (not *claimed* to have read, actually sat down and *read*) Hemingway or Fitzgerald. Even though H. P. Lovecraft was basically unknown during his lifetime, he's had far greater influence on pop culture than the literary greats who were his contemporaries.

And, as we'll see, the influence of the staunch atheist Lovecraft has bled over into the metaphysical realm. Maybe it's fitting that the principalities and powers aligned against their Creator would find an atheist a most useful tool.

While Lovecraft was beginning his career as a writer, across the ocean another man fascinated with arcana and the influence of old gods on our world was hearing voices from beyond. Edward Alexander "Aleister" Crowley, born 1875 in Warwickshire, England, traveled to Cairo in 1904 with his new bride, Rose Kelly. While there, Crowley, who'd been a member of the Order of the Golden Dawn about five years earlier, set up a temple room in their apartment and began performing rituals to invoke Egyptian deities. Eventually, something calling itself Aiwass, the messenger of Hoor-Paar-Kraat (known to the Greeks as an aspect of Horus, Harpocrates, the god of silence), answered. Over a period of three days, April 8–10, 1904, Crowley transcribed what he heard from the voice of Aiwass.

> The Voice of Aiwass came apparently from over my left shoulder, from the furthest corner of the room....
>
> I had a strong impression that the speaker was actually in the corner where he seemed to be, in a body of "fine matter," transparent as a veil of gauze, or a cloud of incense-smoke. He seemed to be a tall, dark man in his thirties, well-knit, active and strong, with the face of a savage king, and eyes veiled lest their gaze should destroy what they saw. The dress was not Arab; it suggested Assyria or Persia, but very vaguely. I took little note of it, for to me at that time Aiwass and an "angel" such as I had often seen in visions, a being purely astral.
>
> I now incline to believe that Aiwass is not only the God or Demon or Devil once held holy in Sumer, and mine own Guardian Angel, but also a man as I am, insofar as He uses a human body to make His magical link with Mankind, whom He loves.[96]

That eventually became the central text for Crowley's new religion, Thelema,[97] which in turn is the basis for *Ordo Templi Orientis*. The OTO is a secret society that, like Blavatsky's Theosophical Society and Freemasonry, believes in universal brotherhood. The primary difference between Thelema and Theosophy is in the nature of the entities sending messages from beyond. Blavatsky claimed to hear from Ascended Masters who were shepherding humanity's evolution; Crowley claimed to be guided by gods from the Egyptian pantheon: Nuit, Hadit, and Ra-Hoor-Khuit.[98]

Aleister Crowley in OTO garb

The irony of all this is that Lovecraft, who denied the existence of Crowley's gods and Blavatsky's mahatmas, may have drawn his inspiration from the same supernatural source.

A key thread woven through the fiction of H. P. Lovecraft was a fictional grimoire, or book of witchcraft, called the *Necronomicon*. The book, according to the Lovecraft canon, was written in the eighth century AD by the "Mad Arab," Abdul Alhazred (Lovecraft's childhood nickname because of his love for the book *1001 Arabian Nights*). Perhaps not surprisingly, inspiration for the invented grimoire came to Lovecraft in a dream,[99] and through his many letters to friends and colleagues, he encouraged others to incorporate the mysterious tome in their works. Over time, references to the *Necronomicon* by a growing number of authors creating Lovecraftian fiction led to a growing belief that the book was, in fact, real. Significantly, one of those who believed in the book was an occultist named Kenneth Grant.

Grant was an English ceremonial magician and an acolyte of Crowley, serving as Crowley's personal secretary toward the end of his life. After Crowley's death, Grant was named head of the OTO in Britain by Crowley's successor, Karl Germer. However, Grant's promotion of an extraterrestrial "Sirius/Set current" in Crowley's work infuriated Germer, who expelled Grant from the organization for heresy.[100]

Lovecraft's fiction inspired some of Grant's innovations to Thelema. Grant said Lovecraft "snatched from nightmare-space his lurid dream-readings of the *Necronomicon*." Instead of attributing the *Necronomicon* to Lovecraft's fertile imagination, Grant took it as evidence of the tome's existence as an astral book.[101] Furthermore, Grant believed others, including Crowley and Blavatsky, had "glimpsed the akashic *Necronomicon*"[102]—a reference to the Akashic records, a Thesophist concept describing a collection of all human thoughts, deeds, and emotions that exist on another plane of reality accessed only through proper spiritual discipline.

Kenneth Grant was perhaps the first to notice the strange parallels between the writings of Lovecraft and Crowley. In *The Dark Lord*, an extensive analysis of Grant's magickal system and Lovecraft's influence on it, researcher and author Peter Levenda documented a number of these similarities.

In 1907, Crowley was writing some of the works that became seminal to the doctrines of Thelema, known as the Holy Books. These include *Liber Liberi vel Lapidus Lazuli*, *Liber Cordis Cincti Serpente*, and other works written between October 30 and November 1 of that year, and *Liber Arcanorum* and *Liber Carcerorum*, written between December 5 and 14 that same year. Lovecraft would have had no knowledge of this, as he was only a seventeen-year-old recluse living at home on Angell Street in Providence, Rhode Island, dreaming of the stars.

Instead, he later would write of an orgiastic ritual taking place that year in the bayous outside New Orleans, Louisiana, and on the very same day Crowley was writing the books enumerated above. The story Lovecraft wrote is entitled "The Call of Cthulhu" and is arguably his most famous work. He wrote the story in 1926, in late August or early September, but placed the action in New Orleans in 1907 and later in Providence in 1925.

How is this relevant? Lovecraft's placement of the orgiastic ritual in honor of the high priest of the Great Old Ones, Cthulhu, and the discovery of a statue of Cthulhu by the New Orleans police on Halloween, 1907 coincides precisely with Crowley's fevered writing of his own gothic prose. In the *Liber*

Liberi vel Lapidus Lazuli, for instance, Crowley writes the word "Tutulu" for the first time. He claims not to know what this word means, or where it came from. As the name of Lovecraft's fictional alien god can be pronounced "Kutulu," it seems more than coincidental, as Kenneth Grant himself noted.

However, this is only the tip of an eldritch iceberg. In Crowley's *Liber Cordis Cincti Serpente*—or "The Book of the Heart Girt with a Serpent"—there are numerous references to the "Abyss of the Great Deep," to Typhon, Python, and the appearance of an "old gnarled fish" with tentacles...all descriptions that match Lovecraft's imagined Cthulhu perfectly—not approximately, but perfectly. Crowley's volume was written on November 1, 1907. The ritual for Cthulhu in New Orleans took place on the same day, month and year.[103]

Now, this could be nothing more than a strange coincidence. Your authors, however, are not coincidence theorists. Levenda, an excellent researcher and a gifted author (more on just *how* gifted shortly), and Kenneth Grant before him, also concluded otherwise.

Both men—the American author and the English magician—were dealing with the same subject matter, and indeed Lovecraft had dated the first appearance of the Cthulhu statue to the same year, month, and day Crowley began writing these sections of the Holy Books. There is no hard evidence that either man knew of the other, although the author believes references to an English satanist in Lovecraft's "The Thing on the Doorstep" could be an allusion to Crowley. In any event, to suggest these two men cooperated or collaborated in any deliberate way would be the height (or depth!) of conspiracy theory.

It may actually be more logical to suggest—as an explanation for some of these coincidences—that darker forces were at work. In fact, it is possible the same forces of which Lovecraft himself writes—the telepathic communication between followers of Cthulhu and the Great Old Ones—were what prompted him to write these fictional accounts of real events. Either Lovecraft was in some kind of telepathic communication with Crowley, or both men were in telepathic communication with…Something Else.[104]

As Christians, your authors are inclined to go with the supernatural explanation. If the Apostle Paul knew his theology, and he did, then we must consider the influence of principalities and powers on our natural world. That's the most likely source of the odd, highly improbable Crowley-Cthulhu connection.

In the early 1970s, Grant would break with the American OTO and form his own Thelemic organization, the Typhonian OTO. The "Sirius/Set current" Grant identified in the 1950s referred to the Egyptian deity Set, god of the desert, storms, foreigners, violence, and chaos. To grasp the significance of Grant's innovation to Crowley's religion, a brief history of the Egyptian god Set is in order.

Set—sometimes called Seth, Sheth, or Sutekh—is one of the oldest gods in the Egyptian pantheon. There is evidence he was worshipped long before the pharaohs, in the pre-dynastic era called Naqada I, which may date as far back as 3750 BC.[105] To put that into context, writing wasn't invented in Sumer until about 3000 BC, around the time of the first pharaoh, Narmer (whom some researchers identify as Nimrod of the Bible).[106]

Set was originally one of the good deities in Egypt. He protected Ra's solar boat, defending it from the evil chaos serpent Apep (or Apophis), who tried to eat the sun every night as it dropped below the horizon. During the Second Intermediate Period, roughly 1750 BC to 1550 BC, Semitic-speaking people called the Hyksos, probably Amorites,[107] equated Set with Baal, the Canaanite storm god.[108] Scholars have discovered that Baal-Set was the patron god of Avaris, the Hyksos capital. But the worship of Baal-Set continued long after the Hyksos were driven out of Egypt. Two centuries after Moses led the Israelites to Canaan, three hundred years after the Hyksos expulsion, Ramesses the Great erected a memorial called the Year 400 Stela to honor the four hundredth year of Set's arrival in Egypt. In fact, Ramesses' father was named Seti, which literally means "man of Set."

Set didn't acquire his evil reputation until the Third Intermediate Period, during which Egypt was overrun by successive waves of foreign invaders. After being conquered by Nubia, Assyria, and Persia, one after another between 728 BC and 525 BC, the god of foreigners wasn't welcome around the pyramids anymore.[109] No longer was Set the dangerous rabble-rouser whose appetite for destruction kept Apophis from eating the sun; now Set was the evil god who murdered his brother, Osiris, and the sworn enemy of Osiris' son, Horus.

By the time of Persia's rise, Greek civilization had begun to flower, and they identified Set with Typhon, their terrifying, powerful serpentine god of chaos. That's the link between Set and Typhon, and this is the entity Kenneth Grant believed was the true source of power in Thelemic magick. That's why the "Sirius/Set current" led to the Typhonian OTO, and that's the destructive, chaos-monster aspect of Set-Typhon we need to keep in view when analyzing the magickal system Grant created by filtering Crowley through Lovecraft.

> Grant's anxiety—as expressed in *Nightside of Eden* and his other works—is that the Earth is being infiltrated by a race of extraterrestrial beings who will cause tremendous changes to take place in our world. This statement is not to be taken quite as literally as it appears, for the "Earth" can be understood to mean our current level of conscious awareness, and extraterrestrial would mean simply "not of this current level of conscious awareness." But the potential for danger is there, and Grant's work—like Lovecraft's—is an attempt to warn us of the impending (potentially dramatic) alterations in our physical, mental, and emotional states due to powerful influences from "outside."[110]

By the 1970s, Lovecraft's work had found a new audience, and his stories were being mined by Hollywood (for example, *The Dunwich*

Horror, starring Dean Stockwell and Sandra Dee, and several episodes of Rod Serling's *Night Gallery*). Then in 1977, a hardback edition of the *Necronomicon* suddenly appeared (published in a limited run of 666 copies!),[111] edited by a mysterious figure known only as "Simon," purportedly a bishop in the Eastern Orthodox Church. According to Simon, two monks from his denomination had stolen a copy of the actual *Necronomicon* in one of the most daring and dangerous book thefts in history.

Apparently, the good bishop wasn't above earning a few bucks by publishing a stolen heretical text.

A mass-market paperback edition followed a few years later. That version has reportedly sold more than a million copies over the last four decades.[112] Kenneth Grant validated the text, going so far as to offer explanations for apparent discrepancies between Crowley and the *Necronomicon*.

> Crowley admitted to not having heard correctly certain words during the transmission of *Liber L*, and it is probable that he misheard the word Tutulu. It may have been Kutulu, in which case it would be identical phonetically, but not qabalistically, with Cthulhu. The (Simon) *Necronomicon* (Introduction, p. xix) suggests a relationship between Kutulu and Cutha.[113]

Simon's *Necronomicon* was just one of several grimoires published in the 1970s that claimed to be the nefarious book. The others were either obvious fakes published for entertainment purposes, or hoaxes their authors admitted to soon after publication. Simon, on the other hand, appeared to be serious.

But here's the thing: People involved with producing the "Simonomicon" have admitted to making it up, and the central figure behind the book's publication was Peter Levenda.

> The text itself was Levenda's creation, a synthesis of Sumerian and later Babylonian myths and texts peppered with names of

entities from H. P. Lovecraft's notorious and enormously popular Cthulhu stories. Levenda seems to have drawn heavily on the works of Samuel Noah Kramer for the Sumerian, and almost certainly spent a great deal of time at the University of Pennsylvania library researching the thing. Structurally, the text was modeled on the wiccan *Book of Shadows* and the *Goetia*, a grimoire of doubtful authenticity itself dating from the late Middle Ages.

"Simon" was also Levenda's creation. He cultivated an elusive, secretive persona, giving him a fantastic and blatantly implausible line of [BS] to cover the book's origins. He had no telephone. He always wore business suits, in stark contrast to the flamboyant Renaissance fair, proto-goth costuming that dominated the scene.[114]

In *The Dark Lord*, Levenda not only analyzed Kenneth Grant's magickal system and documented the synchronicities between Crowley and Lovecraft, he validated the supernatural authenticity of the fake *Necronomicon* he himself created! But make no mistake—that doesn't mean the *Necronomicon* is fake in the supernatural sense.

We can conclude that the hoax *Necronomicons*—at least the Hay-Wilson-Langford-Turner and Simon versions—falsely claim to be the work of the mad Arab Abdul Alhazred, but in so falsely attributing themselves, they signal their genuine inclusion in the grimoire genre. The misattribution is the mark of their genre, and their very falsity is the condition of their genuineness. The hoax *Necronomicons* are every bit as "authentic" as the *Lesser Key of Solomon* or the *Sixth and Seventh Books of Moses*.[115]

In other words, while the published editions of the *Necronomicon* were obviously invented long after the deaths of H. P. Lovecraft and Aleister Crowley, they are still genuine tools for the practice of sorcery. And, as Grant and Levenda suggest, they share a common origin point somewhere in the spirit realm.

Simon's *Necronomicon* arrived on the wave of a renewed interest in the occult that washed over the Western world in the 1960s and 1970s. Interestingly, it was a French journal of science fiction that helped spark the revival, and it did so by publishing the works of H. P. Lovecraft for a new audience. *Planète* was launched in the early 1960s by Louis Pauwles and Jacques Bergier, and their magazine brought a new legion of admirers to the "bent genius." More significantly for our study, however, was the book Pauwles and Bergier coauthored in 1960, *Les matins des magiciens* (*Morning of the Magicians*), which was translated into English in 1963 as *Dawn of Magic*.[116]

> The book covered everything from pyramidology (the belief that the Egyptian pyramids held ancient secrets) to supposed advanced technology in the ancient world. Likewise, the authors praised Arthur Machen, the Irish author of horror fiction, about surviving Celtic mythological creatures, and they discussed the genius of H. P. Lovecraft in the same breath as the scientist Albert Einstein and psychoanalyst Carl Jung. From Lovecraft, Bergier and Pauwles borrowed the one thought that would be of more importance than any other in their book. As we have seen, *Morning of the Magicians* speculates that **extraterrestrial beings may be responsible for the rise of the human race and the development of its culture, a theme Lovecraft invented.** (emphasis added)[117]

The success of Pauwles and Bergier inspired others to run with the concepts they'd developed from the writings of Lovecraft. The most successful of these, without question, was Erich von Däniken's *Chariots of the Gods?*, the best-selling English-language archeology book of all time.[118]

You can say one thing at least for von Däniken. He wasn't shy about challenging accepted history:

> I claim that our forefathers received visits from the universe in the remote past, even though I do not yet know who these

extraterrestrial intelligences were or from which planet they came. I nevertheless proclaim that these "strangers" annihilated part of mankind existing at the time and produced a new, perhaps the first, *homo sapiens*.[119]

The book had the good fortune of being published in 1968, the same year Stanley Kubrick's epic adaptation of Arthur C. Clarke's *2001: A Space Odyssey* hit theaters. The film, based on the idea that advanced alien technology had guided human evolution, was the top-grossing film of the year, and was named the "greatest sci-fi film of all time" in 2002 by the Online Film Critics Society.[120] By 1971, when *Chariots of the Gods?* finally appeared in American bookstores, NASA had put men on the moon three times and the public was fully primed for what von Däniken was selling.

It's hard to overstate the impact *Chariots of the Gods?* has had on the UFO research community and the worldview of millions of people around the world over the last half century. In 1973, *Twilight Zone* creator Rod Serling built a documentary around *Chariots* titled *In Search of Ancient Astronauts*, which featured astronomer Carl Sagan and Wernher von Braun, architect of the Saturn V rocket.[121] The following year, a feature film with the same title as the book was released to theaters. By the turn of the twenty-first century, von Däniken had sold more than sixty million copies of his twenty-six books, all promoting the idea that our creators came from the stars.[122]

This, in spite of the fact that von Däniken told *National Enquirer* in a 1974 interview that his information came not through archeological fieldwork but through out-of-body travel to a place called Point Aleph, "a sort of fourth dimension" outside of space and time.[123]

Right. Might that be the same cosmic place Kenneth Grant found the ethereal *Necronomicon*?

The claims of von Däniken, to be kind, don't hold water. His theories have been debunked in great detail,[124] and he's even admitted to just making stuff up,[125] but lack of evidence has never stopped crazy ideas for long. And now, thanks to a new generation of true believers,

Ancient Aliens and its imitators are still mining von Däniken gold five decades after his first book hit the shelves.

Ancient alien evangelists have effectively proselytized the American public since *Chariots of the Gods* went viral nearly fifty years ago. As noted earlier, more adults in the US believe in ETI than in the God of the Bible. Interestingly, serious UFO researchers are disturbed by the impact of the ancient alien meme on their work.

MUFON, the Mutual UFO Network, which calls itself "the world's oldest and largest UFO phenomenon investigative body,"[126] has gone all in with ancient aliens in recent years. The group now openly supports pseudoscientific and New Age (in other words, occultic) interpretations of the UFO phenomenon instead of sticking to what can be supported by evidence. For example, the theme of MUFON's 2017 national convention was "The Case for a Secret Space Program," which was described by one critic as "blatantly unscientific and irrational."[127]

The conference featured among its speakers a man who claims he was recruited for "a '20 & Back' assignment which involved age regression (via Pharmaceutical means) as well as time regressed to the point of beginning service." In plain English, he claims he served twenty years in an off-planet research project, and then was sent back in time to a few minutes after he left and "age-regressed" so no one would notice he's twenty years older than the rest of us.[128]

Seriously.

Another speaker claimed he was pre-identified as a future president of the United States in a CIA/DARPA program called Project Pegasus, which purportedly gathered intel on past and future events, such as the identities of future presidents. He also claimed Barack Obama was his roommate in 1980 in a CIA project called Mars Jump Room,[129] a teleportation program that sent trainees to a secret base on the red planet.[130]

The content of MUFON's 2017 symposium was so over the top that Richard Dolan, a longtime advocate for ETI disclosure, felt it was necessary to publicly explain why he'd sit on a MUFON-sanctioned discussion panel with men who claimed, without any corroboration whatsoever, they'd been part of a "secret space program."

When I learned I would be on a panel with Corey [Goode], Andy [Basiago], Bill [Tompkins], and Michael [Salla], I phoned Jan [Harzan, MUFON's executive director] and politely asked him what was he thinking. I mentioned my concern about MUFON's decision to bring in individuals with claims that are inherently impossible to verify. MUFON, after all, is supposed to have evidence-based standards.[131]

Maybe it shouldn't surprise us that MUFON has morphed from an "evidence-based" organization to one that actively promotes unverifiable claims at its national convention. As controversy grew over the theme of MUFON's 2017 symposium, it was revealed that MUFON's "Inner Circle," a group that provides "advisory guidance" to MUFON because its members—thirteen in all, a curiously coincidental number—have "shown unparalleled generosity towards MUFON by donating in excess of $5,000 in a single donation," included New Age teacher J. Z. Knight.[132]

Knight was born in Roswell, New Mexico (of course), in March 1946, just about the time Aleister Crowley devotees Jack Parsons and L. Ron Hubbard wrapped up their magickal ritual the Babalon [sic] Working to bring the Whore of Babylon to Earth. Knight claims to channel the spirit of Ramtha the Enlightened One, a warrior who lived thirty-five thousand years ago in the mythical land of Lemuria. Knight says Ramtha fought against the tyrannical Atlanteans before eventually bidding his troops farewell and ascending to heaven in a flash of light.[133]

Ten years after Ramtha's first appearance, Knight founded Ramtha's School of Enlightenment (RSE), through which she's become a very wealthy woman by selling counseling sessions based on the wisdom of the ancient Lemurian warrior. (While Ramtha has no need for creature comforts, Ms. Knight apparently likes nice things.) As of 2017, the school employed eighty full-time staff,[134] and annual profits from book and audio sales ran into the millions.[135] According to Knight, Ramtha's teachings can be boiled down to mind over matter: "Ramtha tells people that if they learn what to do, the art of creating your own reality is really a divine act. There's no guru here. You are creating your day. You do it yourself."[136]

That said, your authors assume that despite having mastered the art of creating her own reality, Ms. Knight still looks both ways before crossing the street.

Three students of RSE produced the 2004 film *What the Bleep Do We Know?*, a low-budget movie that twisted quantum physics into pseudoscientific New Age propaganda. Of course, Ramtha's doctrine of changing the physical world through proper spiritual discipline was the heart of the film.[137] Despite criticism from actual physicists, *Bleep* has grossed nearly $16 million in theaters to date.[138]

The attention attracted by MUFON's bizarre symposium on the "secret space program," coupled with the disclosure of some of the aberrant views of its state leadership and inner circle—not just occult, but racist[139] (which was far more damaging to the organization)—apparently led to a restructuring after 2017. There is no mention of an inner circle at MUFON's website any longer, and while they tout a Science Review Board under the heading "Our People," no names are given as members of that board, and what appears to be a link to a page titled "The Scientific Method" goes nowhere.

It sounds bizarre when we step back and summarize things, but there's no way to make this sound rational. The horror fiction of Lovecraft, inspired by the spirits behind nineteenth- century occultists like Helena Blavatsky (and possibly the *same* spirit that communicated with Aleister Crowley), was filtered through the French science-fiction scene in the 1960s, adapted by a Swiss hotelier named von Däniken, recycled as "archeology" around the time of the first moon landings, and blossomed into a scientistic religion that replaces God with aliens.

Wow.

To paraphrase our friend, Christian researcher and author L. A. Marzulli: The ancient alien meme is real, burgeoning, and not going away.

And the old gods are using it to set the stage for their return.

CHAPTER 9

GOVERNMENT
AND ET

By Derek Gilbert

Our goal in writing this book is not to document the crazy cults that have emerged since the beginning of the modern UFO era in 1947. There are plenty, and frankly they're so obvious that you, as a discerning reader, don't need us to tell you how far removed from reality they are. Some are relatively harmless, and others are not—like the Heaven's Gate cult that convinced thirty-nine of its members to commit suicide in late March of 1997 in the belief they'd be taken aboard a spacecraft trailing Comet Hale-Bopp.

It's more important that we look at how the ancient astronaut/alien meme has influenced our society in subtler ways. It's shaping the beliefs of people who have been convinced by media and academia that the Bible cannot be true, so we must look elsewhere for answers to the Big Questions.

As Christians, this kind of spiritual propaganda shouldn't surprise us. And yet it does, because too many churches have been lured by principalities and powers—fallen angels and their demonic minions—into a Modernist or Postmodernist worldview, either looking to science as the only tool for revealing spiritual truth or buying into the absurd, self-refuting notion that absolute truth doesn't exist at all.

What should concern American evangelicals is not the role played by the UFO researchers in spreading the ETI disclosure meme. That's why they're interested in the phenomenon in the first place. We expect that from them. No, what's bothersome is that the government of our purportedly Christian nation has deployed a variety of agencies and operatives to sell the existence of ETI over the last seventy years.

It began early in the modern UFO era. About two weeks before the crash at Roswell, New Mexico, made headlines, a harbor patrolman named Harold A. Dahl anchored in Maury Island Bay, Washington, with his son, their dog, and two crewmen. At two o'clock in the afternoon on June 21, 1947 (the summer solstice, coincidentally), they spotted half a dozen odd, metallic, doughnut-shaped craft hovering a couple thousand feet above them. According to Dahl, one of the ships seemed to be in trouble, with the other five circling around it as it lost altitude. A small explosion showered Dahl's boat with hot metal, killing his dog and injuring his son. Dahl beached the boat and took some pictures of the craft, which took off in the direction of Canada.[140]

His boat's radio was jammed, so Dahl headed back to Tacoma, got treatment for his son's injured arm, then took his camera and some of the metal fragments to his boss, twenty-seven-year-old Fred L. Crisman.

The Maury Island incident has gone down in the books as a hoax. Whether it is or isn't is beyond the scope of this book. The important point—unless you're a coincidence theorist—is that more than twenty years later, Crisman, a former officer in the OSS (the Office of Strategic Services, the forerunner of the Central Intelligence Agency, CIA), was subpoenaed by New Orleans District Attorney Jim Garrison in the trial of businessman Clay Shaw,[141] who'd been charged with being part of the conspiracy to kill President John F. Kennedy.[142] Some thought

Crisman was one of the three tramps picked up by Dallas police in the railyard near Dealey Plaza,[143] although evidence suggests he wasn't in Dallas that day.[144] In spite of that, Garrison apparently believed Crisman was one of the trigger men on the grassy knoll.[145]

Here's where things get even weirder: A few days after the Maury Island incident, Kenneth Arnold of Boise, Idaho, a successful businessman, deputy federal marshal, experienced pilot, and member of an Idaho Search and Rescue Team—in other words, an excellent witness—was flying home from Washington when he spotted a formation of nine UFOs north of Mount Rainier moving at upwards of 1,200 miles per hour. Needless to say, that's not a speed any known aircraft could reach in 1947.

Fred Crisman, even though he wasn't a witness to whatever Harold Dahl claimed he saw, reached out to the editor of *Amazing Stories* magazine, Raymond Palmer. Palmer had already been in touch with Arnold, offering him an advance for an interview about his UFO encounter. After hearing from Crisman, who'd had a pair of letters to the editor published in *Amazing Stories* in the previous year,[146] Palmer persuaded Arnold to fly from Boise to Tacoma, Washington, to meet with Dahl and check out the Maury Island incident. Oddly, when he arrived, Arnold found all the hotels in Tacoma fully booked—until he tried the most expensive place in town and discovered a reservation in his name, although no one seemed to know who made it.[147]

The odd series of events apparently gave Arnold the feeling the situation was a setup, possibly an intelligence op to discredit both him and Harold Dahl. So, he contacted the two Army intelligence officers who'd debriefed him after his initial report, Captain William Davidson and 1st Lieutenant Frank M. Brown. They flew to Tacoma immediately, arriving that afternoon and discussing the case with Arnold and United Airlines pilot Captain Emil J. Smith,[148] who had likewise been invited by Arnold. The two pilots had become friends after Smith and his crew reported five "somethings" over Idaho the night of July 4, 1947,[149] flying wings or discs similar to what Arnold had seen two weeks earlier near Mount Rainier.

After meeting with Arnold, Smith, Crisman, and Dahl, the intelligence officers seemed to think the Maury Island sighting was a hoax, and they prepared to fly back to Hamilton Field in California late the night of July 31 because their B-25 bomber was scheduled to fly in the first Air Force Day celebration the next day.

Sadly, Davidson and Brown never made it back to their base:

> At the airport, an odd thing happened, one which has plagued UFO researchers for years. Crisman, the man the intelligence officers seemed to think was nothing more than an oddball hoaxer, turned up at the last minute and gave the men a heavy box which he claimed was filled with the debris from the damaged UFO. To Arnold, who was there, the contents looked like a bunch of rocks. The men stowed the box in the trunk of their car and left for the airport, catching their flight. They never made it back to base. Both Davidson and Brown were killed. The enlisted men on board parachuted to safety after the left engine caught fire—according to the report of one of the survivors—and the two officers remained with the aircraft for a full ten minutes before the B-25 bomber crashed to earth. No one has any idea why the two intelligence officers would have remained with the plane and not parachuted themselves; or why they did not radio a distress call.[150]

It's important to note that Davidson and Brown were preparing to fly their B-25 out of Tacoma at around two o'clock in the morning. What are the odds that Fred Crisman just happened to be driving by the airport at that time of night?

A report filed by the FBI's Butte, Montana, field office designated SM-X (for "Security Matter X"—real-life *X Files!*) noted that Arnold remembered Crisman calling him and Smith at their hotel in the morning to tell them about the deadly crash, and wondering how Crisman knew who was on the B-25 before the Army had released any information to the press. And as for the press: Journalists for the United Press office in Tacoma were getting reports from someone who sat in the meetings between Crisman, Dahl, Arnold, Smith, and the Army intelligence officers, because bits of conversation were quoted back to Arnold and Smith verbatim.[151]

It's not within the scope of this book to unravel the Maury Island case, an incident that's still not settled in the minds of UFO researchers more than seventy-five years later. The big question is this: What was Fred Crisman really doing in Tacoma that summer?

The UFO sightings by Kenneth Arnold and E. J. Smith were only two among dozens in the Pacific Northwest, and literally hundreds across the country, in June and July of 1947. On June 24 alone, *seventeen* reports of UFOs eventually surfaced in the Northwest from Boise, Idaho, to Bellingham, Washington.

Crisman's behavior after Dahl's UFO sighting was odd, to say the least. And what conceivable path could lead him from the first "flap" of the modern UFO era to the Kennedy assassination?

In 1967, Harold Dahl authored an odd addendum to the Crisman chronicle in a note to UFO researcher Gary Leslie:

> There is a TV series running now that I swear is based in the main on the life of F. Lee Crisman. I know him better than any living man and I know of some of the incredible adventures he has passed through in the last twenty years. I do not mean that his life has been that of this TV hero on *The Invaders* show… but there are parts of it that I swear were told to me years ago by Mr. Crisman…and I know of several that are too wild to be believed…even by the enlightened attitude of 1967.[152]

Dahl made Crisman sound like the mysterious Cigarette Smoking Man from *The X-Files*. That may have been by design. Crisman may even have written Dahl's letter himself[153] to divert attention from what he was really doing in the Seattle area after World War 2.

[Crisman's] involvement with Maury Island may have had to do with covering up top-secret radar-fogging discs or the dumping of nuclear waste from the nearby Hanford pluto-nium reactor. Crisman wanted people to believe the [UFO] scenario, however. In early 1968, he corresponded with well-known UFO researcher Lucius Farish as the contact person for a group he called Parapsychology Research, under the pseud-onym Fred Lee. The alias, which only dropped his last name, provided Crisman with a means to discuss himself in the third person, telling Farish: "Mr. Crisman is probably the most informed man in the United States on UFOs and also one of the hardest to find—as the FBI has learned several times."[154]

Even more bizarre is Fred Crisman's link to another far-reaching conspiracy, "the Octopus," a case that's attracted new attention in 2024 because of *The Octopus Murders*, a four-part Netflix docuseries. "The Octopus" was the name given by investigative journalist Danny Caso-laro to a network of shadowy groups that overlapped the intelligence community (IC), global bankers, the military-industrial complex, and the theft of powerful case management software called PROMIS by the Justice Department during the Reagan administration. Central to Casolaro's investigation was an electronics and computer genius named Michael Riconosciuto, who claimed he'd modified PROMIS at the request of a friend of former Attorney General Ed Meese to allow secret back-door access by the government.

As it happens, Crisman worked for a Tacoma advertising agency owned by Riconosciuto's father, Marshall, thus linking the earliest UFO sightings of the modern era, the Kennedy assassination, and major figures in the Iran-Contra scandal, the 1980 October surprise,[155] the savings and loan crisis of the 1980s and 1990s, and other global conspiracies too convoluted to get into here.

To give you a hint of the type of games being played: Casolaro was found dead, his wrists brutally slashed, in a motel room in August 1991. His death was officially ruled suicide.[156] Riconosciuto was convicted early the next year of seven drug-related charges and received a minimum twenty-year sentence,[157] despite his claim that the video evidence presented by the prosecution was faked. Riconosciuto was released from custody in 2017 after twenty-six years in prison.

Back to Fred Crisman: As strange as his story is, he wasn't the only spook linked to early UFO accounts and the Kennedy assassination. You see, the FBI agent who filed the SM-X report on the Maury Island case was Special Agent Guy Banister.[158]

Banister is well known to John F. Kennedy assassination researchers. He retired from the FBI in 1954 and, after a stint with the New Orleans Police Department, set up a private detective agency that may have served as a front to supply weapons used by Cuban exiles in 1961's disastrous Bay of Pigs invasion.[159] Banister's mistress later said she was present when he advised Lee Harvey Oswald to set up a local pro-Castro Fair Play for Cuba Committee office in the same building as Banister's agency.[160]

In the 1940s, during the first wave of the modern UFO era, Guy Banister served as the Special Agent in Charge of the FBI's Butte, Montana, field office, which had jurisdiction over several western states. Declassified FBI documents obtained through Freedom of Information Act requests include several telexes marked SM-X sent by Banister from Butte to Washington, DC, all related to UFO sightings.[161]

The assassination of JFK had fingerprints of the IC all over it. But what were they doing with UFO reports back in the 1940s? And why has the involvement of American intelligence agencies (and presumably those of other nations) continued to the present day?

The key question is *cui bono?*—"who benefits?". For example, the Roswell crash was either an extraterrestrial craft (note: we authors don't think so) or an advanced project being developed by the US military. Either way, it did *not* benefit the government of the United States to tell the truth. If it was an ETI, then the United States wouldn't want to share any technology it might harvest from an alien ship with other nations; if it was a secret military project, then the Pentagon certainly didn't want anyone to know about it, especially if Nazi scientists smuggled into America via Operation Paperclip were involved.[162]

Deception in war is a very old art, going back at least to the time of the great Chinese military strategist Sun Tzu. During the Second World War, the Pentagon created a task force called Joint Security Command to preserve secrecy around planned military operations.

> Joint Security Control (JSC) was founded during WW2 as the US deception planning counterpart to the British deception organization knows as the London Controlling Section (LCS). Together, JSC and LCS perfected the art of strategic wartime deception, initially in North Africa but then throughout the theater of the European war, including the deception planning that contributed to the success of D-Day....
>
> In May of 1947, JSC received a revised charter, one that authorized it to continue its deception mission not just under wartime conditions but also during times of peace. JSC was tasked with preventing important military information from falling into the hands of the enemy, to control classified information through proper security classification, to correlate, maintain and disseminate all of the information furnished to JSC by the War and Navy Department Bureau of Public Relations, and finally the very important mission of cover and deception planning and implementation.[163]

Note the JSC's revised charter was issued less than two months before the UFO outbreak of June–July 1947, which included the Roswell crash. A declassified FBI memo dated July 21, 1947, related how a Colonel Carl Goldbranson of the War Department's Intelligence Division had sent a telegram on July 5 to Army Air Force Major Paul Gaynor, a public relations officer, advising him to contact "[redacted] Illinois who may have important information concerning [UFOs'] origin."[164] Major Gaynor had been quoted in a United Press story dated July 3 as saying the Army Air Force had dropped its investigation into flying saucers because of a lack of concrete evidence.[165]

Independent researcher and author James Carrion, a former international director of the Mutual UFO Network, a former signals intelligence analyst for the US Army, and an IT manager, has established that Col. Goldbranson was a member of the JSC since at least 1943, specifically working on "Cover, Deception, and Task Force Security."[166] The July 21 memo is important because it documents that a member of a military unit responsible for strategic deception, operating just below the Joint Chiefs of Staff, had asked the FBI to investigate UFO reports. Thus, we have FBI agent Guy Banister sending telexes marked SM-X to J. Edgar Hoover.

If, as we believe, the ET hypothesis is the least likely explanation for the wave of modern UFO sightings that began in the summer of 1947, then the motives of intelligence agencies to spin a compelling cover story become clearer. Blaming odd lights and strange shapes in the sky on an extraterrestrial intelligence gets curious eyes looking at a target as far removed from the government as one can get. Is it better for the public to believe we're being visited by ETIs or for word to get around about tests on a new high-tech fighter, bomber, or drone?

Cases like the Paul Bennewitz affair, in which a businessman whose company supplied equipment to the US Air Force was fed bogus information by an agent of the Air Force Office of Special Investigations to convince him that Earth was being colonized by aliens working from an underground base near Dulce, New Mexico, highlight the impact the intelligence community has had on the UFO phenomenon.

Bennewitz was a physicist by training. He lived in New Mexico within sight of Kirtland Air Force Base, home to the Manzano Nuclear Weapons Storage Facility, and Sandia National Labs, a research site that mainly tests non-nuclear components of nuclear weapons. In the late 1970s, Bennewitz became convinced that strange lights in the sky over Kirtland were the advance team of a race of hostile aliens preparing to invade. He began using his skills as a physicist and an inventor to monitor anomalous radio emissions from Kirtland.

He also began writing letters to people he thought should know what was happening in New Mexico, which brought him to the attention of the United States military. There was concern that someone as bright as Bennewitz might unintentionally expose something the Pentagon didn't want the Kremlin to know. And thus, the Air Force Office of Special Investigations (AFOSI) got involved.[167]

Having learned the essential parts of Bennewitz's theories— very ironically from the man himself, by actually breaking into his home while he was out and checking his files and research notes—that aliens were mutilating cattle as part of some weird medical experiment; that they were abducting American citizens and implanting them with devices for purposes unknown; that those same aliens were living deep underground in a secure fortress at Dulce, New Mexico; and that we were all very soon going to be in deep and dire trouble as a direct result of the presence of this brewing, intergalactic threat, the Air Force gave Bennewitz precisely what he was looking for—a confirmation that his theories were all true, and more.

Of course, this was all just a carefully-planned ruse to bombard Bennewitz with so much faked UFO data in the hope that it would steer him away from the classified military projects of a non-UFO nature he had uncovered. And, indeed, it worked.

When Bennewitz received conformation (albeit carefully controlled and utterly fabricated confirmation) that, yes, he had stumbled upon the horrible truth and that, yes, there really was an alien base deep below Dulce, the actions of the Intelligence community had the desired effect: Bennewitz became increasingly paranoid and unstable, and he began looking away from Kirtland (the hub of the secrets that had to be kept) and harmlessly towards the vicinity of Dulce, where his actions, research, and theories could be carefully controlled and manipulated by the Government.[168]

No, there is not an underground alien base at Dulce, New Mexico. It's a government PSYOP (psychological operation) (or rather, a MISO; "Military Intelligence Support Operation" is now the preferred term). Paul Bennewitz was gaslighted by the AFOSI with the help of prominent ufologist William Moore, coauthor of the first major book on the Roswell phenomenon, 1980's *The Roswell Incident*. Moore admitted to his role in the Bennewitz affair in a presentation to the 1989 MUFON national convention, but he justified it by claiming he'd used the opportunity to search for information that might expose government knowledge about the alien origin of UFOs—in other words, to work as a sort of double agent.[169]

Oddly enough, this revelation only reinforced the faith of true believers in the ETI meme. The government wouldn't try to discredit a prominent ufologist like Paul Bennewitz if he wasn't onto something, would they?

Maybe not, but what Bennewitz was on to had more to do with Russians than aliens. And the government deception worked beautifully. Not only did it distract attention from whatever the Air Force wanted to keep hidden at Kirtland Air Force Base, it established the Dulce base as a fixture in UFO lore.

To be blunt, the UFO research community has assisted this deception by being willing dupes. The low standard of evidence required for wide acceptance makes it easy for stories like the Dulce base to spread. French researcher Jacques Vallée illustrated this point in his 1991 book, *Revelations: Alien Contact and Human Deception*:

"Why doesn't anybody know about [Dulce]?" I asked.

"It's underground, hidden in the desert. You can't see it."

"How large is it?"

"The size of Manhattan."

"Who takes out the garbage?"

The group looked at me in shock. There is a certain unwritten etiquette one is supposed to follow when crashed saucers and government secrecy are discussed; you must not ask where the information comes from, because informants' lives would be in danger, presumably from hired assassins paid by the Pentagon, the kind who try to hit the tires of fully-loaded gasoline trucks speeding through refineries. And you are *not* supposed *to point out contradictions in the stories.* Questions must always be directed at the higher topics, such as the philosophy of the aliens, or their purpose in the universe—not the practical details of their existence. In other words, *it is not done* to ask any question that has a plain, verifiable answer.[170]

What about contactees and abductees? Surely, not all their cases are fake. True enough. But most of the time, their stories appear to be grounded in emotional or psychological issues that have nothing to do with ETIs.

As Jack Brewer documents in his book *The Greys Have Been Framed: Exploitation in the UFO Community*, accounts obtained from abductees under hypnosis are unreliable, to put it mildly. Hypnosis is not a trustworthy method of retrieving memories, and it may in fact be harmful.[171] Sadly, as Brewer notes:

Traumatized individuals are then at risk of sustaining deeper emotional damage while failing to seek qualified professional treatment. Such professional treatment is often discouraged within the UFO community in lieu of compiling so-called evidence of fantastic encounters with extraterrestrials.[172]

Contactees may have various reasons for concocting stories of ETI encounters, from just wanting to feel special to out-and-out delusions resulting from psychosis. But too often, treatment comes second to hearing new "evidence" of ETs' existence.

The intelligence community doesn't have to work very hard to push the ETI meme. The UFO community is doing that on its own.

Now, there are, without question, cases that can't be explained away as delusions, hoaxes, or intelligence ops. Joe Jordan, cofounder of CE4

Research Group and MUFON's national director for South Korea, has compiled hundreds of accounts of "alien" abductions that have been stopped by victims who called on the Name of Jesus. And, according to Jordan, this happens consistently. Now, why would that be if the abductors were, say, aliens from Zeta Reticuli? The logical answer, if one is open to a supernatural explanation, is that the alien abduction phenomenon is primarily *spiritual*—in other words, demonic.

But that isn't an answer the UFO community wants to hear, either, which is why Jordan calls it "the unwanted piece of the UFO puzzle."[173]

For all the interest in ETIs and the continuing popularity of science fiction in pop culture, there is no concrete evidence that genuine extraterrestrials are visiting Earth, if they exist at all. So why the deception? In part, spooks and military men find it a useful cover story for things they'd rather not tell the rest of us.

On a spiritual level, there is a darker agenda.

In 2010, researcher and author Nick Redfern published *Final Events and the Secret Government Group on Demonic UFOs and the Afterlife*, which he calls "probably my most controversial book to date."[174] It tells the story of an interdepartmental think tank inside the United States government nicknamed the Collins Elite. The group, according to Redfern's source, had been tasked with analyzing the UFO phenomenon, and it reached a disturbing conclusion: UFOs aren't extraterrestrial, they're demonic. Worse, the Collins Elite reportedly believes "the phenomenon 'feeds' upon a poorly understood form of energy contained in the human soul. In other words, we are being reared, nurtured, and finally digested, just like cattle."[175]

Furthermore, according to Redfern's account, the Collins Elite believed the soul-sucking "aliens" had anticipated that discerning Christians might recognize them for what they are. They countered that development by manipulating the ETI disclosure movement to make believers look foolish by convincing the public that extraterrestrial life is real. Members of the Collins Elite then reportedly settled on an odd strategy for dealing with the crisis—establishing a Christian theocracy in America. Somehow, according to Redfern, this shadowy, unofficial government agency decided imposing pharisaical laws on the United States would save the world from these infernal entities.[176]

How that's supposed to work isn't explained. Redfern admits to being agnostic on matters spiritual, so he can be excused for not grasping the theology involved, but if the story of the Collins Elite is true—and bear in mind Redfern's sources are mainly secret informants—then the US government is in serious need of people who've opened a Bible at least once in their lives. In his review of *Final Events*, Dr. Michael Heiser concluded:

> In my mind, the most disturbing thing about the book is that highly-placed insiders within the intelligence community could think so poorly—especially if they are Christians....
>
> What is the theological logic of this? That if the ruling elite are Christians, the demons will be powerless? Or that if a majority of US citizens are Christians, then God can or will act? (This makes God capricious to say the least ["I won't intervene against evil unless enough humans measure up"] or powerless to act unilaterally ["I cannot intervene against evil unless enough humans measure up"]). You can have that God. And how small-minded is this approach—to presume that the fate of humanity lies in the hands of the Church in the United States? What a muddled theological mess.[177]

But maybe that was the whole point of putting out the story of the Collins Elite. As Redfern notes elsewhere, the United States government has been thinking about how to use religious ideas as propaganda for a long time.[178] A 1950 RAND Corporation report commissioned by the Air Force, "The Exploitation of Superstitions for Purposes of Psychological Warfare," details examples of how closely held beliefs were manipulated by operatives for various governments.[179] The RAND report appeared just as the UFO phenomenon hit its stride in the US.

Predictably, the publication of *Final Events* seeded the notion among skeptics and atheists that evangelical Christians are willing to use the UFO phenomenon to justify "a concentration camp vision of America based in ancient Jewish law."[180] Those opposed to such a view of America's future will probably be hostile to anything that looks like it moves the ball toward that goal line.

Now, since you're reading this book, the odds are you, like us authors, laugh out loud at the idea that Christians are going to take over this or any other national government any time soon. Look at the culture around us, then ask yourself: Is this a society that's going to vote a truly godly government into power?

When we analyze the story of the Collins Elite, which serves as an appropriate summary of the history of the modern UFO phenomenon, the most likely explanation is this: Once again, human agents for the principalities and powers arrayed against humanity carried out an op to use ETI disclosure to advance the kingdom of darkness.

CHAPTER 10

THE NINE

By Derek Gilbert

Without a doubt, *Star Trek* has been one of the most influential entertainment franchises in history. Kirk, Spock, McCoy, Scotty, and others are iconic characters, recognized around the world. Oddly enough, though, through the series creator Gene Roddenberry, the starship *Enterprise* is linked to CIA mind-control experiments, a group of "aliens" who claim to be the creators of humanity, and—here we go again—the assassination of John F. Kennedy.

Let's back up to World War 2. During the war, Andrija Puharich, the son of immigrants from the Balkans, attended Northwestern University outside Chicago where he earned a bachelor's degree in philosophy in 1942 and his MD in 1947. Through an invitation from a well-off family friend who'd married into the Borden dairy family, Puharich found himself in Maine in early 1948, where he established a research institute to pursue his interest in parapsychology, the Round Table Foundation of Electrobiology, usually shortened to the Round Table.[181]

An early member of the Puharich Round Table was Aldous Huxley, author of *Brave New World* and *The Doors of Perception*, a book about his experiences with mescaline (and the book that inspired rock singer Jim Morrison to name his band The Doors). Puharich financed his research with gifts from donors, one of whom was Henry Wallace, who had been vice president under Franklin D. Roosevelt. Wallace, a 32nd-degree Freemason, persuaded Roosevelt to add the reverse of the Great Seal of the United States—the pyramid and the all-seeing eye—to the dollar bill.[182]

This book isn't big enough to hold a full account of what Puharich was up to for the US Army in the 1950s,[183] but the upshot is he was apparently researching parapsychology and chemical substances that might stimulate the human mind to reach into realities beyond those we can normally perceive with our natural senses. And at one of his gatherings in Maine, on New Year's Eve in 1952, Puharich and his Round Table, working with a Hindu channeler named Dr. D. G. Vinod, conducted a séance that apparently made contact with something calling itself The Nine.[184] Thus began a truly breathtaking chapter in America's hidden programs that searched for ways to weaponize the occult.

Some months later, on June 27, 1953, the night of the full moon, Puharich gathered around him what was to be a core group of the Round Table Foundation for another session with Vinod. The membership of this group of nine members—á la The Nine—is illuminating. Henry Jackson, Georgia Jackson, Alice Bouverie, Marcella Du Pont, Carl Betz, Vonnie Beck, Arthur Young, Ruth Young, and Andrija Puharich. Dr. Vinod acted as the medium.

Imagine the Fellowship of the Ring, with government funding and a security classification that was, well, "cosmic."[185]

This group included old money—*very* old money. The DuPont name is obvious, but some of the others were no less prominent. Alice

Bouverie was an Astor, a descendent of John Jacob Astor and the daughter of Col. John Jacob Astor IV, who built the Astoria Hotel and went down with the Titanic. Arthur Young was the designer of the Bell helicopter; his wife had been born Ruth Forbes. Yes, the *Forbes* magazine Forbes. Carl Betz was an actor at the beginning of his career in 1953 who later enjoyed success in Hollywood, best known as Donna Reed's television husband from 1958 to 1966 on *The Donna Reed Show*.

Ruth Young's previous marriage had been to another old-money family that traced its roots back to the early days of the American colonies, George Lyman Paine. The Youngs' son, Michael Paine, married a woman named Ruth Hyde, and in 1963, Michael and Ruth Paine became friends with a young couple newly arrived from Russia: Lee and Marina Oswald.

Yes, *that* Lee Oswald. Lee Harvey.

It's so implausible that it reads like the setup to a joke: "A DuPont, an Astor, and a Forbes/Paine walk into a government-funded séance…" But who or what were they talking to?

And why was the monkey god there?

Dr. Vinod sat on the floor, the nine members of the group in a circle around him, with a copper plate on his lap, prayer beads in his hands, and a small statue of "Hanoum," a Hindu god that the author believes to be Hanuman, the Monkey King. If this is so, it is interesting in that Hanuman was a human being, a minister, before becoming divine due to his devotion and courage. The half-human, half-divine image is one that becomes more important and more obvious as this study progresses. Another important aspect of Hanuman is his depiction in much Indian art as holding an entire mountain in one hand (and a club in the other). When—in the Ramayana and during the battle of Rama and Ravana—Lakshmana was mortally wounded, Hanuman raced to a mountain covered with different healing herbs. Not knowing which one Lakshmana required, Hanuman simply brought the entire mountain. Hanuman—as well as his fellow monkey-men, the Vanaras of southern India—is often shown with his hand in front of his mouth, signifying "silence" as well as obedience, in much the same way western occultists depict Harpocrates. In this sense, replete with silence, obedience, a club, and a mountain of herbs, Hanuman might easily have been the patron saint of MK-ULTRA.[186]

What an interesting coincidence, if you're a coincidence theorist. Remember that Aleister Crowley believed *The Book of the Law* was dictated to him by Aiwass, the messenger of Hoor-Paar-Kraat, known to the Greeks as Harpocrates, the god of secrets and silence.

Anyway, The Nine disclosed that they wanted the Round Table to lead a spiritual renewal on Earth, and eventually revealed that they were extraterrestrials orbiting the planet in a giant, invisible spacecraft.

Consider that the group assembled that night included highly intelligent, very successful people. And Puharich later wrote, "We took every known precaution against fraud, and the staff and I became thoroughly convinced that we were dealing with some kind of an extraordinary extraterrestrial intelligence."[187] In other words, if this was a hoax, it worked on some very smart people.

On the other hand, the decades-long career of Andrija Puharich suggests it may also have been a case of "leading the witnesses," in a sense. He appears to have been a seeker who, like Fox Mulder in *The X-Files*, really wanted to believe.

But it was more than that. The Nine declared, "God is nobody else than we together, the Nine Principles of God."[188]

So, The Nine claimed to be extraterrestrial *and* divine. And while the Round Table was hearing from The Nine, Aleister Crowley's acolyte Kenneth Grant was developing his occult system based on an ET god from Sirius.

Dr. Vinod returned to India a short time later and contact with The Nine was interrupted for more than fifteen years. Then, in 1971, Puharich discovered Israeli psychic Uri Geller.

Geller, best known for his alleged power to bend silverware with his mind, became for a time the new link to The Nine. Through Geller, The Nine informed Puharich that his life's mission was "to alert the world to an imminent mass landing of spaceships that would bring representatives of The Nine."[189]

Well, that group of space gods never arrived. Geller moved on in 1973, compelling Puharich to find someone else to bridge the gap between Earth and the giant, invisible craft allegedly orbiting it. He eventually connected with former race car driver Sir John Whitmore and Florida psychic Phyllis Schlemmer, who became the authorized spokesperson for their contact within The Nine, who finally identified himself as "Tom."[190]

Puharich, Whitmore and Schlemmer then set up Lab Nine at Puharich's estate in Ossining, New York. The Nine's disciples included multi-millionaire businessmen (many hiding behind pseudonyms and including members of Canada's richest family, the Bronfmans), European nobility, scientists from the Stamford Research Institute and at least one prominent political figure who was a personal friend of President Gerald Ford.[191]

Another member of Lab Nine in 1974 and 1975 was *Star Trek* creator Gene Roddenberry, who reportedly wrote a screenplay based on The Nine. Some suggest concepts from the channeling sessions Roddenberry attended surfaced in the early *Star Trek* movies and in the series *Star Trek: The Next Generation* and *Star Trek: Deep Space Nine*. The latter series featured a prominent subplot in which the commander of the space station Deep Space 9, Starfleet officer Benjamin Sisko, was chosen as the Emissary of an alien race worshipped as gods, called the Prophets, by the people of planet Bajor. The Prophets reveal potential futures to the Bajorans through orbs, which cause visions in those selected for the experience. There are many parallels between the role of Commander Sisko as the Emissary and the mission The Nine purportedly planned for Uri Geller and the other members of Lab Nine.

Before Lab Nine folded in 1978, the identities of Tom and the Other Eight were finally revealed: Tom was Atum,[192] he said, the creator of the Great Ennead, the Egyptian gods worshipped at Heliopolis, near modern-day Cairo. Besides Atum, the Ennead included his children Shu and Tefnut; their children Geb and Nut; and their children Osiris, Isis, Set, Nephthys, and sometimes the son of Osiris and Isis, Horus.[193]

Connecting dots between Andrija Puharich, who was almost certainly a CIA asset during much of the time he conducted parapsychological research,[194] and the volunteers of his Round Table and Lab Nine, we can link the United States government (specifically the US Army and CIA during the period of mind-control research projects like Bluebird and MKUltra),[195] members of upper-class society from the East Coast and Canada, the creator of the most successful science-fiction entertainment franchise in history, extraterrestrials, and gods. And not just any gods—the pantheon that included the chaos god, Set, who Crowleyite Kenneth Grant believed was the spirit of the age.

Oh, yes—and the Kennedy assassination.

How do we wrap our heads around this? Considering that Puharich probably conducted this research for the government and that he led the witnesses, suggesting to Geller and at least one of his successors while they were under hypnosis that they were being contacted by The Nine,[196] it appears that this was a long PSYOP to stir up belief in the existence of ETIs and the return of the old gods—in this case, from outer space.

To what end? For Puharich and his superiors, maybe it was an experiment in group dynamics, or maybe a test of how people would react to the imminent arrival of extraterrestrial visitors. Or maybe, as with the Paul Bennewitz case, it was an intelligence op to misdirect the wealthy members of Lab Nine and their social circles toward an ETI explanation for any unexplained aerial phenomena and away from secret government projects.

As Christians, we must look past the human actors in movements like these. In the case of The Nine, how did the charade benefit the entities that spoke to Vinod, Geller, and Schlemmer? Frankly, it's difficult to identify a specific goal other than spreading spiritual confusion. Certainly, seeding these ideas through influential members of high society and the military-industrial complex would be one way to do it. It's one thing to mock Blue-collar Bubba when he claims aliens from Sirius are about to land, but it's a different story when the one spreading the ET gospel is from one of the wealthiest families in the world or a successful industrialist who's proven to be a productive member of society.

But spreading confusion about the Big Questions—where did we come from, why are we here, where do we go when we die—may be enough for the principalities, powers, thrones, and dominions. See, the rebellious gods don't care what you believe as long as it's not this: Jesus is the way, and the truth, and the life, and no one comes to the Father except through Him (John 14:6).

And for the record: He's not from Sirius.

CHAPTER 11

HOLLYWOOD AND ET

By Derek Gilbert

The media has played a key role in promoting this new faith. Without the reach of the Internet, cable television, and Hollywood, it's doubtful the gospel of ET would have spread as far and as fast as it has.

They probably wouldn't characterize themselves this way, but the regulars on cable TV "alien hunter" shows are essentially, as Dr. Michael Heiser calls them, televangelists for the ET religion. *Ancient Aliens* is, incredibly, now in its twentieth season on the History Channel.

Do you remember when the History Channel still broadcast programs about history? Sadly, real history is as popular on television as it was in high school. So, programmers have turned to so-called reality shows, rehashing old cases about UFOs and alien contact, turning accounts of encounters with unexplained lights in the sky into a very nice living for the programs' hosts and producers.

We humans love a mystery, and other television networks have followed the History Channel's lead over the last decade with varying degrees of success. Programs about the paranormal and unexplained are featured on National Geographic, SyFy, Animal Planet, and the Travel Channel. Mystery sells. And nothing is more mysterious than unexplained lights in the sky and persistent stories of those who claim to have been aboard the ships.

The most popular and influential program catering to the hunger for the ET gospel is undoubtedly *Ancient Aliens*. It was launched by the History Channel in 2010 as a successor to *UFO Hunters*, which aired in 2008 and 2009. A number of other programs featuring the UFO phenomenon have come and gone since the turn of the century— *UFO Chasers*, *UFOs Declassified*, *UFO Files*, *Hangar 1*, and *Unsealed: Alien Files* to name a few—but *Ancient Aliens* is still plugging along in 2024, a one-time top-ten cable show with about 1.2 million adult viewers in its Friday-night time slot during its heyday.[197] Although viewership has dropped by nearly half since then, with most of the recent episodes just repackaged segments from previous seasons,[198] by the time you read this, some 250 episodes of *Ancient Aliens* will have delivered the subtle message that the Bible's account of humanity's origins is incomplete.

In retrospect, the shift from UFOs to "ancient aliens" was a brilliant programming decision. There are only so many ways to make jittery mobile phone videos of blurry lights in the night sky look interesting. Famous cases like Roswell, Kecksburg, and the Phoenix Lights have been analyzed as often as the Kennedy assassination. Without new information on old events, which isn't likely, or spectacular new cases to investigate, the UFO conversation runs out of material quickly.

By tying the UFO phenomenon to unsolved mysteries of the past, the producers of *Ancient Aliens* opened a gold mine of material. Everything from the pyramids to cults and mystery religions were suddenly fair game. Borrowing heavily from the work of Erich von Däniken and Zecharia Sitchin, *Ancient Aliens* has linked extraterrestrial intelligences to everything from ancient Sumer to cyclopean architecture and Freemasonry.

And, of course, the Bible. This, too, is no accident. Researcher and author Jason Colavito observed:

> *Ancient Aliens* stopped being about space aliens years ago and is now a sort of propaganda arm for New Age religion, which explains why it is so much more interested in the mystery of consciousness than actual evidence for the existence of space aliens.... Over the years *Ancient Aliens* has become *Theosophy: The Series.*[199]

Colavito is exactly right.

The beauty of this approach is that the producers of *Ancient Aliens* don't have to prove a thing. A medieval painting, an inscription from the ancient Near East, or an odd-looking prehistoric petroglyph is all they need to build another episode. Host Giorgio Tsoukalos begins so many statements with, "Could it be...," or, "Is it possible...," that the show has become a parody of itself.

A classic example is the fascination ancient astronaut believers have with biblical prophet Ezekiel's wheel:

> As I looked, behold, a stormy wind came out of the north, and a great cloud, with brightness around it, and fire flashing forth continually, and in the midst of the fire, as it were gleaming metal....
>
> Now as I looked at the living creatures, I saw a wheel on the earth beside the living creatures, one for each of the four of them. As for the appearance of the wheels and their construction: their appearance was like the gleaming of beryl. And the four had the same likeness, their appearance and construction being as it were a wheel within a wheel. When they went, they went in any of their four directions without turning as they went. And their rims were tall and awesome, and the rims of all four were full of eyes all around. And when the living creatures went, the wheels went beside them; and when the living

creatures rose from the earth, the wheels rose. Wherever the spirit wanted to go, they went, and the wheels rose along with them, for the spirit of the living creatures was in the wheels. When those went, these went; and when those stood, these stood; and when those rose from the earth, the wheels rose along with them, for the spirit of the living creatures was in the wheels. (Ezekiel 1:4, 15–21, ESV)

The analysis by Tsoukalos? "It reads much more like an encounter with some type of extraterrestrial craft that was misinterpreted as some type of a divine event."[200]

That's true only if you weren't reading it in Mesopotamia about 2,600 years ago. The imagery described by Ezekiel was common back then. The subjects of Nebuchadnezzar would have known exactly what they were seeing—a royal throne and its divine guardians.

What's even more significant about Ezekiel's vision is the location. The prophet mentions that he "was among the exiles by the Chebar canal" when "the heavens were opened, and [he] saw visions of God" (Ezekiel 1:1). That's not unusual, but Ezekiel goes on to repeat the location *seven more times* in his book, often referring to "the vision that I had seen by the Chebar canal" (Ezekiel 43:3). Why? What was so significant about the Chebar canal?

The waterway, most likely a silted-up canal today called the Shatt en-Nil, was a channel that left the Euphrates River north of Babylon and flowed southeastward for about sixty miles through Sumer, rejoining the river south of Uruk (biblical Erech).[201] Between Babylon and Uruk, it flowed through the ancient city of Nippur, where references to the *naru Kabari* ("Great Canal") have been found on cuneiform tablets dated to the fifth century BC,[202] about 150 years after the time of Ezekiel.

Nippur was the home of the Ekur ("Mountain House"), the temple of the god Enlil, so named because of the god's main epithet, *kur-gal* ("Great Mountain").[203] Nippur, or Nibru in Sumerian, became the center of Mesopotamian religion after the rise of the Akkadian Empire in the twenty-fourth century BC.[204] The Ekur was where the Mesopotamian "divine council" convened to decree the fates of the people under their domain.[205]

Although Enlil was replaced at the top of the pantheon by the chief god of Babylon, Marduk, around the time of the judges in Israel (ca. 1200 BC),[206] his cult continued for many years thereafter. As argued in my book *The Second Coming of Saturn*, references to Enlil are salted throughout the Old Testament, most notably in his identity as Molech, the detestable underworld god who demanded child sacrifice, but also in the book of Zechariah, where Enlil is openly mocked by God: "Who are you, O great mountain? Before Zerubbabel, you shall become a plain" (Zechariah 4:7).

The point of Ezekiel's vision is this: He was called as a prophet when the throne room of God appeared in the sky directly over the temple that served as the meeting place for the gods of Babylon!

The UFO interpretation of Ezekiel 1 is modern, but it isn't new. *The Spaceships of Ezekiel*, a 1974 book by Josef P. Blumrich, capitalized on the growing popularity of von Däniken's *Chariots of the Gods*, with the added marketing appeal that Blumrich wrote the book while he was "chief of NASA's systems layout branch of the program development office at the Marshall Space Flight Center."

Except that he wasn't:

One of the reasons so many people have (and still do) think Blumrich's book is worth referencing is that he claimed (and so his followers are fond of repeating) that he was a NASA engineer. He wasn't. As Jason Colavito demonstrated a long time ago, documentation exists from the U.S. State Department that shows the State Department could find no evidence that Blumrich was affiliated with NASA. Frankly, it wouldn't matter if Blumrich was an engineer. His ideas are based on desperate and uninformed misreadings of the biblical text anyway. We know what Ezekiel saw because his descriptions mirror ancient Babylonian iconography that we can look at today because of archaeologists. The imagery is no mystery, nor is its meaning.

So, once again, the uncritical thinkers in the ancient astronaut orbit (and I do mean orbit) were duped by a "researcher" that lied to them. You have to wonder how many times this has to happen before some of these folks wake up. The ancient astronaut theory is primarily supported by industrious but duplicitous researchers offering fraudulent research to an emotionally and psychologically primed audience. It's actually pretty sad.[207]

So, in a nutshell, Blumrich was a fake and Tsoukalos got things backwards. We think Ezekiel saw a UFO because our twenty-first century worldview misinterprets divine imagery from the sixth century BC. Sadly, people who say they take the Bible seriously aren't any better prepared to understand what the prophet saw than Giorgio Tsoukalos. Even those who've studied Ezekiel usually haven't read up on Mesopotamian religious imagery. Evangelists of the ET religion disregard what the ancient Mesopotamians believed because—well, because *aliens*.

That's behind the continued popularity of the work of the late Zecharia Sitchin. Sitchin, who passed away in 2010, claimed Mesopotamian iconography showed the existence of a forgotten planet called Nibiru beyond Neptune. This planet, Sitchin said, follows a highly elliptical orbit into the inner solar system about every 3,600 years with catastrophic consequences. He also equated the Anunnaki, the gods of Sumer, with the biblical Nephilim, asserting that they arrived on Earth some 450,000 years ago to mine gold in Africa.

Here's the funny bit: Sitchin appears to have conflated the Sumerian name of Enlil's home city, Nibru, with the Akkadian word *Nibiru* (also transliterated *Nebiru* and *Neberu*), an astronomical term referring to the planet Jupiter (or Mercury, in one text), the god Marduk, or a star distinguished from Jupiter.[208]

Bible scholar Michael S. Heiser, whose passing in 2023 was a great loss to academia in general and Christian theology in particular, concluded this about Sitchin's scholarship:

1) Nibiru is called a star.
2) Nibiru is called a planet—nearly always Jupiter-Marduk, but once Mercury, and never anything beyond Pluto or the known planets.
3) The Sumerians, by their own records, knew of only five planets (and accepted the sun and moon as planets).
4) Nibiru is never mentioned in any respect with the Anunnaki; it is never said to have been or be inhabited.
5) Nibiru is both a "fixed star" in some relationship to constellations (whether a member or just in proximity is unknown) that "holds" them in their courses, but is also described as "changing position" and "crossing" the sky at times.
6) Nibiru was seen every year, which demolishes Sitchin's view of a 3,600 year cycle for it.[209]

Sitchin's theories are behind much of the Planet X angst that clogs up the Internet. Heiser, who could actually read Sumerian, thoroughly debunked Sitchin's theories, even going so far as to post his personal tax returns to show he wasn't trying to profit by publicly challenging Sitchin.[210] That hasn't stopped Sitchinites from continuing to spread the idea that the gods of the ancient world were astronauts from outside the solar system looking for wealth, riches, or just some shore leave on Sol III.

All manner of ancient mysteries are explained away with, "Well, we don't know—so it must be aliens." For example, one of the more convincing stories we're told about our ancestors is that they couldn't possibly have moved the stones used to build the pyramids, the temple at Baalbek, or Machu Picchu because our modern cranes can't lift that kind of weight today. What we're *not* told is that between 1768 and 1770, the Russians transported the heaviest stone ever moved by humans, the 1,500-ton Thunder Stone, nearly four miles overland to the center of St. Petersburg without animal or machine power.

Think about that. While the American colonies slowly marched toward their war for independence, four hundred Russians with rope, timber, and a bunch of six-inch diameter bronze spheres moved a block of granite that weighed as much as sixty-five fully loaded tractor-trailers across six kilometers of dry land in nine months. So just because we don't know exactly how people moved big blocks of stone four thousand years ago, it doesn't follow that it must have been aliens.

Yet as factually void as the show is, people still watch *Ancient Aliens*. And the lack of response from the Church to the ancient alien meme isn't helping. Ignoring the UFO phenomenon hasn't made it go away. More than a third of American adults believe we're being visited by ETs.[211] Only 4 percent believe in God as He's described in the Bible.[212]

In other words, we're in the middle of an information war, and pop culture is on the side of the "aliens."

Science fiction is popular entertainment. Five of the twenty highest-grossing movies of all time (adjusted for inflation) are from the *Star Wars* series (two of which were the top-grossing films of 2015 and 2016). 1977's *Star Wars Episode IV*, which was actually the first film of the *Star Wars* franchise on the big screen, was number two on the list, surpassed only by the 1939 classic *Gone with the Wind*. Other top-grossing films featuring aliens include *E.T.: The Extraterrestrial* (number four all-time) and *Avatar* (number fifteen).[213] Other films from the last twenty years like *Star Trek: Beyond, X-Men: Apocalypse, Transformers: Age of Extinction, Guardians of the Galaxy, Star Trek into Darkness, Thor: The Dark World, MIB 3, Transformers: Dark of the Moon, Thor, Avatar, Transformers: Revenge of the Fallen, Star Trek,* and *Indiana Jones and the Kingdom of the Crystal Skull* were all among the top twenty films for their year of release, and all incorporated alien contact in one way or another.

In the early years of sci-fi cinema, *The Day the Earth Stood Still* featured Gort, a robot with lasers in his eyes, and an iconic flying saucer that set the table for contemporary UFO iconography. On television, we've been entertained over the last sixty years by *Star Trek* and its spinoffs, *Doctor Who*, *The X-Files*, *Babylon 5*, *Stargate SG-1* and its spinoffs (which featured a strong "the old gods were ancient aliens" theme), and anthology series that often featured ETIs like *The Twilight Zone* and *The Outer Limits*.

The ETs weren't always friendly, but the theme of alien contact has been a Hollywood staple for decades. Thanks to Tinseltown, we know what aliens are supposed to look like, the type of craft they fly, and the role of government in covering it all up. It's been repeated and rehashed so often the tropes have taken on lives of their own.

No wonder so many of us take the existence of extraterrestrial intelligence as a given. We've been conditioned to accept it as reality for a very long time.

CHAPTER 12

SCIENCE FICTION AND THE ET GOSPEL

By Derek Gilbert

I f H. P. Lovecraft used horror to introduce the idea of contact with an alien "other" to the masses, the growing popularity of science fiction in the twentieth century established ET as a stereotype in popular entertainment. It's hard to imagine, but our great-grandparents would have had no idea what the phrase "little green men" was supposed to mean.

Nineteenth-century forerunners like Jules Verne and H. G. Wells demonstrated that fiction based on speculative science would sell. Verne's 1865 *From the Earth to the Moon* was the first major work to feature space travel; in 1898, Wells produced the first ET invasion story with his classic *The War of the Worlds*. Another Welles—Orson— transformed *The War of the Worlds* into a compelling radio drama on Halloween Eve in 1938, although the story that the program caused a national panic is, sadly, a myth. (Newspapers lost a lot of advertising revenue to the new medium during the Great Depression and took advantage of an opportunity to slam radio—an early example of "fake news.")[214]

The popularity of the genre took off in the 1920s with the arrival of the first pulp magazines that featured science fiction, such as *Amazing Stories*, *Weird Tales*, *Astounding Stories*, and *Wonder Stories*. The golden age of science fiction arrived in 1937 when John W. Campbell took over as editor of *Astounding Science Fiction*. Campbell is widely considered the most influential editor of the early years of the genre, publishing first or early stories by Isaac Asimov, Lester del Rey, Robert Heinlein, A. E. Van Vogt, and Theodore Sturgeon, thus helping launch the careers of many of the biggest names in twentieth-century science fiction.

Despite insisting that his writers research the science behind their stories, Campbell had an interest in parapsychology that grew over the years. Writers learned that topics like telepathy helped them sell stories to *Astounding*.[215] In 1949, Campbell discovered L. Ron Hubbard and published his first article on Dianetics, which Campbell described as "one of the most important articles ever published."[216] He suggested to some that Hubbard would win the Nobel Peace Prize for his creation.

Three years before selling Campbell on Dianetics, Hubbard participated in an event that falls smack into the "you can't make this stuff up" category: From January to March 1946, Hubbard and Jack Parsons, rocket engineer and one of the founders of the Jet Propulsion Laboratory, performed a series of sex magick rituals called the Babalon [sic] Working. It was intended to manifest an incarnation of the divine feminine, a concept based on the writings of Aleister Crowley and described in his 1917 novel *Moonchild*.

So, through L. Ron Hubbard and Joseph Campbell, science fiction fans were connected to the Two Degrees of Aleister Crowley just as readers of gothic horror were through the works of H. P. Lovecraft and his successors.

Campbell managed to capture the paranoia and dread that marked Lovecraft's work in his classic 1938 novella *Who Goes There?* The story has been adapted for the big screen three times—1951's *The Thing from Another World* (featuring a young James Arnett, TV's Matt Dillon, as the creature), 1982's *The Thing*, starring Kurt Russell, and a 2011 prequel, also titled *The Thing*.

The Kurt Russell film, set in Antarctica, draws on key Lovecraftian themes—an ancient extraterrestrial that poses an existential threat to all life on Earth, the loss of self as one is assimilated by the monster, and a claustrophobic setting. *The Thing* was set at an Antarctic research station, where the bitter cold confines most of the action to the interior of the base. The paranoia-inducing monster imitates its victims perfectly (similar to the ETs in the 1956 classic *Invasion of the Body Snatchers*), which causes the base scientist, played by Wilford Brimley, to snap when he realizes just how quickly the creature could destroy the Earth if it escapes the Antarctic—which makes Brimley's character an awful lot like the protagonists in many of Lovecraft's stories.

Even the setting near the South Pole recalls Lovecraft, whose classic novella *At the Mountains of Madness* introduced a theme that's been revisited over the years in films like *The X-Files* and *Alien vs. Predator*—there's something beneath the ice down there that shouldn't be disturbed.

> It is absolutely necessary, for the peace and safety of mankind, that some of earth's dark, dead corners and unplumbed depths be let alone; lest sleeping abnormalities wake to resurgent life, and blasphemously surviving nightmares squirm and splash out of their black lairs to newer and wider conquests.[217]

Not coincidentally, UFO enthusiasts claim to find alien craft half-buried in the Antarctic on a regular basis these days.

The point is that by the time Campbell began to elevate science fiction out of the swamp of pulp fiction in the late 1930s, the concept of unfriendly (or uncaring) ETIs intervening in Earth's affairs was already several decades old. By the late 1940s, it was already fodder for kiddie cartoons; Marvin the Martian (and his Uranium PU-36 Explosive Space Modulator) debuted in 1948, just one year after Kenneth

Arnold's UFO sighting at Mount Rainier and the famous crash near Roswell, New Mexico.

In the decades since, science fiction has become, in the words of Dr. Michael S. Heiser, "televangelism for the ET religion."[218] People looking in from outside the genre may assume sci-fi is all rockets, ray guns, and lasers, but a lot of it is theological. Films like *Prometheus*, *Mission to Mars*, *Knowing*, and *2001: A Space Odyssey*, for example, conflate space travel, extraterrestrial intelligence, and religion by offering answers to the Big Questions the world's religions have been addressing since the beginning of time—where we come from, why we're here, and where we go when we die.

Human interaction with ETIs has been a stock premise for television for decades, sometimes played for drama and sometimes for laughs. And the mix of space travel and religion has never been off-screen for long. The original *Star Trek* reimagined the gods of Greece and Rome as powerful aliens when they encounter Apollo in the second-season episode, "Who Mourns for Adonais?"

Other entries in the *Star Trek* franchise likewise explored religious themes. The pilot episode of *Star Trek: The Next Generation* introduced Picard's godlike nemesis, Q, who eventually appeared in a dozen episodes of *TNG*, *Star Trek: Deep Space Nine (DS9)*, and *Star Trek: Voyager*. A major plot arc of *DS9* involved Commander Sisko's role as the Emissary of the Prophets, the "wormhole aliens" worshipped as gods on the planet Bajor.

The 1994 film *Stargate* kicked off a long-running science-fiction franchise that centered on the return of the old gods to Earth. In the *Stargate* universe, the deities of the ancient Near East were parasitic, technologically advanced ETIs called the Goa'Uld who ruled the Earth thousands of years ago as gods. The movie follows a team of explorers who travel through a stargate to discover a world controlled by a brutal entity posing as the Egyptian sun god Ra, whose spaceship just happens to look a lot like the Great Pyramid of Giza.

The television series *Stargate SG-1* and its spinoffs continued that theme. The Norse pantheon was introduced in the series as the Asgard, whose appearance inspired stories of the alien greys (that look just doesn't work for Thor), and who, contrary to their reputation among ET contactees, side with humanity in the war against the Goa'Uld. (The 1947 Roswell panic was presumably an accident.)

In other words, the *Stargate* franchise built an entire alternate history for the main religions of the world: basically, they were all aliens. We don't recall how they explained why the "gods" stopped visiting Earth for a couple thousand years, and of course they never touched the third rail of Hollywood, Jesus. Considering what the series did to the pagan gods, it's just as well.

SG-1 ran from 1997 through 2007, surpassing *The X-Files* as the longest-running science-fiction television series in North America until it was passed by *Smallville* (a series featuring another godlike ETI, Superman) in 2011.

Battlestar Galactica had two series runs, the first in 1978–79, and the second, which produced seventy-five episodes between 2003 and 2009. It's notable for being a not-too-subtle dramatization of Mormon theology, including a council of twelve, marriage for "time and eternity," and a planet named Kobol. Religion was a prominent theme in the reboot, too; the twelve "Lords of Kobol" were the gods of the Greco-Roman pantheon (Zeus, Hera, Apollo, Ares, Athena, Poseidon, etc.), and the twelve occupied planets of the human race were named for the signs of the zodiac.

Interestingly, the Cylons, sentient robots who rebelled against their human masters, were depicted as monotheistic, following a religion that looked a lot like a cross between Christianity and Judaism—basically Christianity minus Christ (well, except for the part where they attempt genocide and nearly destroy the entire human race).

The reimagined series introduced a new element: humanoid Cylons so lifelike they're indistinguishable from humans. As the series developed, it was revealed that there were only seven models, but a multitude of copies of each. Model Number One, Cavil, deceives the other Cylons by hiding the identities of the five remaining humanoid Cylon models. Finding the Final Five becomes a major plot line in the series, and their revelation to the human fleet is a major turning point that leads humanity to salvation on a new Earth.

Interestingly, that Cylon plot twist draws from a number of Western occult traditions, especially as they've been syncretized into Theosophy. Madame Blavatsky wrote in *The Secret Doctrine* that seven "rays" together form all energy and all forms produced by it—in other words, you, us, and everything around us. Somehow these "rays" are also intelligent beings called the Dhyan Chohans.

Since at least the early 1970s, however, some New Age leaders like Elizabeth Clare Prophet have been teaching on the "five secret rays," which "promote an action of detail, the final sculpturing of the mind and consciousness in the perfect image of the Christ."[219]

It's difficult to pin down what exactly inspired the writers of the reimagined *Battlestar* to add the "final five" plot line, but we don't believe the parallel to current New Age thinking is a coincidence.

Remember, we're not coincidence theorists.

Comic heroes have also mined human theology for story arcs. Beyond the obvious, such as Marvel making a superhero out of the Norse storm god Thor (who was a cognate for Jupiter, Zeus, Baal, and the ancient Sumerian storm god Ishkur—in other words, same god with different names), researcher and author Christopher Knowles makes a strong case in his book, *Our Gods Wear Spandex: The Secret History of Comic Book Heroes,* for comic book heroes as a modern rebranding of ancient mythological archetypes.

> This culture is far more influential (and insidious) than most realize. Most contemporary action movies take their visual language from comic books. The rhythm of constant hyper-violence of today's action movies comes straight from Jack Kirby. Elvis Presley idolized Captain Marvel Jr., to the point of adopting his hairstyle....
>
> Although most of us don't realize it, there's simply nothing new about devotion to superheroes. Their powers, their costumes, and sometimes even their names are plucked straight

from the pre-Christian religions of antiquity. When you go back and look at these heroes in their original incarnations, you can't help but be struck by how blatant their symbolism is and how strongly they reflect they belief systems of the pagan age. What even fewer people realize is that this didn't occur by chance, but came directly out of the spiritual and mystical secret societies and cults of the late nineteenth century—groups like the Theosophists, the Rosicrucians, and the Golden Dawn. These groups turned their backs on the state cult of Christianity and reached back in time to the elemental deities of the ancient traditions.[220]

Popular movies based on comics or graphic novels featuring the ETI/religion theme include the *Transformers* franchise, *X-Men Apocalypse*, and the *Guardians of the Galaxy* films. The common thread: ETIs exist, they're coming to Earth, and it's either going to be awesome or apocalyptic when they get here.

And how have eighty years of pop culture pushing the ETI meme shaped our ideas about contact? Seth Shostak, lead astronomer for the SETI (Search for Extraterrestrial Intelligence) Institute, hits the nail on the head:

> I think we are ready for ET contact in some sense, because the public has been conditioned to the idea of life in space by movies and TV. And if you go into a classroom with a bunch of 11 year olds and ask them, "How many of you kids think there are aliens out there?" they all raise their hands! Why? Is it because their parents have been educating them about astrobiology? No. It's because they've seen them on TV!...
>
> I think that Hollywood is by far the biggest term in the equation of the public's reaction to confirmation of alien life.[221]

Exactly. But it's a concept that's been drawn from nineteenth-century occult groups and filtered through pulp magazines, sci-fi novels, radio dramas, cartoons, comic books, graphic novels, movies, and television, packaged as popular entertainment, and sold as a worldview to the last four generations. How long before an official announcement that the ETIs—the old gods—are finally back?

One last thing: Isn't it odd the lead astronomer of the group searching for ETIs is named for the chaos god, Seth (Set)? And that the group's acronym, SETI, is Egyptian for "man of Set?" Should we be concerned that Set-Typhon, the dark lord of chaos, is the one Aleister Crowley's successor Kenneth Grant believed is the spirit of our age—and that he's apparently reaching out to Earth from somewhere in the direction of Sirius?

Most likely it's just coincidence. It's probably fine.

CHAPTER 13

UFOS
GO MAINSTREAM

By Derek Gilbert

On November 14, 2004, two F/A-18F pilots from the aircraft carrier USS *Nimitz*, on a routine training mission over the Pacific about one hundred miles west of San Diego, were asked to investigate a strange radar signal. The account of what the pilots saw was featured in a story published December 16, 2017, by the *New York Times*, along with disclosure of a secret Pentagon program that investigated UFO sightings between 2007 and 2012.

The story was picked up by mainstream media around the world, which, for the first time, appeared to take UFOs and the possibility of extraterrestrial life seriously. That touched off widespread speculation over whether the existence of ETs was finally about to be confirmed.

The main source for the *Times* article was Luis Elizondo, a former Defense Intelligence Agency official who ran the secret program, the Advanced Aerospace Threat Identification Program, from the fifth floor of the C Ring at the Pentagon.[222] Twenty-two million dollars to fund the program was inserted into Defense Department budgets at the request of retired Sen. Harry Reid, most of which, the *Times* reported, was paid to Bigelow Aerospace, to which the Pentagon outsourced its UFO research. The company is owned by Robert Bigelow, a billionaire friend and supporter of Reid. Bigelow also owns Skinwalker Ranch, the alleged site of numerous paranormal events, and he's a longtime believer in the existence of extraterrestrial life.

Here's the short version of what's been dubbed the "USS *Nimitz* UFO Incident":

According to F/A-18 pilot Cmdr. David Fravor, the radio operator on the guided missile cruiser USS *Princeton*, they'd been tracking strange radar signals for a couple of weeks. Objects appeared suddenly at eighty thousand feet, then dropped to twenty thousand feet, where they stopped and hovered. "Then they either dropped out of radar range or shot straight back up."[223]

Fravor and his wingman, Lt. Cmdr. Jim Slaight, found an oval-shaped object about forty feet long hovering about fifty feet above the ocean, directly over something just below the surface of the water. The pilots couldn't see the submerged object, but it was big enough that waves broke over it, causing the sea to "churn."[224]

As Cmdr. Fravor descended for a closer look, the mysterious craft began to climb, almost as if to meet him. Fravor turned toward it—and then it took off. "It accelerated like nothing I've ever seen," he told the *Times*.[225]

After communicating with the operations officer on the *Princeton*, Fravor and Slaight agreed to meet at a rendezvous about sixty miles away, at a site called the cap point. Then the *Princeton*'s radio operator called back: "Sir, you won't believe it, but that thing is at your cap point."[226]

According to Fravor, the F-18s were still at least forty miles away. The object had covered the distance in less than a minute. Even if the travel time is rounded up to exactly one minute, that's a speed of 3,600 miles per hour—more than *three times faster* than the maximum speed of the F/A-18F Super Hornets flown by Fravor and Slaight.

Also puzzling is how the thing knew to go to the cap point. By the time the pilots arrived there a few minutes later, the object was gone.

Oddly, the thing never showed up on either pilot's onboard radar. A second flight of four Super Hornets from their squadron, VFA-41 "Black Aces," was directed to where Fravor and Slaight had encountered the object. These planes were equipped with forward-looking infrared (FLIR) sensors, which enabled one of the crews to record video of the mysterious object.[227] That's the video clip posted by the *Times*.

Whatever the thing was, the incident almost certainly wasn't a hoax. The object was seen or detected by the crews of six Navy F/A-18s, a Marine Corps F/A-18, an E-2C Hawkeye airborne early-warning aircraft, and the radar crew on the USS *Princeton*.[228]

So, what was it? And what was in the ocean directly beneath the thing? Fravor estimated the area of churning water at between fifty and one hundred meters (about 160 to 320 feet) in diameter![229]

To this day, no one knows. There are a few things to consider, however. First, the incident wasn't exactly a secret before the *New York Times* published its story at the end of 2017. In February of 2007, a user at the conspiracy forum Above Top Secret posted a transcript of what appears to be a genuine event summary from Carrier Air Wing 11.[230]

Then, in March of 2014, the encounter was written up for a website called Fighter Sweep. Paco Chierci, a fellow fighter pilot, wrote that he'd heard the story directly from Cmdr. Fravor sometime around 2007, by which time the video from the F/A-18's infrared sensor had been leaked to YouTube.

Curiously, by the time Chierci wrote his article, the video was no longer online.

Last month when I called Dave to refresh my memory before sitting down to write this bizarre encounter, he informed me that the video had been removed from YouTube. He told me that a government agency with a three-letter identifier had recently conducted an investigation into the AAVs and had exhaustively interviewed all parties involved.

All of the seven flight crew, including 6 aircrew from VFA-41 and Cheeks from VMFA-232. The Fire Control Officer and Senior Chief from Princeton, and the radar operator on the E-2. They even queried the crew of the USS Louisville, a Los Angeles-class Fast-Attack submarine that was in the area as part of the Nimitz Carrier Strike Group who reported there were no unidentified sonar contacts or strange underwater noises on that day.[231]

A three-letter identifier? DIA, perhaps?

Let's ask some obvious questions: Since video of the *Nimitz* incident has been floating around the Internet for ten years, why is it getting attention from mainstream media *now*? What's changed? Remember, when watching or reading news, the timing of a story's release is often more important than the story itself.

In October 2017, Luis Elizondo left his career as an intelligence officer for the US government and took a new job as chief of Global Security for To the Stars Academy of Arts and Science (TTS Academy), now called To the Stars Incorporated, a company that launched October 11, 2017.

The timeline of his job change means Elizondo and TTS Academy were in talks prior to his resignation from the Department of Defense. (It also means he waited five years to resign after funding for his program was cut off.) Just eight weeks after his departure from government service, Elizondo was featured in the *Times* article. And within a month of the *Times* story, he was interviewed about UFOs by CNN, CBS, NPR, HLN, and political commentator Glenn Beck, among others.

TTS Academy's mission, according to its website, was to be "a powerful vehicle for change by creating a consortium among science, aerospace and entertainment that will work collectively to allow gifted researchers the freedom to explore exotic science and technologies with the infrastructure and resources to rapidly transition them to products that can change the world."[232] In other words, it will promote the idea that ETs exist and are here to help in the "transformation" of humanity (whatever that means).

Now, maybe Elizondo just wanted the world to know that "the truth is out there," to borrow a phrase. He told CNN's Erin Burnett, "There is very compelling evidence that we may not be alone."[233]

On the other hand, Elizondo might have been trying to use a persuasive piece of UFO video as a marketing hook to attract investors to the new company.

Still, why would one man get this kind of attention for a topic the mainstream media usually plays for laughs? A look at some of Elizondo's colleagues is revealing.

There was a very large intelligence community presence at To the Stars Academy. Other than the president and interim CEO, Tom DeLonge, former guitarist and lead singer of the rock band Blink-182, most of the visible members of the team had long careers with American intelligence agencies or defense contractors. For example:

- Dr. Hal Puthoff (VP Science & Technology): Directed the Stanford Research Institute's experiments in remote viewing in the 1970s and 1980s, part of the Stargate Project for the CIA and DIA.
- Jim Semivan (VP Operations): Retired in 2007 from the CIA; since retirement, consults for CIA on tradecraft training (teaching spies how to spy).
- Steve Justice (Aerospace Division director): Recently retired after thirty-one years as program director for Advanced Systems from Lockheed Martin Advanced Development Programs, the "Skunk Works" that developed secret aircraft like the U-2 and the stealth fighter.
- Chris Mellon (National Security Affairs advisor): Deputy Assistant Secretary of Defense for Intelligence in the Clinton and Bush administrations.

- Dr. Paul Rapp (brain function & consciousness consultant): "Past honors include a Certificate of Commendation from the Central Intelligence Agency for 'significant contributions to the mission of the Office of Research and Development.'"
- Dr. Norm Kahn (national security & program management consultant): Thirty-year career with the Central Intelligence Agency, culminating in developing and directing the intelligence community's Counter-Biological Weapons Program.[234]

You get the picture. From the media's viewpoint, these men are credible sources. UFO stories coming from them carry weight. From our perspective, however, their backgrounds raise additional questions. The American intelligence community has been embedded in the modern UFO phenomenon since the end of World War 2.

Now, there are a couple plausible explanations for loading up the company with intelligence community professionals. They may have experience that makes them uniquely qualified to analyze the UFO occurrences. Maybe these people are leveraging that experience to launch an exciting new private venture. We can't blame them for that; the private sector presumably pays better than government service.

Maybe these people are true believers who feel the time is now to share the "truth" about UFOs. And, for some reason, these career professionals, with decades of experience at the highest levels of the intelligence and defense industries, decided partnering with the former guitarist and lead singer for a popular rock band was the best way to do it. (Wait—what?)[235]

But there's another explanation. People like this have been connected to encounters with unidentified craft since 1947—to shape what the public thinks about UFOs and the existence of ETIs.

You might ask why the intelligence community would encourage belief in UFOs and ETIs. Good question. From the Pentagon's point of view, is it better for the Kremlin to think we've invented a new aircraft that can make 3,600 miles an hour or to believe Earth is being visited by ETs?

That may seem flippant, but it's true. It's documented fact that the Department of Defense command tasked with "strategic deception," Joint Security Control, contacted the Army Air Force's public relations staff in July of 1947, just a few weeks after Roswell, to advise them on addressing the UFO issue.[236]

That leads to a key point: Just because those F/A-18 pilots can't identify what they saw *doesn't mean the craft is extraterrestrial*. It may have been an experimental drone. And while those Navy and Marine Corps pilots are professionals and patriots, if they didn't need to know about a secret project, the government agency conducting the test isn't going to tell them what it was.

But even if that unidentified craft wasn't one of ours (and by "ours" we mean "human"), that *still* doesn't mean it's extraterrestrial.

The difficulty of space travel has been vastly understated by movies and television. Wormholes and warp drive are convenient devices used by writers to explain away the time and energy requirements of interstellar travel, but they are science *fiction*. It's one reason serious, secular UFO researchers like Jacques Vallée, John Keel, and J. Allen Hynek came to believe UFOs are more likely extra*dimensional* rather than extra*terrestrial*.

And now you're speaking our language. We Christians know Earth has been visited by nonhuman entities who seem to defy the laws of physics for thousands of years. The UFO phenomenon is real—it's just not what most people in the UFO community think it is.

We're not saying those pilots in 2004 saw an angel or angelic craft. We *are* saying we need to apply more critical thinking to UFO accounts. "We don't know, ergo aliens," is not an example of thoughtful analysis.

Summing up: There is no evidence that the 2004 *Nimitz* UFO was extraterrestrial. That it's been featured by mainstream media twenty years later is a curiosity, especially considering the nature of the group behind the re-release of the video. Their motive for pushing the incident into the spotlight may be as simple as profiting from the publicity. Or they may be true believers spreading the ET gospel. Or it might be the intelligence community doing what the intelligence community does—spread disinformation in the service of government.

Or—considering that we wrestle not against flesh and blood—it might be in the service of principalities, powers, and cosmic rulers over this present darkness.

Jesus commanded us to love God with all our hearts, souls, and *minds*. Asking intelligent questions when the media serves up stories like this is one of the ways we do it.

CHAPTER 14

THE FIGHT THAT SHOWS NO PITY: TRANSHUMANISM AND THE QUEST FOR IMMORTALITY

By Derek Gilbert

For mankind, whatever life it has, be not sick at heart,
be not in despair, be not heart-stricken!
　　The bane of mankind is thus come, I have told you,
what was fixed when your navel-cord was cut is thus come, I
have told you.
　　The darkest day of mortal man has caught up with you,
the solitary place of mortal man has caught up with you,
the flood-wave that cannot be breasted has caught up with you,
the battle that cannot be fled has caught up with you,
the combat that cannot be matched has caught up with you,
the fight that shows no pity has caught up with you!
　　　　　　　　　　　　　　　　　—*Epic of Gilgamesh*[237]

More than five thousand years ago, the legendary Sumerian king Gilgamesh embarked on a single-minded quest to procure the secret of immortality. According to the story, he was so distressed by the death of his best friend, Enkidu, and obsessed with overcoming his own mortality that he tracked down the Sumerian Noah, Utnapishtim the Far-away, for advice.

A thousand years or so after Gilgamesh succumbed to the fate that awaits us all, around 2000 BC, Amorites overwhelmed the native Sumerian and Akkadian rulers of the Fertile Crescent. By 1900 BC, the time of Abraham, Amorites controlled nearly every kingdom and city-state from the Persian Gulf to the Levant—modern Iraq, Syria, Jordan, Lebanon, and Israel. By the time of Jacob, Amorites had taken over northern Egypt, too.

The Amorites added ancestor worship to the magical and religious practices of the Sumerians, but with a twist. It appears the kings of the Amorites believed they descended from the gods who ruled before the Flood—the ones who, in Babylonian, Hurrian, Hittite, Greek, and Roman cosmology (as well as the Bible),[238] were locked away in an underworld prison reserved for supernatural threats to the divine order, a place called Tartarus or the Abyss.[239]

Now, flash forward four thousand years to today: In the West, we've been so indoctrinated by positivism, which teaches science is the only reliable tool for finding truth, that we're more likely to believe the old gods were alien astronauts than supernatural beings. But the quest to unlock the secret of immortality continues. The modern transhumanist movement holds out the same promise offered to Adam and Eve in Eden: To paraphrase, "Ye shall not surely die; your eyes shall be opened, and ye shall be as gods."

As Christians, we reject positivism. We're not anti-science, but admittance to our club requires believing that an invisible, all-powerful deity spoke everything into existence; that He manifested as a fully divine *and* fully human man in a dusty province of the Roman Empire about two thousand years ago; that He died for our sins; and that then, three days later, He literally rose from the dead. There is no way to mesh those beliefs with a worldview based on only what can be observed and quantified with our limited human senses.

Transhumanism is a growing movement that wants to fundamentally transform human physiology through cutting-edge technology, with the goal of achieving eternal life through science. In other words, transhumanists are trying to weld together two diametrically opposed worldviews—one based on the supernatural and the other that denies its existence.

Two generations before Gilgamesh, a Sumerian king named Enmerkar dominated the ancient Near East. Both men ruled from the city of Uruk in what is today southeastern Iraq—which, you might have noticed, is just a different spelling of the city's name. In the Bible, it's spelled a third way—Erech, which, along with Babel, was "the beginning of [Nimrod's] kingdom." From there, the kings of Uruk ruled nearly the entire Fertile Crescent, the land between the Euphrates and Tigris rivers in what is now Iraq, Syria, and southern Türkiye. Scholars call this the Uruk Expansion, a period between about 4000 BC and 3100 BC. Logically, Nimrod and Gilgamesh fit somewhere in that time frame.

Scholars generally consider Gilgamesh a historical character. A team of German archeologists mapped Uruk in 2001 and 2002 using cesium magnetometry, and among their discoveries was the outline of a building, in what was the bed of the Euphrates River more than four thousand years ago, that fits the description of the burial crypt of the legendary king.[240]

Gilgamesh may be responsible for bringing back knowledge that had been lost beneath the waters of the Great Flood. According to the Book of 1 Enoch, a group of angelic beings, called "Watchers" by the Hebrews, descended to the summit of Mount Hermon and made a pact to corrupt humanity.[241] As Dr. Michael Heiser noted in *Reversing Hermon*, there was more to the visit of the Watchers than producing monstrous offspring. The rebellious angels brought with them information humankind was not meant to possess—sorcery, charms, the cutting of roots and plants for mixing potions, metalworking and making weapons, makeup (presumably for seduction), and reading fortunes in the movement of the stars. In short, the Watchers lured humanity into evil, and "all the earth was filled with the godlessness and violence that had befallen it."[242]

The legendary king was referred to on a Mesopotamian cylinder seal as "master of the *apkallu*,"[243] and by the time of Hammurabi the Great, who was probably a contemporary of Isaac and Jacob, Gilgamesh was viewed as the one who had returned to humankind the pre-Flood knowledge of the *apkallu*, which was the Akkadian name for the beings the Hebrews called the Watchers.[244]

The Old Babylonian text of the Gilgamesh epic establishes another link between Gilgamesh and the Watchers. To make a name for himself, Gilgamesh and his drinking buddy Enkidu decided to kill Humbaba, the monster who guarded the Cedar Forest. In a sense, the pair aimed for a sort of immortality by performing a great deed.

The Old Babylonian text of the epic locates the cedar forest on the peaks of "Hermon and Lebanon."[245] After killing Humbaba, the two friends "penetrated into the forest, [and] opened the secret dwelling of the Anunnaki."[246] The Anunnaki, who were originally the great gods of Mesopotamia, had become underworld judges of the dead by the time of Abraham,[247] which suggests the Anunnaki, the *apkallu*, and the Watchers are the same group of supernatural rebels.[248] Marduk, after defeating the chaos-dragon Tiamat, decreed the Anunnaki, or at least half of them, should relocate permanently to the nether realm.[249] The Hittites, who lived north of Mesopotamia in what is now Turkey, identified the Anunnaki as primordial deities of the underworld, possibly "an earlier generation of gods who had retired or were banished by the younger gods now in charge."[250]

It's important to note these entities are the same ones put forward by the followers of Zecharia Sitchin as space travelers who were mistaken for gods by the people of Mesopotamia five thousand years ago. And this history is relevant because Gilgamesh, despite his desperate effort to avoid "the bane of mankind," died anyway—and upon his death, according to the legend, joined the Anunnaki in the underworld as governor of the dead.

Gilgamesh, in the form of his ghost, dead in the underworld, shall be the governor of the Netherworld, chief of the shades![251]

Without realizing it, today's transhumanists are replicating the quest of Gilgamesh for the secret of immortality. Most transhumanists are atheists, which makes their mission easier to understand. If you believe you cease to exist the moment your physical existence ends, you might be driven to extraordinary lengths to avoid death. And since atheists don't even have a sorcerer, spirit, or Satan to try to bargain with, they're left with nothing but natural science to solve the insurmountable problem of mortality. Over the last hundred years, and especially since the turn of this century, this has led to the rise in the worldview called transhumanism.

What is transhumanism, exactly? According to leading bioethicist Wesley J. Smith, it is "an emerging social movement that promotes the technological enhancement of human capacities toward the end of creating a utopian era in which 'post humans' will enjoy absolute morphological freedom and live for thousands of years."[252]

Transhumanists themselves are more direct in describing their goals and the means of attaining them:

> Biology mandates not only very limited durability, death and poor memory retention, but also limited speed of communication, transportation, learning, interaction and evolution... transhumanists everywhere must support the revolutionary movement against death and the existing biological order of things.[253]

In short, transhumanists believe God's design is inherently flawed, so we humans must get busy "speeding up evolution and becoming true masters of our destiny."[254]

Zoltan Istvan, who ran for president in 2016 as a candidate for the Transhumanist Party, which he founded, distilled the objectives of transhumanism into a philosophy he calls Teleological Egocentric

Functionalism. Istvan summarized those ideas with his Three Laws of Transhumanism:

1) A transhumanist must safeguard one's own existence above all else.
2) A transhumanist must strive to achieve omnipotence as expediently as possible—so long as one's actions do not conflict with the First Law.
3) A transhumanist must safeguard value in the universe—so long as one's actions do not conflict with the First and Second Laws.[255]

The first of Istvan's laws runs headfirst into Jesus' description of true love: "Greater love hath no man than this, that a man lay down his life for his friends" (John 15:13). That, right there, should be a deal-breaker for Christians who try to reconcile transhumanism with faith in Jesus Christ.

It's no surprise that Istvan is an atheist. His three laws make perfect sense to those who believe there's no God and no existence after death. Even the actions of Jethro Knights, the protagonist of Istvan's novel *The Transhumanist Wager*, are understandable, if chilling. To rid the world of the corrosive superstition of religion, as Istvan sees it, Knights and his team of super geniuses form a new, independent nation called Transhumania, and then they proceed to destroy the Vatican, the Ka'aba in Mecca, and the Wailing Wall in Jerusalem, among other iconic religious and cultural sites around the world.

Further, Knights has no problem with adopting a eugenics program that would have made Hitler proud:

We need to divert the resources to the genuinely gifted and qualified. To the achievers of society—the ones who pay your bills by their innovation, genius, and hard work. They will find the best way to the future. Not the losers of the world, or the mediocre, or the downtrodden, or the fearful. They will only drag us down, like they already have.[256]

To be fair, even other transhumanists are put off by *The Transhumanist Wager*. Transhumanism means different things to different people, and not all transhumanists are ready to exterminate the "unfit."

The Transhumanist Wager has only one idea—a fascistic interpretation of the meaning of transhumanism in which the complexity of every other current of human thinking, including transhumanism itself, is reduced to a cartoon.[257]

You may be wondering at this point why we're even discussing the concept of transhumanism in a book that examines God, gods, and extraterrestrials. Actually, a Venn diagram of worldviews touched on in this book would show a considerable degree of shared ideas between transhumanists and true believers in "ancient aliens."

For example, over the last two hundred years, a philosophy called "cosmism" emerged in Russia that blended Orthodox Christianity with Eastern and Western philosophic traditions.[258] In a nutshell, the cosmists believed in harnessing science to overcome death, with a goal of resurrecting dead ancestors to create a united humanity worthy of colonizing and governing the universe.[259]

It's not a coincidence that cosmism began to emerge alongside the Industrial Revolution. It must have seemed like the explosion of technology would inevitably lead to a solution for the most vexing problem in human history, death. At the same time, the Age of Enlightenment, which preceded the Industrial Revolution by about a century, laid the philosophical groundwork for positivism, which has gradually pushed a transcendent, omnipotent, omniscient Creator out of our society and replaced him with scientists, engineers, and technocrats.

After four hundred years of the intelligentsia declaring the death of God, and seventy-five years of indoctrination through pulp fiction, television, pseudo-archeology, and Hollywood, the secular West is just about ready to receive a false messiah from space. After all, if the gods of ancient Sumer were just aliens from Nibiru, then all we need to become as gods, fulfilling the promise of the serpent in Eden, is better tech.

Seriously. Children today practically come out of the crib with a smart phone. What are they going to trust—the seemingly magical technology they've lived with since birth or a dust-covered book Mom puts on the coffee table to impress visitors?

Obviously, whether one believes in God is a key factor in whether one thinks living forever through technology is a good idea. We make no claim to the gift of prophecy, but we feel confident in predicting that if advances in genetics, robotics, artificial intelligence, and nanotechnology ever succeed in bringing virtually unlimited lifespans to humanity, it will not create the heaven on Earth transhumanists are looking for.

As with every breakthrough in medicine, science, and technology, it will be reserved for the military or the wealthy, at least at first. Lt. Col. Robert Maginnis (US Army–Ret.) and journalist Annie Jacobsen have explored the potential military uses of cutting-edge tech in their books *Future War* and *The Pentagon's Brain*. If there are perceived advantages to restricting radical life-extension technologies for the military, you can bet civilians won't see them.

If the private sector does get access to medical miracles, the wealthy will be the beneficiaries. Consider education: Isn't it in the best interest of society to provide the highest quality education for every child? Of course it is. So, why do the wealthy send their children to expensive, top-notch learning academies that are out of reach for the poor and middle classes?

Because they can. Be honest—if you could do that for your kids and grandkids, wouldn't you?

Now, ask a transhumanist: Why do they think physical and mental upgrades that offer godlike power and near immortality will be available for everybody? Who gets to upgrade? To repeat the words Zoltan

Istvan's fictional transhumanist hero, Jethro Knights: "Not the losers of the world, or the mediocre, or the downtrodden, or the fearful. They will only drag us down, like they already have."[260]

Which begs the question: Who decides on who deserves to upgrade? Human nature being what it is, transhumanism's promise of immortality would bring back the eugenics programs of the last century, which sought to improve humankind by removing the unfit from the gene pool. Already, transhumanists—unwittingly, we assume, because it's hard to believe they'd do this on purpose—have adopted the motto of the International Eugenics Congresses held in 1912, 1921, and 1932: "Self-directed evolution."[261]

How quickly we forget.

Next question: If science somehow overcomes the problems of death and distribution and rolls out the miracle of immortality to everyone on Earth, does that really look like heaven? Imagine a world where most of the people, who do *not* subscribe to a biblical standard of morality, are immortal, and therefore no longer restrained from doing things that might have gotten them killed previously.

Put another way, imagine a world where Adolf Hitler, Josef Stalin, and Charles Manson could never die—and where others, who might have been too afraid of dying to live out their vile fantasies, no longer have that check on their behavior.

That's more like hell than heaven.

Now some speculation: For several years, we've considered the possibility that an autonomous artificial intelligence might be used by Antichrist to give life to the image of the Beast (Revelation 13:15). While this sounds like science fiction, it's not a new idea.

More than a hundred years ago, theologian E. W. Bullinger put forward the very same idea in his commentary on the book of Revelation:

> Nikola Tesla, the Hungarian-American electrician, boldly declares (in *The Century* magazine for June, 1900), that he has a plan for the construction of an automaton which shall have its "own mind," and be able, "independent of any operator, to

perform a great variety of acts and operations as if it had intelligence." He speaks of it, not as a miracle, of course, but only as an invention which he "has now perfected."

But again we say we care not how it is going to be done. God's word declares that it will be done, and we believe it.... We already hear of talking machines; with "a little" Satanic power thrown in, it will be a miracle very easily worked.[262]

Bullinger was not without controversial beliefs. He was an ultradispensationalist,[263] a believer in the cessation of the soul between death and resurrection,[264] and a member of the Universal Zetetic Society—a flat-earther.[265] Regardless, Bullinger's 1903 observation about the potential prophetic application of Tesla's research was profoundly insightful and relevant to our discussion of the transhumanist movement.

The human body in general, and the brain especially, is a bioelectrical machine. An electroencephalogram measures electrical activity in the brain to diagnose disorders such as epilepsy.[266] As Christians, we know (or we should) that this bioelectrical device can be overwhelmed and controlled by an external entity—it's what we call "demonic possession." Is it possible, then, that an autonomous, electrical superintelligence could provide a substrate for "the image of the Beast"?

Speculative, yes. We can't say with certainty that artificial intelligence will produce the false miracle that is the resurrected Beast or an army of demonically possessed super soldiers, but it is a fact that leading transhumanists see their goal as transcendence—rising above the limits of our flawed (they think) biology. Inventor Ray Kurzweil, Google's director of engineering, foresees what he calls the Singularity, "a future period during which the pace of technological change will be so rapid, its impact so deep, that human life will be irreversibly transformed."[267]

Kurzweil and his followers mean that literally. They foresee what Dr. Kurzweil calls the Sixth Epoch of Evolution. In his view, we're now in the final stages of Epoch 4 (humans working with technology) and we're about to enter Epoch 5, where biology and technology merge to create higher forms of life. Epoch 6 is when "the Universe wakes up," and virtually immortal human-machine hybrids go forth into the universe, presumably to be fruitful and multiply.[268]

You can see the influence of the Russian cosmists on today's transhumanists. A couple of generations ago, French Jesuit Pierre Teilhard de Chardin, a paleontologist by training and philosopher by nature, put forward a similar idea. In his 1959 book, *The Phenomenon of Man*, Teilhard theorized that creation was evolving to ever-higher levels of complexity toward something he called "the Omega Point." At some future date, he believed, a sphere of sentient thought surrounding the Earth he called "the noosphere" joins with itself, human thought unifies, and "our ancient itch to flee this woeful orb will finally be satisfied as the immense expanse of cosmic matter collapses like some mathematician's hypercube into absolute spirit."[269]

In other words, mind merges with matter and the universe wakes up. Teilhard's Omega Point and Kurzweil's Singularity are the same thing.

Although Teilhard's writings were cited with a warning by the Vatican in 1962, the Pontifical Council for Culture recently approved a petition asking Pope Francis to remove it. The council expressed its desire for the pope to "acknowledge the genuine effort of the pious Jesuit to reconcile the scientific vision of the universe with Christian eschatology."[270] The problem is that any such reconciliation of science and the Bible is neither scientific nor biblical. There is no evidence to support Teilhard's theory of a noosphere as a "living thinking machine with enormous physical powers,"[271] and believing in his Omega Point, and likewise the transhumanist Singularity, requires throwing out the book of Revelation and then deleting every other end-times prophecy in the Bible.

Transhumanists believe the Singularity will be humanity's crowning achievement, our great evolutionary leap forward to finally exceed the limits of our biology—in other words, apotheosis; finally realizing the promise from the garden to "be as gods." This is a sad delusion.

Transhumanism is nothing more than the ill-fated quest of Gilgamesh with a sci-fi veneer.

Now, the search will unquestionably yield benefits. We are not technophobes. Medical advances are a good thing, but they are *restoration*, not *transformation*. An artificial knee is not the first installment in a full-body immortality upgrade.

According to the epic, when Gilgamesh died, he was laid to rest in a tomb of stone in the bed of the Euphrates River. He probably didn't go to his eternal rest alone:

> His beloved wife, his beloved children, his beloved favorite and junior wife, his beloved musician, cup-bearer and…his beloved barber, his beloved…his beloved palace retainers and servants and his beloved objects were laid down in their places as if…in the purified (?) palace in the middle of Uruk.[272]

Scholars have debated the meaning of that text for the last hundred years, but tombs of the wealthy at the Sumerian city of Ur, dated at least five hundred years after the probable time of Gilgamesh, included as many as sixty-five servants and retainers who were killed to provide their late master or mistress with the comforts they'd been accustomed to in life.[273] It's possible this was a tradition that extended back to the kingdom of Uruk ruled by Gilgamesh, and by Nimrod before him.

The secret of immortality that eluded Gilgamesh will not be revealed to those who today unknowingly follow his footsteps. Technology, even if shared by our "space brothers" through a modern update on the pre-Flood knowledge resurrected by the legendary king, will not spare us the fate of all flesh since sin and death entered the world. The good news is that you are already an immortal being. The question you need to ask is where you plan to spend eternity.

Here's a helpful bit of advice: Do not look to so-called extraterrestrials for the answer.

CHAPTER 15

TRUE DISCLOSURE

By Derek Gilbert

G od has blessed us humans with a marvelous ability to think—to reason, to "search out a matter," which the Bible tells us "is the glory of kings" (Proverbs 25:2). Jesus even told us we are to love the Lord our God with all of our hearts, souls, and *minds*. Yet far too many Christians settle for two out of three, happily swallowing strange ideas based on nothing more than the unsubstantiated claims of dynamic leaders.

Well, we all have a right to believe whatever we want. Just remember that some bad choices have eternal consequences.

God—Yahweh, the God of the Bible—made sure He left behind evidence for the hope we have in Jesus: eyewitness testimonies, archeological discoveries, and even the activities of demons themselves argue for the truth of the Gospel.

Over the centuries, the principalities and powers Paul warned us about have played a long game, cultivating philosophies and doctrines opposed to their Creator. As human understanding of science grew, the Enemy and his cohorts shifted from portraying themselves as the true creators and masters of humanity to convincing the world, especially in the scientistic West, that there are no gods, only highly advanced extraterrestrials. And since, per Clarke's Third Law, "any sufficiently advanced technology is indistinguishable from magic," those so-called ETIs have become, by definition, the gods we thought we knew.

Let's give credit where it's due: This strategy is brilliant. It appeals to our human vanity. If our gods are gods only because they have better gizmos, then we, too, can someday be as gods. Fantastic! Where do we sign up?

The principalities and powers, rather than compelling us to accept them as our masters at the point of a sword (or a ray gun), have spooled out line over the centuries, patiently waiting while more and more of us took their bait. Through spiritualists like Swedenborg and the Fox sisters, modern gnostics like Blavatsky and Bailey, occultists like Crowley and Grant, and storytellers from Lovecraft to Roddenberry (and we might add von Däniken, Sitchin, and Tsoukalos to that category), a compelling message has been spread throughout the technologically advanced Western world: The spirit realm is real; we know who created you and where you go when you die; and your mission until then is to "work in the light."

In other words, the spirits behind this movement have created an alternate science-fiction religion. How do we know this? Because it's a faith that promises to answer the Big Questions: Where do we come from? Why are we here? What happens to us when we die?

Remember, people who believe ETIs are visiting the Earth outnumber truly biblical Christians in America three to one. The Enemy's deception is working.

So, the recent fascination with "official disclosure" of the existence of extraterrestrials is something Christians must be prepared to address. The fact that we're not is an indictment of the lack of discernment in the Church today. Not only do we fail to recognize the Enemy, but most American Christians also don't even acknowledge the Enemy's existence.

God save us.

Knowingly or otherwise, the Enemy's plans have been aided and abetted by the United States government, or at least by elements within it. The intelligence community's use of UFOs as a convenient cover story is a matter of public record. Evidence for the IC's role in famous cases like Maury Island, Roswell, and Dulce (the Paul Bennewitz affair), to pick the most obvious, and the highly improbable links between people connected to early UFO sightings and the assassination of John F. Kennedy, suggest critical thinkers should at least ask whether "official disclosure" might also be an intelligence op—especially since we know the US military command specifically tasked with creating convincing deceptions, Joint Security Control, has been positively linked to the UFO phenomenon.

The big question, of course, is *cui bono?*—"who benefits?". Who wins when the public buys into the idea that our gods are ETIs and they're coming back, if they're not here already, to help us join the Great White Brotherhood, the Galactic Federation, or whatever their club is called?

If you have a supernatural worldview, which should be your default setting if you're a Christian, the answer to that question should be obvious.

The issue here is that ETIs aren't coming back. *They're already here.* They never left. The UFO research community, which has a black hole where its critical thinking should be, accepts the existence of aliens as a good thing. Why? The Age of Discovery, which was obviously named by the Europeans who did the discovering, was devastating for the native peoples who were "discovered." Why should we expect first contact to be like *E.T.* when it might be more like *War of the Worlds* or *Independence Day*?

As to that, why do UFO researchers believe these so-called ETIs? Assuming the channelers in touch with The Nine, Ashtar Command, or Ramtha the Enlightened One are hearing from *something* and not just playing us for fools, why do they think these entities are telling the truth? If they *are* hostile, would they tell us?

And if they're friendly, why don't they just open a hailing frequency? Why are they so coy? They've allegedly crossed interstellar space; why haven't they mastered radio technology? Can't they use a webcam? Couldn't they flash a laser at us? Tap out some Morse code? Wave flags? Send smoke signals? Land on the National Mall and announce, "*Klaatu barada nikto*"?[274]

Why do those who eagerly await official disclosure ignore such basic, common-sense questions? Is it possible that Seth Shostak, chief astronomer for SETI, is spot on when he says we've been conditioned by Hollywood—propagandized, in other words—to think positively about our first contact with something that claims to be a traveler from another world? (And should we be worried that the acronym of the group trying to communicate with space aliens means "man of Set"—the chaos god?)

"Conspiratorial crazy talk," some will say. Maybe, but only if we ignore Paul's warning to the church of Ephesus. This massive, coordinated, and wildly successful propaganda campaign isn't run by humans. Principalities, powers, thrones, dominions, rulers, authorities, and cosmic powers—ranks of an angelic hierarchy—are our true opponents. And if you consider the influence and motives of the rebellious denizens of the unseen realm, the "spiritual forces of evil in the heavenly places," then a PSYOP like this is exactly the kind of thing we should expect. *And no wonder, for even Satan disguises himself as an angel of light* (2 Corinthians 11:14).

Beware, you lightworkers who serve the Ashtar Command. You know not what you do.

This gets to the heart of our book. When we look at the evolution of the ideas behind the belief that God, or the "gods," are extraterrestrials, the picture that emerges is much darker than they realize. For all of their claims to spiritual enlightenment, the New Agers who dominate the official disclosure movement are mostly ignorant of the roots of their doctrines, a condition one scholar calls "source amnesia."[275]

To repeat, we are not coincidence theorists. It is no accident the communications humanity has received from alleged ETIs so far have come through channelers instead of radios, telephones, or video screens. It is not an irrelevant detail that the accounts of "alien" abductees are very similar to those of victims of satanic ritual abuse.[276]

It is also not a coincidence that Aleister Crowley, his successor Kenneth Grant, and the Round Table of CIA asset Andrija Puharich believed they were hearing from gods worshipped in Egypt three thousand years ago—and specifically, in the case of Crowley and Grant, the Egyptian god of chaos, Set.

Consider this: The gods of the ancient world are real. That's not a guess, that's biblical.[277] Those small-g gods are under a death sentence with no hope of a pardon. God has also decreed that those who put their faith in Jesus Christ will one day judge the angels (1 Corinthians 6:3). The only thing left for the rebellious *elohim*, the fallen angels who dared to rebel against their Creator, is to drag as much of His creation as they can into the Lake of Fire with them when they go.

And the conflict between the Creator and Chaos has been ongoing since before the creation of the Garden of Eden. As we noted earlier, we read in Genesis 1:2 that the Spirit of God hovered over the face of the waters—waters that contained "the deep," the abyss, *tehom*, or Tiamat, the Sumerian chaos dragon. That's the entity named Leviathan in the Bible.

Remember that occultist Kenneth Grant believed the god he channeled was Set, Egypt's dark lord of chaos. Set was called "Typhon" by the Greeks, hence Grant's religion, the Typhonian Order.

Grant further believed horror author H. P. Lovecraft had tapped into that same spirit, which revealed to Lovecraft the dangerous grimoire, the *Necronomicon*. Given the common theme in Lovecraft's stories of cosmic horror, often built around the imminent return of old, extraterrestrial gods with no love for, or even awareness of, humanity, it's hard to argue with Grant's conclusion.

And, as bizarre as it sounds, it was the fiction of H. P. Lovecraft, and thus the spirit(s) behind it, that inspired Erich von Däniken to write the book that launched the ancient astronaut theory.

In short, our culture's fascination with ancient aliens is the result of a supernatural deception in the long war between the god of chaos—Leviathan—and Yahweh.

While Yahweh defeated Leviathan before creating humanity by crushing its heads (Psalm 74:14), it is not dead. Its future destruction is guaranteed, however. On the Day of the Lord, "He will slay the dragon that is in the sea" (Isaiah 27:1), and when He creates the new heaven and the new earth, the sea—chaos—will be no more (Revelation 21:1).

Creation is far more complex and a whole lot weirder than we've been taught. Our God spoke the universe into existence and all that's in it, including the small-g gods who rage and plot against Him (and us). We shouldn't be afraid to address the question of whether we're being visited by ETIs or how to respond to a future announcement that aliens have just landed in front of the United Nations building. The universe is a huge place. Speculating on the possibility of other inhabited worlds is fascinating. But it can lead people without a biblical anchor down paths to destruction.

Based on the evidence that's been made public and the chain of ideas leading from the ancient Greek philosophers to the modern UFO phenomenon, we don't believe ET has come calling. Ever. True believers in the existence of ETIs have been duped by smoke and shadows, buying into a spiritual deception wrapped in a pseudoscientific veneer.

It's a pity. They've sided with the junior varsity team. Our God not only created them, He created the stuff He made them with. That's the God who captains our army. And you, dear reader, were created as His "imager"—His moral agent on Earth. No matter what happens to you or to the world, that's a job title you never lose.

Ancient astronaut theorists, New Agers, and atheists longing for answers to the Big Questions that don't involve the God of the Bible will keep pushing the governments of the world to disclose what they know about extraterrestrial intelligences. The principalities and powers behind the thrones of this world may well oblige them someday with an event that *looks* like official disclosure.

Just remember: You are created in the image of God. You are His Image-bearer on Earth. That's a specific set of attributes inherent in, unique to, and inseparable from the human race.[278] The arrival of something claiming to be from Zeta Reticuli *does not change your status.* It does not change the need for a Savior or the plan of salvation. It doesn't change who Jesus is or why He died, and it sure doesn't change the established historical fact of His Resurrection and the victory it achieved over the Fallen.

In short, although we don't think this will ever happen, the legitimate discovery of an extraterrestrial intelligence should have no impact whatsoever on your Christian faith.

The disclosure of ETIs, ancient astronaut theory, and the old lie that is the New Age are just tactics by the small-g gods to lure unsuspecting and undiscerning humans to destruction. They deny the authority, identity, or existence of God, and offer instead the false promise they first rolled out in the Garden: "Ye shall be as gods" (Genesis 3:5).

So, when you encounter the topic of official disclosure, please remember: We follow the One who created everything. Christian doctrine—and your worldview—is big enough to handle the "what ifs."

After all, we own the definitive Book on the supernatural. The answers are in there…if we just look.

NOTES

1   Though this story received a lot of coverage from many platforms, one article that succinctly captured the basic facts and included several links to user-uploaded videos can be accessed at the following: Reuters Fact Check, "Video Shows a Goodyear Blimp, Not a UFO or Alien Spacecraft," February 15, 2023, *Reuters*, last accessed April 17, 2024, https://www.reuters.com/article/factcheck-ufo-alien-highway/fact-check-video -shows-a-goodyear-blimp-not-a-ufo-or-alien-spacecraft-idUSL1N34V1RS/.

2   Zurlo, Gina, "The Annual Statistical Table for World Christianity 2024: Fragmentation and Unity," *Princeton Theological Seminary, Overseas Ministries Study Center*, last accessed May 15, 2024, https://omsc.ptsem.edu/the-annual-statistical-table/#:~:text =Weidentifysomeofthe,Charismatics)Cand47C000denominations.

3   Fleck, Anna, "More American Now Believe in Aliens," October 14, 2022, *Statista*, last accessed April 17, 2024, https://www.statista.com/chart/28466/how-many-us-adults -believe-in-aliens/.

4   Kennedy, Courtney, Arnold Lau, "Most Americans Believe in Intelligent Life Beyond Earth; Few See UFOs As a Major National Security Threat," June 30, 2021, *Pew Research Center*, last accessed April 17, 2024, https://www.pewresearch.org/short-reads /2021/06/30/most-americans-believe-in-intelligent-life-beyond-earth-few-see-ufos-as -a-major-national-security-threat/. Out of the 46 percent of Americans who believe military-reported UFOs represent a threat to US national security, 36 percent said it's a "minor threat" while 10 percent said "major."

5   Buchholz, Katharina, "Are UFO Sightings Taking Off Again?" June 30, 2023, *Statista*, last accessed April 17, 2024, https://www.statista.com/chart/8452/ufo-sightings-are-at -record-heights/.

6   Martin, Walter, et al., *The Kingdom of the Occult* (Nashville, TN: Thomas Nelson, 2008), 366–369.

7   Clark, Jeffrey, "Harvard Physicist Searching for UFO Evidence Says Humanity Will View Alien Intelligence Like 'God,'" August 14, 2023, *Fox News*, last accessed April 17, 2024, https://www.foxnews.com/media/harvard-physicist-searching-ufo-evidence -says-humanity-will-view-alien-intelligence-like-god, video timestamp: 2:36–3:55.

8   Loeb, Abraham, "Advanced Extraterrestrials as an Approximation to God," January 26, 2019, *Scientific American*, last accessed April 18, 2024, https://www.scientificamerican .com/blog/observations/advanced-extraterrestrials-as-an-approximation-to-god/.

9   Howell, Donna, and Allie Henson, *Dark Covenant: How the Masses Are Being Groomed to Embrace the Unthinkable While the Leaders of Organized Religion Make a Deal with the Devil* (Crane, MO: Defender Publishing, 2021), 40–41.

10 Randles, Jenny, and Hough, Peter, *The Complete Book of UFOs* (New York: Sterling, 1996), 230–235.

NOTES

11 The reference of angels as the "sons of God" is peppered in several places throughout the Old Testament (Genesis 6:2, 4; Job 1:6; 2:1; 38:7). Though some have questioned whether this term is in reference to human men, Job 1:6 and 2:1 appear to make such a conclusion impossible. For more reading on this particular topic, including in-depth reflections by a renowned Hebrew Bible scholar regarding the holes in other leading arguments, see Dr. Michael Heiser's *Unseen Realm* and *Angels*.

12 Though we will not be addressing these sites at length in this work, many of these cities raised in worship of the fallen angels still exist. Secular archeologists frequently acknowledge that the ancients behind the building of such sites as Gobekli Tepe, Baalbek, Catalhoyuk, and others left carvings in stone of the "gods" they worshipped in an era earlier than the Flood of Noah's day. Gobekli Tepe was intentionally backfilled at an early point, and many scholars who compare that evidence with the timing of the Flood identify the backfill as an attempt by the ancients to protect their story of the "gods" (fallen angels) from being swept away by the waters of the Flood that re-layered the Earth's surface so their unholy religion would be unearthed again when the waters of Noah's day ceased. Such "gods" as those in view amidst these archaic stones scattered about our current world seamlessly intertwine with the Bible's narrative of the fallen angels. For more reading on this topic, consider Dr. Michael Heiser's *Unseen Realm*, *Angels*, *Demons*, and *Reversing Hermon*, as well as many works by Dr. Thomas R. Horn (including a book he wrote alongside Donna Howell entitled *Before Genesis*) and Derek Gilbert.

13 Bullinger, Ethelbert W., *The Companion Bible: Being the Authorized Version of 1611 with the Structures and Notes, Critical, Explanatory and Suggestive and with 198 Appendixes*, vol. 2 (Bellingham, WA: Faithlife, 2018), 28.

14 Ibid.

15 Barnes, Albert, *Barnes Notes on the Whole Bible* (E4 Group; Kindle edition), Kindle locations 3503–3505, emphasis added.

16 Some mainstream teachings within the Church insist upon a biblical interpretation that views the angels at fault for only one fall account amidst their kind—a sort of "they learned their lesson and would/could never fall again" approach. Though I have certainly heard these arguments and find them interesting, the conclusions born from this interpretation do not align with the permanency of the gift of free will; if God gives one of His creatures a mind and free will, it does not match His character to take that away, rendering a mindless drone who worships Him forever without question. Scholars deeply entrenched in parsing the Hebrew of the Old Testament, both in modernity and throughout history, have repeatedly identified multiple fall accounts of angels within Scripture. For a deeper treatment of this issue, including at least *three separate* accounts of angels utilizing their free will to forsake God and the Messiah's role in reversing that malady, see: Dr. Michael Heiser, *Reversing Hermon: Enoch, the Watchers, and the Forgotten Mission of Jesus Christ* (Crane, MO: Defender Publishing, 2017).

17 For example: *Unearthing the Lost World of the Cloudeaters*, especially the chapter, "The Truth about the Great Smithsonian Cover-Up." This book, alongside many others, shows a time when scientists discovered bizarre ancient remains in our soil and *transparently reported them to the public*. Among those discoveries were giant, humanlike bones with double rows of teeth. Archeologists went from telling the world giants

were real and providing proof to hiding all evidence and insisting, per John Powell of the Smithsonian, that any and all of our resources used to study these findings were a waste of precious funds. The infamous "Powell Doctrine" solidified this stance and essentially wrapped all past discovery in red tape. Unfortunately for *them*, years and years of annual reports published up to that point were, and are, still in circulation, and it was from those annual reports that anyone can build a case for a cover-up in high places that obscures the truth of Genesis 6:4 from us today.

18 Dr. Michael Heiser deeply tackled this connection in many of his works, which have been well received among scholars, including those who maintain more mainstream, nondenominational teaching (such as those behind the highly regarded Logos Bible Software). For more information regarding how and why the origin of demons links to the disembodied spirits of the now-deceased Nephilim from Genesis, see his following titles: *Unseen Realm, Reversing Hermon, Angels,* and *Demons.*

19 Merriam-Webster, "alien," "extraterrestrial," *Merriam-Webster's Collegiate Dictionary,* 11th Edition (Merriam-Webster, Inc.; 2014, Kindle Edition), Kindle locations 42270–42282 (for "alien") and 148712–148716 (for "extraterrestrial").

20 Findlater, ed., Andrew, "Alien," *Chambers' Etymological Dictionary of the English Language* (London; Edinburgh: W. & R. Chambers, 1900), 11.

21 Microsoft Copilot. https://www.bing.com/search?q=extraterrestrial&form=ANSPH 1&refig=1aa8296acadc42379e7b633ef7e7584f&pc=U531&showconv=1

22 Koehler, Ludwig et al., *The Hebrew and Aramaic Lexicon of the Old Testament* (Leiden: E.J. Brill, 1994–2000), 1066.

23 Sproul, R. C., "The Meaning of the Holiness of God," YouTube video, https://youtube /K96e1tK7eN4?si=hLYx4_DmxkH7z7yw.

24 Citations are as they appeared in the original correspondence from Dr. Lake.

25 Howell, Donna, *Before Genesis: The Unauthorized History of Tohu, Bohu, and the Chaos Dragon in the Land Before Time* (Crane, MO: Defender Publishing; 2023), 32.

26 Stewart, Don, "What Are We to Make of the Idea That Jesus Was an Alien from Another Planet?" *Blue Letter Bible Online,* last accessed May 16, 2024, https://www .blueletterbible.org/Comm/stewart_don/faq/accusations-against-jesus-answered/16 -what-are-we-to-make-of-the-idea-that-jesus-was-an-alien.cfm.

27 Powell, Doug, *Holman QuickSource Guide to Christian Apologetics* (Nashville, TN: Holman Reference, 2006), 281.

28 Doyle, Shaun, "Was Jesus an Alien?" February 10, 2018, *Creation Ministries International,* last accessed May 16, 2024, https://creation.com/was-jesus-an-alien.

29 Ibid.

30 Ibid.

31 Martin, Walter, et al., *The Kingdom of the Occult* (Nashville, TN: Thomas Nelson, 2008), 373–379.

32 Ibid.

33 Hoff, Paul. *Genesis, 6th edition.* (Springfield, MO: Global University, 2015) 58.

34 Ibid., p. 58.

35 Genesis 6:5, *Blue Letter Bible.* 2024. Last accessed May 31, https://www.blueletterbible .org/kjv/gen/6/1/t_conc_6005.

36 "Top Ten Most Terrible Events in History," *The Top Tens.* 2024. Last accessed May 31, 2024. https://www.thetoptens.com/history/most-terrible-events/.

37   Sostak, Seth. "Space Aliens Are Breeding with Humans, University Instructor Says. Scientists Say Otherwise." *NBC News*. May 15, 2019. Last accessed May 31, 2024. https://www.nbcnews.com/mach/science/space-aliens-are-breeding-humans-university -instructor-says-scientists-say-ncna1008971.

38   Ibid.

39   "Empirical." *Merriam-Webster Dictionary*. 2024. Last accessed May 31, 2024. https:// www.merriam-webster.com/dictionary/empirical.

40   Davison, Andrew. "We Believe in Miracles, So Why Not Aliens?" *Christianity Today*. December 4, 2023. Last accessed May 31, 2024. https://www.christianitytoday.com/ct /2023/november-web-only/ufo-uap-alien-extraterrestrial-astrobiology-theology-christ.html.

41   Wenk, Gary. "Why Do Humans Keep Inventing Gods to Worship?" *Psychology Today*. July 6, 2021. Last accessed May 31, 2024. https://www.psychologytoday.com/us/blog /your-brain-food/202107/why-do-humans-keep-inventing-gods-worship.

42   Kluger, Jeffrey. "Religion: Is God in Our Genes?" *Time Magazine*. October 25, 2004. Last accessed May 31, 2024. https://time.com/archive/6739753/religion-is-god-in-our-genes/.

43   Venable, Hannah. "Is the 'Need to Worship' Part of the Human Condition?" July 23, 2013. Last accessed May 31, 2024. https://diatothaumazein.com/2013/07/23/is-the -need-to-worship-part-of-the-human-condition/.

44   Ibid.

45   *The Inner Journey*. "The Human Need to Worship." Feb. 9, 2019. Last accessed May 31, 2024. https://innerjourneyblog.weebly.com/current-blog/the-human-need-to-worship.

46   Frost, Jacqui. "Inside the 'Secular Churches' That Fill a Need for Some Nonreligious Americans," January 11, 2024. Last accessed May 31, 2024. https://www.cbsnews.com /news/secular-churches-atheist-congregations-sunday-assembly-worship-oasis/.

47   Ibid.

48   Ibid.

49   "Agnostic," *Dictionary.com*. Last accessed May 31, 2024. https://www.dictionary.com /browse/agnostic.

50   Ibid.

51   "Atheist," *Merriam Webster Dictionary*. Last accessed May 31, 2024. https://www.merriam -webster.com/dictionary/atheist.

52   Lipka, Michael; Tevington, Patricia; & Starr, Kelsey Jo. "8 Facts about Atheists," *Pew Research*. February 7, 2024. Last accessed May 31, 2024. https://www.pewresearch.org /short-reads/2024/02/07/8-facts-about-atheists/#:~:text=About%20three%2Dquarters% 20of%20U.S.,to%20our%20summer%202023%20survey.

53   Ibid.

54   Ibid.

55   Ecklund, Elaine Howard, and David R. Johnson, "Spiritual Atheist Scientists," *Varieties of Atheism in Science* (New York, 2021; online edn, Oxford Academic, 19 Aug. 2021), https://doi.org/10.1093/oso/9780197539163.003.0005, accessed 23 Apr. 2024.

56   Lipka, et. al, "8 Facts."

57   Kluger, "Religion: Is God in Our Genes?"

58   B., Nick. "Higher Power for Atheists and Agnostics: 6 Alternatives to God." *The Freedom Center: Addiction Treatment*. September 15, 2021. Last accessed May 31, 2024. https:// www.thefreedomcenter.com/higher-power-for-atheists-and-agnostics-6-alternatives-to-god/.

NOTES

59 Edgar, Robert; Hackett, Neil; Jewsbury, George; et. al., *Civilizations Past & Present, 12th edition*. (Upper Saddle River, NJ: Pearson Education, Inc. 2008) 550.

60 Ibid.

61 Ibid.

62 Ibid.

63 Ambrosino, Brandon. "If We Made Contact with Aliens, How Would Religions React?" BBC. December 16, 2016. Last accessed May 31, 2024. https://www.bbc.com/future/article/20161215-if-we-made-contact-with-aliens-how-would-religions-react.

64 Sagan, Carl. (1994). *Pale Blue Dot: A Vision of the Human Future in Space*, (New York, NY: Ballantine Books) 50.

65 Estes, Douglas. "Love Thy Extraterrestrial Neighbor." *Christianity Today*. November 20, 2019. Last accessed May 31, 2024. https://www.christianitytoday.com/ct/2019/november-web-only/love-thy-extraterrestrial-neighbor-aliens-astrobiology.html.

66 Graham, Billy. "Answers: If There Is Intelligent Life on Other Planets, Does God Love Those Creatures as Much as He Does Us, Whatever They Are Like? Did Jesus Have to Visit Those Planets Also, So They Could Learn About God?" *Billy Graham Evangelistic Association*. June 1, 2004. Last accessed May 31, 2024. https://billygraham.org/answer/if-there-is-intelligent-life-on-other-planets-does-god-care-about-those-creatures-as-much-as-he-does-us/.

67 Murphy, James. *Barnes Notes: Genesis*. 1873. (Grand Rapids, MI: Baker Book House) 84.

68 "Vicegerent," *Merriam Webster Dictionary*. 2024. Last accessed May 31, 2024. https://www.merriam-webster.com/dictionary/vicegerent.

69 Murphy, James. *Barnes Notes: Genesis*. (Grand Rapids, Michigan: Baker Book House, 1873) 107.

70 Davison, "We Believe in Miracles, So Why Not Aliens?"

71 Spurgeon, Charles. "Man's Thoughts and God's Thoughts." *The Spurgeon Center: For Biblical Preaching at Midwestern Seminary*. February, 1866. Last accessed May 31, 2024. https://www.spurgeon.org/resource-library/sermons/mans-thoughts-and-gods-thoughts/#flipbook/.

72 Davison, Andrew. "We Believe in Miracles, So Why Not Aliens?"

73 Brzozowski, Nick. "Do Christians Believe in Aliens? What 12 Christian Leaders Say About Aliens," *Anchor Church*. July 6, 2021. Last accessed June 1, 2024. https://www.anchorchurchil.com/post/what-12-christian-leaders-say-about-aliens.

74 Fulks, Jeffrey; Petersen, Randy; & Plake, John Farquhar. "State of the Bible." *Research from American Bible Society*. 2022. Last accessed June 1, 2024. chrome-extension://efaidnbmnnnibpcajpcglclefindmkaj/https://1s712.americanbible.org/state-of-the-bible/stateofthebible/State_of_the_bible-2022.pdf.

75 Routledge, Clay, PhD, "5 Scientifically Supported Benefits of Prayer," June 23, 2014, *Psychology Today*. https://www.psychologytoday.com/blog/more-mortal/201406/5-scientifically-supported-benefits-prayer, retrieved 7/20/17.

76 Lactantius, *On the Anger of God*, 13.19.

77 https://web.archive.org/web/20171127001718/ http://www.noetic.org/about/overview, retrieved 5/3/24.

78 Stefanidakis, Rev. Simeon. "Emanuel Swedenborg (1688–1772)." https://fst.org/spiritual-teachings/emanuel-swedenborg/. Retrieved 5/3/24.

79 https://web.archive.org/web/20170504164100/ http://www.swedenborg.com/product
/life-planets/, retrieved 5/3/24.

80 Doctrine and Covenants 130:22. https://www.lds.org/scriptures/dc-testament/dc
/130.22?lang=eng#21, retrieved 5/3/24.

81 *The Pearl of Great Price*, Moses 1:29–34. https://www.lds.org/scriptures/pgp/moses
/1.29-34?lang=eng#28. Retrieved 5/3/24.

82 https://newsroom.churchofjesuschrist.org/article/2023-statistical-report-church-jesus
-christ. Retrieved 2/24/24.

83 Margaret Fox Kane, quoted in Davenport, Reuben Briggs. *The Deathblow to Spiritualism.* (New York: G. W. Dillingham, 1888) 75–76.

84 Ibid., p. 77.

85 Zusne, Leonard; Jones, Warren. *Anomalistic Psychology: A Study of Magical Thinking.*
(Lawrence Erlbaum Associates, 1989) 212.

86 Carroll, Bret E. *The Routledge Historical Atlas of Religion in America.* (New York: Routledge, 2000) 74.

87 Hess, David J. *Science in the New Age: The Paranormal, Its Defenders and Debunkers,
and American Culture.* (Madison, WI: University of Wisconsin Press, 1993) 20.

88 Blavatsky, Helena P. *The Key to Theosophy.* (London: Theosophical Publishing Society,
1889) 43.

89 Kuhn, Alvin Boyd. *Theosophy: A Modern Revival of Ancient Wisdom.* (PhD thesis).
American religion series: Studies in religion and culture. (Whitefish, MT: Kessinger
Publishing, 1992 [originally published 1930]), 63–64.

90 Colavito, Jason. *The Cult of Alien Gods: H. P. Lovecraft and Extraterrestrial Pop Culture*
(Kindle locations 364–366). Kindle Edition.

91 https://truthxchange.com/about-2/vision/, retrieved 5/3/24.

92 Cain, Sian. "Ten Things You Should Know about HP Lovecraft," *The Guardian*,
August 20, 2014. https://www.theguardian.com/books/2014/aug/20/ten-things-you
-should-know-about-hp-lovecraft. Retrieved 5/22/24.

93 Ibid.

94 Harms, Daniel, and John Wisdom Gonce. *The Necronomicon Files: The Truth behind
Lovecraft's Legend.* (Boston, MA: Weiser Books, 2003) 5.

95 One of the most well-known pop culture references to Lovecraft is the Arkham Asylum, which has been featured since the mid-1970s in the Batman comics, cartoons,
movies, and video games. Arkham was named for a fictional town in Massachusetts
created by Lovecraft, the home of Miskatonic University, which features prominently
in many of Lovecraft's stories.

96 Crowley, Aleister. *The Equinox of the Gods*, chapter 7. https://hermetic.com/crowley
/equinox-of-the-gods/remarks-on-the-method-of-receiving-liber-legis?redirect=1,
retrieved 5/22/24.

97 Thelemapedia.org. http://www.thelemapedia.org/index.php/The_Book_of_the_Law,
retrieved May 22, 2024.

98 Hutton, Ronald. *The Triumph of the Moon: A History of Modern Pagan Witchcraft.*
(Oxford: Oxford University Press, 2006) 178.

99 Colavito, Jason. "Inside the Necronomicon," 2002. https://jcolavito.tripod.com/lost
civilizations/id25.html, retrieved 5/22/24.

100 O'Neill, Declan. "Kenneth Grant: Writer and Occultist Who Championed Aleister Crowley and Austin Osman Spare." *The Independent.* March 4, 2011. http://www.independent.co.uk/news/obituaries/kenneth-grant-writer-and-occultist-who-championed-aleister-crowley-and-austin-osman-spare-2231570.html. Retrieved 5/22/24.

101 Harms and Gonce, pp. 109–110.

102 Ibid.

103 Levenda, Peter. *The Dark Lord: H. P. Lovecraft, Kenneth Grant, and the Typhonian Tradition in Magic* (Nicolas-Hays, Inc.) 97–98. Kindle Edition.

104 Ibid., pp. 102–103.

105 te Velde, Herman (1967). "Seth, God of Confusion: A Study of His Role in Egyptian Mythology and Religion." *Probleme der Ägyptologie* 6. Translated by van Baaren-Pape, G. E., 2nd ed. (Leiden: E. J. Brill) 7.

106 See chapter 4 of Derek Gilbert's book *The Great Inception.*

107 Ryholt, Kim. *The Political Situation in Egypt During the Second Intermediate Period c.1800–1550 B.C.*, (Museum Tuscalanum Press, 1997) 128.

108 Allon, Niv. "Seth Is Baal—Evidence from the Egyptian Script." *Egypt and the Levant* XVII, (2007) 15–22.

109 te Velde. pp. 139–140.

110 Levenda, op. cit. (p. 75). Nicolas-Hays, Inc. Kindle Edition.

111 Colavito, 2002.

112 Levenda, p. 8.

113 "Remembering Kenneth Grant's Understanding of the Necronomicon Tradition," https://warlockasyluminternationalnews.com/2011/02/18/remembering-kenneth-grants-understanding-of-the-necronomicon-tradition/. Retrieved 5/22/24.

114 Cabal, Alan. "The Doom That Came to Chelsea," *Chelsea News*, June 10, 2003. https://www.nypress.com/the-doom-that-came-to-chelsea/. Retrieved 5/22/24.

115 Clore, Dan. "The Lurker on the Threshold of Interpretation: Hoax Necronomicons and Paratextual Noise." *Lovecraft Studies*, No. 42–43. Autumn 2001. http://www.geocities.ws/clorebeast/lurker.htm. Retrieved May 22, 2024.

116 Colavito, *Cult of Alien Gods*, Kindle location 1227.

117 Ibid., Kindle locations 1296–1300.

118 Ibid., Kindle location 1338.

119 Von Däniken, Erich (1968). *Chariots of the Gods: Unsolved Mysteries of the Past.* (New York: Berkley Books) viii.

120 "2001: A Space Odyssey Named the Greatest Sci-Fi Film of All Time by the Online Film Critics Society," June 12, 2002. https://web.archive.org/web/20061126071451/http://ofcs.rottentomatoes.com/pages/pr/top100scifi. Retrieved 5/22/24.

121 Von Braun was one of the 1,600 or so Nazi scientists, engineers, and technicians secretly brought to the US after the war during Operation Paperclip.

122 Colavito, Kindle location 1346.

123 Sheaffer, Robert (1974). "Erich von Däniken's 'Chariots of the Gods': Science or Charlatanism?" Originally published in *NICAP UFO Investigator*. https://www.debunker.com/texts/vondanik.html. Retrieved May 22, 2024.

124 See, for example, Chris White's excellent three-hour film *Ancient Aliens Debunked*, available free at AncientAliensDebunked.com.

125 "Erich von Daniken: Fraud, Lies and Bananas." *Forgetomori,* April 8, 2012. http://forgetomori.com/2012/aliens/erich-von-daniken-fraud-lies-and-bananas/. Retrieved May 22, 2024.

126 http://www.mufon.com. Retrieved August 23, 2017.

127 Sheaffer, Robert. "MUFON Unravels". *Bad UFOs,* August 1, 2017. https://badufos.blogspot.com/2017/08/mufon-unravels.html. Retrieved May 22, 2024.

128 https://www.mufonsymposium.com/corey-goode. Retrieved August 26, 2017 (page now defunct).

129 https://www.mufonsymposium.com/andrew-bassagio. Retrieved August 26, 2027 (page now defunct).

130 Salla, Dr. Michael E. (December 26, 2015). "Jump Room to Mars: Did CIA Groom Obama & Basiago as Future Presidents?" *Exopolitics.org.* https://exopolitics.org/jump-room-to-mars-did-cia-groom-obama-basiago-as-future-presidents/. Retrieved May 22, 2024.

131 Dolan, Richard (July 18, 2017). "On Corey, Andrew, and the Whistleblowers." https://www.facebook.com/notes/richard-dolan/on-corey-andrew-and-the-whistleblowers/1394366947350897/. Retrieved August 26, 2017 (page now defunct).

132 Whalen, Andrew. "What If Aliens Met Racists? MUFON Resignations Highlight Internal Divisions in UFO Sightings Organization." *Newsweek,* April 29, 2018. https://www.newsweek.com/ufo-sightings-mufon-2018-john-ventre-alien-extraterrestrial-905060. Retrieved February 9, 2024.

133 Knight, Judy Zebra. *Ramtha, the White Book* (Yelm, WA: JZK Publishing, 2005).

134 Iwasaki, John. "JZ Knight Not Faking It, Say Scholars—But They Bristle at the Idea She's Buying Them." *Seattle Post-Intelligencer,* February 10, 1997, p. B1.

135 Brenner, Keri. "Disillusioned Former Students Target Ramtha." *The Olympian,* January 27, 2008. Via the Cult Education Institute. https://www.culteducation.com/group/1113-ramtha-school-of-enlightenment/17846-disillusioned-former-students-target-ramtha-.html. Retrieved February 9, 2024.

136 Ibid.

137 Gorenfeld, John. "'Bleep' of Faith," *Salon,* September 16, 2004. https://www.salon.com/2004/09/16/bleep_2/. Retrieved February 9, 2024.

138 Box Office Mojo. http://www.boxofficemojo.com/movies/?id=whatthe.htm. Retrieved February 9, 2024.

139 "Former MUFON State Director Resigns, Cites Cult Leader Involvement," *UFO Watchdog,* July 24, 2017. http://ufowatchdog.blogspot.com/2017/07/former-mufon-state-director-resigns.html. Retrieved February 9, 2024.

140 Levenda, Peter. *Sinister Forces—The Nine: A Grimoire of American Political Witchcraft* (Walterville, OR: TrineDay, 2005), Kindle Edition, Kindle Location 5562.

141 Orleans Parish Grand Jury Testimony of F. Lee Crisman, November 21, 1968. https://archive.org/details/OrleansParishGrandJuryTestimonyOfF.LeeCrisman21Nov1968. Retrieved April 25, 2024.

142 Ibid.

143 Knight, Peter. *Conspiracy Theories in American History: An Encyclopedia* (Santa Barbara, CA: ABC-CLIO, 2003) 690.

144 Best, Emma. "FBI's Real-life 'X-Files' Documents Strange Connection between UFOs and the JFK Assassination." *Muckrock,* December 5, 2016. https://www.muckrock

.com/news/archives/2016/dec/05/fbis-real-x-files-documents-strange-connection-bet/. Retrieved April 25, 2024.

145 Thomas, Kenn. *JFK & UFO: Military-Industrial Conspiracy and Cover-Up from Maury Island to Dallas* (Port Townshend, WA: Feral House, 2011), Kindle Edition, p. 13.

146 Ibid., p. 32.

147 Levenda, Kindle location 5636.

148 Ibid., Kindle location 5667.

149 "5 Discs Sighted by United Flight." http://www.nicap.org/470704emmett_dir.htm. Retrieved April 25, 2024.

150 Levenda, Kindle locations 5569–5678.

151 Best.

152 Gulyas, Aaron John. *The Paranormal and the Paranoid: Conspiratorial Science Fiction Television* (Lanham, MD: Rowman & Littlefield, 2015), 30.

153 Thomas, p. 15.

154 Ibid.

155 That's the nickname given to allegations of a secret agreement between Ronald Reagan's 1980 presidential campaign and the government of Iran to hold on to American hostages, who'd been kidnapped from the US Embassy in Tehran on November 4, 1979, until after the election, making incumbent President Jimmy Carter look weak to voters. Reagan won the election, although it's never been proven that Reagan's team made a deal with Iran.

156 Ridgeway, James, and Vaughan, Doug. "The Last Days of Danny Casolaro," *The Village Voice*, October 15, 1991, p. 34ff.

157 "Jury Says Guilty—Man Claims Frame-Up but Faces 20-Year Term after Verdict On Seven Drug-Related Charges." *Seattle Times*, January 19, 1992. https://web.archive.org/web/20120612013320/http://community.seattletimes.nwsource.com/archive/?date=19920119&slug=1471110. Retrieved April 25, 2024.

158 Best; Levenda, Kindle locations 5682–5683.

159 Kelly, William "The Houma Bunker Raid Revisited." *JFKcountercoup*, May 20, 2009. https://jfkcountercoup.blogspot.com/2009/05/houma-bunker-raid-revisted.html. Retrieved April 25, 2024.

160 "Guy Banister." https://spartacus-educational.com/JFKbannister.htm. Retrieved April 25, 2024.

161 Levenda, Kindle location 5699.

162 Which is a plausible scenario. See "The 1947 Roswell UFO Crash," http://www.roswellufocrash.com. Retrieved April 25, 2024.

163 Carrion, James. "Human Deception at Play during the UFO Wave of 1947," August 20, 2016. https://web.archive.org/web/20160824012258/http://historydeceived.blogspot.com/2016/08/human-deception-at-playduring-ufo-wave.html. Retrieved April 25, 2024.

164 Ibid.

165 "AAF Drops Flying Disc Probe for Lack of Evidence." *Waco News-Tribune*, July 4, 1947, p. 3.

166 Carrion.

167 Coppens, Philip. "Driving Mr. Bennewitz Insane." https://www.eyeofthepsychic.com/bennewitz/. Retrieved April 25, 2024.

168 Redfern, Nick. "UFOs: The Project Beta Scandal." *Mysterious Universe*, April 22, 2012. https://web.archive.org/web/20120425035542/http://mysteriousuniverse .org/2012/04/ufos-the-project-beta-scandal/. Retrieved April 24, 2024.

169 Donovan, B. W. *Conspiracy Films: A Tour of Dark Places in the American Conscious* (Jefferson, NC: McFarland, 2011), 104–105.

170 Vallee, Jacques. *Revelations: Alien Contact and Human Deception* (New York: Ballantine Books, 1991), 53.

171 Brewer, Jack. *The Greys Have Been Framed: Exploitation in the UFO Community* (North Charleston, SC: CreateSpace, 2016), Kindle location 378.

172 Ibid., Kindle locations 210–212.

173 http://www.alienresistance.org/ce4.htm. Retrieved April 25, 2024.

174 Redfern, Nick. "Feeding the UFO Phenomenon." *Mysterious Universe*, September 18, 2013. https://web.archive.org/web/20130925033915/http://mysteriousuniverse.org /2013/09/feeding-the-ufo-phenomenon/. Retrieved April 25, 2024.

175 Ibid.

176 Michael S. Heiser, "Review of Nick Redfern's Final Events." *DrMSH.com*, November 27, 2010. https://drmsh.com/review-of-nick-redferns-final-events/. Retrieved April 25, 2024.

177 Ibid.

178 Redfern, Nick. "A Religious Deception?" *Mysterious Universe*, October 1, 2011. https://web.archive.org/web/20111002004219/http://mysteriousuniverse.org/2011 /10/a-religious-deception/. April 25, 2024.

179 Pilkington, Mark. "RAND, Superstition, and Psychological Warfare." *Mirage Men*, November 3, 2010. https://miragemen.wordpress.com/2010/11/03/rand-superstition -and-psychological-warfare/. Retrieved April 25, 2024.

180 http://www.talk2action.org/comments/2010/10/2/142824/582/9?mode=alone;show rate=1#9, retrieved 4/25/24.

181 Levenda, Peter. *Sinister Forces*, Kindle locations 7603–7604.

182 Melanson, Terry. "The All-Seeing Eye, The President, The Secretary and The Guru." *Illuminati Conspiracy Archive*, July 2001. https://www.conspiracyarchive.com/NWO /All_Seeing_Eye.htm. Retrieved April 25, 2024.

183 For that we recommend Peter Levenda's *Sinister Forces: The Nine*.

184 Levenda, Kindle locations 7734–7737.

185 Levenda, Kindle locations 7765–7769.

186 Levenda, Kindle locations 7809–7815.

187 Puharich, Andrija. *Uri; a Journal of the Mystery of Uri Geller* (Garden City, NY: Anchor Press, 1974)18.

188 Penre, Wes. "The Council of Nine." *Fortean Times*. Republished at UriGeller.com: http://www.urigeller.com/plan-nine-outer-space/. Retrieved August 22, 2017.

189 Ibid.

190 Ibid.

191 Ibid.

192 Ibid.

193 Dunand, Françoise, and Zivie-Coche, Christiane. *Gods and Men in Egypt: 3000 BCE to 395 CE*. Translated by David Lorton (Ithaca: Cornell University Press, 2004).

NOTES

194 Penre.

195 Ibid.

196 Ibid.

197 Welch, Alex. "Friday Cable Ratings: 'Live PD' and Clippers vs Lakers Game Land High," July 10, 2017, *TV by the Numbers*. http://tvbythenumbers.zap2it.com/daily-ratings/friday-cable-ratings-july-7-2017/. Retrieved July 16, 2017.

198 Colavito, Jason. "Review of Ancient Aliens S20E05: 'The Top Ten Alien Codes.'" *JasonColavito.com*, February 2, 2024. https://www.jasoncolavito.com/blog/review-of-ancient-aliens-s20e05-the-top-ten-alien-codes. Retrieved February 23, 2024.

199 Colavito, Jason. "Review of Ancient Aliens S12E10 'The Akashic Record.'" *Jason Colavito.com*, July 14, 2017. http://www.jasoncolavito.com/blog/review-of-ancient-aliens-s12e10-the-akashic-record. Retrieved July 16, 2017.

200 Transcribed from video clip: https://www.youtube.com/watch?v=CDeGGZVxUGg. Retrieved July 16, 2017.

201 Thompson, Henry O. "Chebar (Place)," ed. by David Noel Freedman, *The Anchor Yale Bible Dictionary* (New York: Doubleday, 1992), 893.

202 Ewing, W. "Chebar," ed. by James Orr, John L. Nuelsen, Edgar Y. Mullins, and Morris O. Evans, *The International Standard Bible Encyclopaedia* (Chicago: The Howard-Severance Company, 1915) 599.

203 Wang, Xinhua. *The Metamorphosis of Enlil in Early Mesopotamia* (Münster: Ugarit-Verlag, 2011), 199.

204 Ibid., p. 201.

205 Mark, Joshua J. "Enlil in the E-kur." *World History Encyclopedia*. Last modified March 06, 2023. https://www.worldhistory.org/article/2181/enlil-in-the-e-kur/. Retrieved February 24, 2024.

206 Schneider, Tammi J. *An Introduction to Ancient Mesopotamian Religion* (Grand Rapids, MI: William B. Eerdman's Publishing Company, 2011), 59.

207 Heiser, Michael S. "The Spaceships of Ezekiel Fraud," April 28, 2013, *Paleobabble*. https://drmsh.com/spaceships-ezekiel-fraud/. Retrieved February 23, 2024.

208 Heiser, Michael S. "The Myth of a Sumerian 12th Planet: 'Nibiru' According to the Cuneiform Sources," p. 5., https://www.sitchiniswrong.com/nibirunew.pdf. Retrieved February 24, 2024.

209 Ibid., p. 13.

210 See www.SitchinIsWrong.com.

211 "More than one third of Americans believe aliens have visited Earth," June 28, 2012, *Christian Science Monitor*. https://www.csmonitor.com/Science/2012/0628/More-than-one-third-of-Americans-believe-aliens-have-visited-Earth. Retrieved February 23, 2024.

212 Barna, George. "Incidence of Biblical Worldview Shows Significant Change Since the Start of the Pandemic." *GeorgeBarna.com*, February 28, 2023. https://georgebarna.com/2023/02/incidence-of-biblical-worldview-shows-significant-change-since-the-start-of-the-pandemic/. Retrieved February 23, 2024.

213 "Top Lifetime Adjusted Grosses," *Box Office Mojo*. http://www.boxofficemojo.com/alltime/adjusted.htm. Retrieved July 16, 2017.

214 Chilton, Martin. "The War of the Worlds Panic Was a Myth." *The Telegraph*, May 6, 2016. https://www.telegraph.co.uk/radio/what-to-listen-to/the-war-of-the-worlds-panic-was-a-myth/. Retrieved April 26, 2024.

215 McCaffery, Larry. "An Interview with Jack Williamson." July 1991. https://www .depauw.edu/sfs/interviews/williamson54interview.htm. Retrieved April 26, 2024.

216 Astounding Science Fiction, April 1950, p. 132.

217 H. P. Lovecraft, "At the Mountains of Madness." *Astounding Stories*, 16, No. 6 (February 1936), 8–32; 17, No. 1 (March 1936), 125–55; 17, No. 2 (April 1936), 132–50. https://www.hplovecraft.com/writings/texts/fiction/mm.aspx. Retrieved April 26, 2024.

218 The title of one of Dr. Heiser's presentations at the Modern Challenges to the ET Hypothesis Conference at the 2017 UFO Festival in Roswell.

219 Prophet, Elizabeth Clare. *The Seven Chohans—On the Path of the Ascension: The Opening of the Retreats of the Great White Brotherhood (Teachings of the Ascended Masters)* (Malibu, CA: Summit University Press, 1973), 193.

220 Knowles, Christopher, and Linsner, Joseph Michael. *Our Gods Wear Spandex: The Secret History of Comic Book Heroes* (San Francisco: Weiser Books, 2007), 18.

221 Graham, Robbie. "SETI Astronomer Says We're Ready for Alien Contact… Thanks to Hollywood." *Mysterious Universe*, July 19, 2017. https://web.archive.org/web/2017 0721202616/http://mysteriousuniverse.org/2017/07/seti-atronomer-says-were-ready -for-alien-contact-thanks-to-hollywood/, retrieved 4/26/24.

222 Cooper, Helene; Kean, Leslie; & Blumenthal, Ralph. "Glowing Auras and 'Black Money': The Pentagon's Mysterious U.F.O. Program." *New York Times*, December 16, 2017. https://www.nytimes.com/2017/12/16/us/politics/pentagon-program-ufo-harry -reid.html. Retrieved April 2, 2024.

223 Cooper, Helene; Kean, Leslie; & Blumenthal, Ralph. "2 Navy Airmen and an Object That 'Accelerated :ike Nothing I've Ever Seen'." *The New York Times*, December 16, 2017. https://www.nytimes.com/2017/12/16/us/politics/unidentified-flying-object -navy.html#story-continues-2. Retrieved April 2, 2024.

224 Ibid.

225 Ibid.

226 Ibid.

227 Mizokami, Kyle. "That Time the U.S. Navy Had a Close Encounter with a UFO." *Popular Mechanics*, K. December 18, 2017. http://www.popularmechanics.com/military /a14456936/that-time-the-us-navy-had-a-close-encounter-with-a-ufo/. Retrieved April 2, 2024.

228 Chierci, Paco. "There I Was: The X-Files Edition." *Fighter Sweep*, March 14, 2015. https://fightersweep.com/1460/x-files-edition/. Retrieved April 2, 2024.

229 Ibid.

230 User "cometa2." (February 13, 2007). "Fighter Jet UFO Footage: The Real Deal." *Above Top Secret*. https://www.abovetopsecret.com/forum/thread265835/pg9#pid2951082. Retrieved February 4, 2024.

231 Chierci.

232 "Mission." To the Stars Academy of Arts and Sciences. https://web.archive.org/web /20171231152554/https://dpo.tothestarsacademy.com/#mission. Retrieved April 2, 2024.

233 Watkins Eli, & Todd, Brian. "Former Pentagon UFO Official: 'We May Not Be Alone'," CNN.com. http://www.cnn.com/2017/12/18/politics/luis-elizondo-ufo-pentagon /index.html. Retrieved February 4, 2024.

234 "The Team." To the Stars Academy of Arts and Sciences. https://web.archive.org/web/2017 1221022557/https://dpo.tothestarsacademy.com/#the-team. Retrieved April 2, 2024.

235 As noted, the company has rebranded as To the Stars, Inc., "an award-winning, vertically integrated entertainment company," which may be better suited to the talents of CEO Tom DeLonge—although CIA veteran Jim Semivan is still on the board of directors. https://tothestars.media/pages/about. Retrieved April 2, 2024.

236 Gilbert, Derek P., & Peck, Josh. *The Day the Earth Stands Still* (Crane, MO: Defender, 2017), 74.

237 George, Andrew. *The Epic of Gilgamesh: The Babylonian Epic Poem and Other Texts in Akkadian and Sumerian* (London: Penguin Books, 2000) 200.

238 "God did not spare angels when they sinned, but cast them into hell and committed them to chains of gloomy darkness to be kept until the judgment" (2 Peter 2:4, esv). The only place in the Bible where we are told of angels sinning is Genesis 6:1–4 (the Watchers/*apkallu* who took human wives and produced the Nephilim). The Greek verb translated "cast them into hell" is *tartarōsas*, which literally means "thrust down to Tartarus." In Greek cosmology, Tartarus was a special place of punishment located as far below Hades (hell) as Earth was below heaven. Since Peter wrote under the guidance of the Holy Spirit, we assume he knew the difference between Tartarus and Hades. It is the only place in the Bible where that word is used, which means it deserves special attention.

239 A word that derives from the older Akkadian, Sumerian, and Hurrian words, *apsu*, *abzu*, and *abi*.

240 Becker, Helmut, and Fassbinder, Jörg. "Magnetometry at Uruk (Iraq): The City of King Gilgamesh," *Archaeologia Polona*, 41 (2003), pp. 122–124.

241 1 Enoch 6:6. Although the scholar Edward Lipinski suggested in his 1971 paper "El's Abode" that "days of Jared" should read "days of the *yarid*," which was a ritual libation—a drink offering for the gods. As Lipinski noted, the summit of Mount Hermon is scooped out, and earlier scholars, such as Charles Clermont-Ganneau in 1903, speculated that this may have been where worshippers poured their liquid offerings.

242 Nickelsburg, George W. E. *1 Enoch: The Hermeneia Translation.* (Minneapolis: Fortress Press, 2012), 26.

243 Greenfield, J. C. "Apkallu," *Dictionary of Deities and Demons in the Bible.* Van der Toorn, K., Becking, B., & Van der Horst, P. W. (Eds.) (Leiden: Brill, 1999), 73.

244 Annus, Amar. "On the Origin of Watchers: A Comparative Study of the Antediluvian Wisdom in Mesopotamian and Jewish Traditions." *Journal for the Study of the Pseudepigrapha*, Vol 19, Issue 4 (2010), pp. 277–320.

245 Lipiński, Edward. "El's Abode: Mythological Traditions Related to Mount Hermon and to the Mountains of Armenia," *Orientalia Lovaniensa Periodica II* (1971), p. 19.

246 Ibid.

247 "Anunna." Ancient Mesopotamian Gods and Goddesses. https://oracc.museum. upenn.edu/amgg/listofdeities/anunna/index.html. Retrieved April 29. 2024.

248 The Titans of Greek and Roman mythology, the "former gods" of the Hittites, and the "primeval gods" of the Hurrians are also to be identified with the rebellious "sons of God" from Genesis 6:1–4. See chapters 1–3 of Derek and Sharon Gilbert's book *Veneration* (Crane, MO: Defender, 2019).

NOTES

249 Pritchard, James B., ed., *The Ancient Near East: An Anthology of Texts and Pictures* (Princeton, NJ: Princeton University Press, 1958) 34.

250 Lieck, Gwendolyn. *A Dictionary of Ancient Near Eastern Mythology* (New York, NY: Routledge, 1998), 141.

251 George, p. 199.

252 Smith, Wesley J. "The Trouble with Transhumanism," Christian Life Resources, https://web.archive.org/web/20140802134649/https://christianliferesources.com/article/the-trouble-with-transhumanism-1191. Retrieved April 29, 2024.

253 Danaylov, Nikola. "A Transhumanist Manifesto (Redux)." Singularity Weblog, March 11, 2016. https://www.singularityweblog.com/a-transhumanist-manifesto/. Retrieved April 29, 2024.

254 Ibid.

255 https://www.zoltanistvan.com/TranshumanistWager.html. Retrieved April 29, 2024.

256 Istvan, Zoltan. *The Transhumanist Wager.* (Futurity Imagine Media LLC, 2013), 127–128.

257 Searle, Rick. "Betting against the Transhumanist Wager." Institute for Ethics and Emerging Technologies, September 16, 2013. https://ieet.org/index.php/IEET2/more/searle 20130916. Retrieved April 29, 2024.

258 Berdyaev, N. A. "The Religion of Resuciative Resurrection." Berdyaev.com. https://web.archive.org/web/20181014115444/http://www.berdyaev.com/berdiaev/berd_lib/1915_186.html. Retrieved April 29, 2024.

259 Koutaissoff, Elisabeth and Minto, Marilyn. "Introduction." In *What Was Man Created For? The Philosophy of the Common Task* (Lausanne: Honeyglen Publishing/L'Age d'Homme, 1990), 18.

260 Istvan.

261 For example, Natasha Vita-More, "Transhuman: A Brief History." https://web.archive.org/web/20030621071821/http://www.natasha.cc/quiz.htm#Transhuman%20History. Retrieved April 29, 2024.

262 Bullinger, E. W. (1903). *The Apocalypse or "The Day of the Lord."* (London: Eyre & Spottiswoode).

263 He believed the Church Age started at Acts 28:28 rather than Pentecost, and Paul's authoritative teaching began after the conclusion of the book of Acts.

264 Bullinger, E. W., *The Rich Man and Lazarus or "The Intermediate State,"* (London: Eyrie & Spottiswoode, 1902).

265 Schadewald, Robert J. *The Plane Truth: A History of the Flat Earth Movement (2000),* http://www.cantab.net/users/michael.behrend/ebooks/PlaneTruth/pages/Chapter_04.html. Retrieved April 29, 2024.

266 Mayo Clinic (2014). "EEG Definition," https://www.mayoclinic.org/tests-procedures/eeg/basics/definition/prc-20014093. Retrieved April 29, 2024.

267 Kurzweil, Raymond. *The Singularity is Near: When Humans Transcend Biology.* (New York: Penguin Books, 2005) 7.

268 Honan, Daniel. "Ray Kurzweil: The Six Epochs of Technology Evolution." Big Think. https://bigthink.com/the-nantucket-project/ray-kurzweil-the-six-epochs-of-technology-evolution. Retrieved April 29, 2024.

269 Draper, Lucy. "Could Artificial Intelligence Kill Us Off?" *Newsweek*, June 24, 2015. https://www.newsweek.com/artificial-intelligenceomega-pointai-603286. Retrieved April 29, 2024.

270 O'Connell, Gerard. "Will Pope Francis Remove the Vatican's 'warning' from Teilhard de Chardin's Writings?" *America: The Jesuit Review*, November 21, 2017. https://www. americamagazine.org/faith/2017/11/21/will-pope-francis-remove-vaticans-warning-teilhard-de-chardins-writings. Retrieved April 29, 2024.

271 Steinhart, Eric. "Teilhard de Chardin and Transhumanism," *Journal of Evolution and Technology*, Vol. 20, Issue 1, 1–22 (2008). http://jetpress.org/v20/steinhart.htm. Retrieved April 29, 2024.

272 "The Death of Gilgamesh: Translation." The Electronic Text Corpus of Sumerian Literature, http://etcsl.orinst.ox.ac.uk/section1/tr1813.htm. Retrieved April 29, 2024.

273 Marchesi, Gianni. "Who Was Buried in the Royal Tombs of Ur? The Epigraphic and Textual Data," *Orientalia*, Nova Series, Vol. 73, No. 2 (2004), 154.

274 That's a reference to *The Day the Earth Stood Still*, a classic 1951 science-fiction film about first contact with an extraterrestrial race.

275 Hammer, Olav. *Claiming Knowledge: Strategies of Epistemology from Theosophy to the New Age* (Leiden and Boston: Brill, 2001), 180.

276 Johnson, Ronald C. "Parallels Between Recollections of Repressed Childhood Sex Abuse, Kidnappings by Space Aliens, and the Salem Witch Hunts." *IPT Journal*, Vol. 6 (1994). http://www.ipt-forensics.com/journal/volume6/j6_1_4.htm. Retrieved April 25, 2024. Scholars may discredit both groups of victims as unreliable witnesses, especially if their memories were "recovered" through hypnotic regression. The point is that abductees and SRA victims share similar experiences which, in our view, is as much spiritual as physical, as evidenced by the many accounts collected by CE4 Research Group of abductions that were stopped in the Name of Jesus.

277 See Psalm 82. And for multiple examples of Bible stories that make more sense in this context, see Derek's book *The Great Inception: Satan's PSYOPs from Eden to Armageddon*.

278 Heiser, Michael S. "Image of God". *Lexham Bible Dictionary* (John D. Barry et al., eds.) (Bellingham, WA: Lexham Press, 2012).